19.95

Shrinking the State
The Political Underpinnings of Privatization

Privatization has spread worldwide during the 1980s and 1990s, and has significantly reshaped the balance between state and market in many countries. This book provides a comparative political analysis of the development, form, character and causes of privatization in three countries: the UK, the USA and France. The authors argue that privatization is a political phenomenon and should be analyzed as such, rather than being seen as an economic response to the growth of the state and the cost of state provision. Privatization frequently has explicit political goals, and has consequences which redistribute costs and benefits to different groups. The book presents a threefold typology of privatization policy – pragmatic, tactical and systemic – and relates it to the experiences of the USA, France and the UK respectively. It will be of interest to students and scholars of politics, economics, public policy and business studies, as well as policy-makers and consultants in the field of privatization.

HARVEY FEIGENBAUM is Professor of Political Science and International Affairs at the George Washington University, Washington DC. He is the author of *The Politics of Public Enterprise* (1985).

JEFFREY HENIG is Professor of Political Science at the George Washington University. He is the author of *Public Policy and Federalism: Issues in State and Local Politics* (1985), and *Rethinking School Choice* (1994).

CHRIS HAMNETT is Professor of Human Geography at King's College London, and was previously Professor of Urban Geography at the Open University. He is the co-author of *Cities, Housing and Profits* (1987), *As Safe as Houses* and *Winners and Losers: The Home Ownership Market in Modern Britain* (1998).

Shrinking the State

The Political Underpinnings of Privatization

Harvey Feigenbaum
Jeffrey Henig
Chris Hamnett

CAMBRIDGE
UNIVERSITY PRESS

PUBLISHED BY THE PRESS SYNDICATE OF THE UNIVERSITY OF CAMBRIDGE
The Pitt Building, Trumpington Street, Cambridge CB2 1RP, United Kingdom

CAMBRIDGE UNIVERSITY PRESS
The Edinburgh Building, Cambridge CB2 2RU, United Kingdom
  http://www.cup.cam.ac.uk
40 West 20th Street, New York, NY 10011-4211, USA
  http://www.cup.org
10 Stamford Road, Oakleigh, Melbourne 3166, Australia

First published 1998

Printed in the United Kingdom at the University Press, Cambridge

Typeset in Plantin 10/12 pt   [SE]

A catalogue record for this book is available from the British Library

ISBN 0 521 63080 0 hardback
ISBN 0 521 63918 2 paperback

Contents

Acknowledgments

This book was the product of a very long gestation period. We started talking about the project in the mid 1980s when the authors first met during Chris Hamnett's sojourn as a Banneker Fellow at the George Washington University. All of us had several projects we were trying to work on at once, so our strategy was to write several articles and to gradually work out our ideas. Fortunately, from the point of view of scholarly interest, although perhaps unfortunately from the point of view of the policy's critics, privatization did not recede as an important political issue.

We are grateful for the insights of a number of eminent scholars who read various drafts. These generous souls included Joel Aberbach, Jonathan Boston, Colin Campbell, Hans-Ulrich Derlien, Yvonne Fortin, Joe Greenberg, John Halligan, Charles Hauss, Peter Katzenstein, Mark Kesselman, Desmond King, Ulrich Klöti, Michael Loriaux, Charles-Albert Michalet, Nicole de Montricher, John Power, Bert Rockman, Jean-Michel Saussois, Peter Self, Lee Sigelman, Stephen C. Smith, Deborah Stone, Ezra Suleiman, George Szablowski, R. Kent Weaver, Graham Wilson, and Joel Wolfe.

We also benefited from the research assistance of Joy Bernardo, Janice Kuhn and Lara Frazier. Research assistance was funded by the Advisory Council on Research through the Institute for European, Russian and Eurasian Studies of George Washington University.

Earlier versions of what became chapters 2, 4 and 5 were published in part in scholarly journals. We are grateful to The Johns Hopkins University Press for allowing us to publish in chapter 2 passages from our article "The Political Underpinnings of Privatization: A Typology," which appeared in *World Politics*, 46, 2 (January 1994). An earlier draft of chapter 4 appeared in *Business in the Contemporary World*, 5, 1 (Winter 1993), while Jeffrey R. Henig's article, "Privatization in the United States: Theory and Practice," *Political Science Quarterly*, 104, 4 (Winter 1989–90) was an early version of chapter 5.

John Haslam of Cambridge University Press has been very helpful in guiding us through the publication process. In addition to being read by the many scholars cited above, the manuscript was read in successive stages by four anonymous reviewers for the Press, who provided useful criticism and helped us avoid errors of fact and judgement. Any errors or defects remaining are, of course, our responsibility.

1 Privatization and theories of state growth

Sometime during the 1980s, a major international political movement was born. Led by Great Britain, scores of nations began – or considered – selling publicly owned enterprises to private corporations or shareholders. While the early plans primarily involved industrialized nations in Western Europe and Japan, privatization rapidly caught on worldwide. Less developed countries, prodded by international lending agencies, began experimenting seriously with asset sales. The United States government,[1] which had stayed mostly on the sidelines while many other countries developed state-owned enterprises, began sifting through its assets looking for something to sell. By the early 1990s, former bastions of state ownership – Russia, Poland, Czechoslovakia, and Hungary – not only had joined the privatization parade but were embarking on some of the most aggressive efforts in the world. According to some, this movement amounts to nothing less than a "revolution."[2]

Privatization, defined broadly as "the shifting of a function, either in whole or in part, from the public sector to the private sector,"[3] involves the increased reliance on private actors and market forces to take over functions or responsibilities that had in recent decades come to be regarded as properly within the governmental sphere. Despite its rather late appearance on the radar screen of public awareness, privatization has recently received plenty of attention from academics, policy-makers, and the international media.[4] Much of this attention, however, is misdirected.

---

[1] Collaborative efforts require compromises, not the least of which involves vocabulary. Political scientists who specialize in studying the United States use the term *government* in the same way that comparativists and geographers use the term *state*. We use these two words interchangeably in this book.

[2] P. Young, "Privatization Around the World," in *Prospects for Privatization*, ed. S. Hanke (New York: The Academy of Political Science, 1987), pp. 190–206.

[3] Stuart Butler, "Privatization for Public Purposes," in *Privatization and Its Alternatives*, ed. William T. Gormley (Madison: University of Wisconsin Press, 1991), p. 17.

[4] E.g., J. Vickers and V. Wright, "The Politics of Industrial Privatisation in Britain," in *The Politics of Privatization in Western Europe* (London: Frank Cass, 1989); J. Vickers and G. Yarrow, *Privatization: An Economic Analysis* (Cambridge, MA: MIT Press, 1988); J. Wolfe, "State Power and Ideology in Britain: Mrs. Thatcher's Privatisation Programme," *Political Studies*, 34 (June 1991), 237–252; Ezra N. Suleiman and John Waterbury, eds., *The*

While there are scores of articles describing privatization initiatives in one country or another, most of these have focused on their immediate fiscal implications.

Aside from events in Eastern Europe – in which discussions about privatization are almost always linked to broader considerations related to democratization and political change – privatization is typically portrayed in narrow, almost apolitical terms, as little more than a vehicle for helping governments balance their budgets, or, at best, improving the overall performance of the economy. While the fiscal dimensions of privatization are important, we believe that privatization can be a harbinger of institutional and societal changes that are much broader in scope.

For us, states represent the institutionalized capacity of societies to deal with their collective problems. As we shall argue below, neither introducing market forces into the state apparatus, nor transferring some functions to private providers, *necessarily* results in a net shrinking of the state. By "shrinking the state" we mean reducing the overall level of state intervention in the society rather than simply reducing the size of the public sector. Shrinking the state affects the context within which actors solve their collective problems, and the rules by which politics is played. Under the circumstances we shall describe, privatization has brought about a major change to the rules.

When viewed from a broader theoretical perspective, we believe that the privatization phenomenon can help us to develop more sophisticated answers to a number of critical questions. How do societies draw the line between public and private responsibility? What causes the nature and scope of the state to change, and how broad is the range of state authority within which contemporary societies may vary? What is the power of broad ideas, such as the economic theories that underpin the privatization movement, to bring about sharp reversals in institutional direction and to realign political interests and power?

The argument that we develop in this book is an outgrowth of our efforts to understand commonalities in the privatization movements as they emerged in Great Britain, the Western European continent, and the United States. Hamnett first became interested in privatization as it became manifest in the sale of council housing in Great Britain.[5]

Political Economy of Public Sector Reform and Privatization (Boulder, CO: Westview, 1990); Sheila B. Kamerman and Alfred J. Kahn, eds., *Privatization and the Welfare State* (Princeton: Princeton University Press, 1989); Paul Starr, "The Meaning of Privatization," in Kamerman and Kahn, eds., *Privatization and the Welfare State*; and Dennis Swann, *The Retreat of the State: Deregulation and Privatization in the UK and US* (Ann Arbor: University of Michigan Press, 1988).

[5] E.g., Richard Harris and Chris Hamnett, "The Myth of the Promised Land: The Social Diffusion of Home Ownership in Britain and North America," *Annals of the Association of American Geographers*, 77 (June 1987), 173–190.

Feigenbaum grappled with the issue first as an outgrowth of research into state enterprises and energy policies in France.[6] Henig approached the topic as an outgrowth of interest in use of market theories to rationalize changes in urban service delivery in the USA.[7] When we first began discussing privatization in the three countries, the differences among them seemed to loom very large.[8] Privatization in Great Britain seemed so much bolder and more dramatic than in the USA, for example. In Great Britain privatization seemed clearly linked to an ideological agenda of the Right, while in France the Socialists found themselves albeit reluctantly adopting some aspects of a privatization platform, and in the USA the movement often was presented in apolitical, technical, and pragmatic terms. And, while the major initiatives in both Great Britain and France came at the national level, in the USA it was local governments that seemed to be carrying the ball. The closer and longer we looked, however, the more we came to see that the differences coincided with important similarities. These similarities had less to do with the specific forms of privatization that were favored in each country (although over time such similarities increased) than with the political dynamic that accompanied them and the implications they held for the future shape of the modern democratic state.

The choice of analyzing privatization and efforts to shrink the state in Britain, France and the USA ultimately had its origin in a chance lunch, over which we met to discuss our interests, rather than in scientific research design. Nevertheless, arguments for comparison of these three countries are founded on more than culinary propinquity. By the standards of Harry Eckstein's notion of a "crucial case,"[9] neither Britain, France nor the USA constitute crucial cases of a theory of "state shrinkage." That is, it is not obvious that a generic explanation stands or falls on the experience in these three countries. Rather, we make the argument for our case selection on four grounds: first, to paraphrase Michael Loriaux, that the USA, Britain and France are important countries;[10] secondly, that these three countries, while sharing similar levels of development, present interesting contrasts in political culture and institutions; thirdly,

---

[6] Harvey Feigenbaum, *The Politics of Public Enterprise* (Princeton: Princeton University Press, 1985).

[7] Jeffrey R. Henig, "Privatization in the United States: Theory and Practice," *Political Science Quarterly*, 104, 4 (1990), 649–670.

[8] Jeffrey R. Henig, Chris Hamnett and Harvey Feigenbaum, "The Politics of Privatization: A Comparative Perspective," *Governance*, 1, 4 (October 1988), 442–468.

[9] Harry Eckstein, "Case Study and Theory in Political Science," in Fred I. Greenstein and Nelson W. Polsby, eds., *Handbook of Political Science*, vol. 7, *Political Science: Scope and Theory* (Reading, MA: Addison-Wesley, 1975), pp. 79–137.

[10] Loriaux used this justification in the introduction to an earlier draft of his very original *France After Hegemony: International Change and Financial Reform* (Ithaca: Cornell University Press, 1991).

that all additional observations increase the validity of conclusions to specific hypotheses; and fourthly, that these countries exhibit a wide range of privatization behaviors which illuminate our typology.[11]

We found much of the literature on privatization ahistorical and somewhat parochial. Privatization appeared to some observers so new and so radically different from the norm – "revolutionary," in Young's terms cited above – that there was little effort to seek to bring it into intellectual contact with the theories and concepts that had evolved during the period of a growing welfare state. Privatization was treated as a paradigm-busting anomaly, with the inference that reigning concepts could be – indeed, must be – discarded. Without gainsaying that which is new and distinctive about privatization, we think that there is much benefit in acknowledging the ways that the privatization phenomenon both informs, and is informed by, some long-standing theoretical debates about the nature of the state and its relationship to society.

For that reason, we begin this book by considering the privatization movement, and its implication that the state is destined to shrink, directly in relation to various theories about why the curve of state intervention was so strongly upward at least until recently. Some theories have implied that the growth of the welfare state was in some ways natural and inevitable – a functional adaptation to evolving societal conditions and needs, or a logical consequence of the political forces unleashed once the public sector grew large and independent enough to develop its own interests and the latitude to pursue them. To those theories, privatization potentially represents a critical anomaly. Yet, as we will suggest, other theories have offered a more contingent and open-ended understanding of the growth of the state. Those theories view interests, ideas, and institutions as interacting in complex ways that belie any simplistic effort to deduce an immutable imperative of either state expansion or contraction.

Ultimately, our efforts to come to terms with privatization in Great Britain, France, and the USA led us to develop what we refer to as a "political typology" of privatization. This typology suggests that some of the distinctions typically drawn among different forms of privatization may distract us from more consequential distinctions relating to political motivations and, ultimately, political consequences. We sketch out that typology and explain its advantages in chapter 2; in chapters 3 to 5 we illustrate the typology more fully by applying it to the three countries that form the foundation of our analysis. In stretching our conceptualization to encompass the differing processes in these three countries, we believe

---

[11] We are especially swayed here by the argument of Gary King, Robert Keohane and Sidney Verba, *Designing Social Inquiry* (Princeton: Princeton University Press, 1994), ch. 6.

that we have generated a framework with even broader applications. Chapter 6 returns to the issues raised in this and the following chapter, and considers what the case studies tell us about the limits and future of privatization, not only in the countries that provide our primary focus, but in some other settings as well.

What is privatization?

US Supreme Court Justice Potter Stewart wrote about pornography that, while he might not be able to define it intelligibly, "I know it when I see it."[12] Some might say the same about privatization. Certainly, many of those writing about privatization have felt it unnecessary to strive for definitional precision. To some, privatization represents a move from government to private ownership. To others, it connotes a reduction in the regulatory role of government. Another group of scholars bounds the concept more narrowly, identifying it with some specific techniques for introducing competitive bidding among private firms to provide publicly defined services. And in some cases, the term is so hospitable as to include any and all tendencies to increase individuals' responsibilities for their own needs (whether such tendencies are the result of deliberate policies or broad societal trends).

It is understandable why those who minted the term initially might frame it so broadly. In the late 1970s, when the term emerged, there was a widely shared presumption that continued governmental expansion was inevitable. In this context an open-ended definition served both analytic and political functions. To those seeking to understand the dynamics of governmental growth, "privatization" drew under one terminological roof a diverse array of largely scattered activities and proposals sharing the characteristic of injecting market mechanisms into areas conventionally perceived to belong to the public realm. Thus, the expansion of public–private partnerships and quasi-governmental bodies, contracting out of public service delivery, efforts to rein in public employee unions, and grass-roots tax revolts could be portrayed as part of an emergent rejection of the welfare state, rather than as simultaneous but discrete enterprises. Beyond whatever analytic enlightenment this recategorization attained, promotion of a broad definition of privatization also served a political purpose for those actively seeking to scale back the governmental apparatus and responsibilities; through terminological linkage, it created the appearance of a broader, more fully established model for change than otherwise was apparent.

[12] *Jacobellis* v *Ohio* [378 U.S. 184 (1964)].

It is our claim that this ambiguity has confounded analysis. What is more, it has done so in a manner that has furthered the interests of those favoring a partial (at least) dismantling of the state. At some times and in some places the assault on the state has been openly proclaimed, but when the targeted programs have sizable and politically resourceful constituencies, anti-state activists have found tactical benefit in ambiguity. Ambiguity about what privatization entails has allowed those with a broad political agenda to point to narrower, limited, and more selective governmental techniques in order to legitimize their more radical stance. Sharper thinking about privatization requires, first of all, some attention to its manifestation in different forms.

Privatization has also had different emphases, largely because of the legacies of previous public policies. Market failures[13] can be corrected either by public enterprise (e.g. a national electric company) or by regulation (e.g., a public utilities commission regulating a private electric company). Europeans have frequently opted for public enterprise to correct market failure or to meet strategic or public needs. On the other hand, American solutions to market failure have rarely taken the form of public enterprise, except at the municipal level, but rather have been found in the public regulation of private monopolies. Privatization in Europe, then, frequently has meant asset sales, while in the USA, other kinds of privatization have been more likely, such as contracting with private firms to provide public functions, as well as increasing the use of market incentives in the public sector. In either case, states historically have taken on new functions because markets have been unable to produce desired goods or services. Thus, states may occasionally move from direct to indirect provision of these goods and services, so that the privatization of a public utility, for example, may be followed by the creation of a new regulatory agency. *In such cases, where states have merely moved from one form of intervention to another to correct market failure, privatization does not necessarily lead to shrinking the state.*

Since political conservatives in the United States and economic neoliberals in Europe have tended to champion not only the dismantling of state institutions, but deregulation and tax-cutting (so that the state will not be able to fund its activities), there is a tendency to lump such initia-

---

[13] "Market failure" is the justification in neoclassical economics for state intervention. It occurs in situations where collective goods are not provided by individuals reacting to market incentives or where there is a tendency toward negative externalities (e.g. pollution) or "natural" monopoly (e.g. public utilities). Economists differ as to when such conditions actually occur, and changes in technology may lead to a supposed potential for competition in areas previously thought to be natural monopolies, such as in telecommunications and electricity provision. For a discussion, see Harvey B. Feigenbaum, *The Politics of Public Enterprise* (Princeton: Princeton University Press, 1985), ch. 1.

tives together. Many of these neoliberal reforms do indeed appeal to the same political clientele.[14] However, too many subjects under the same microscope tend to obscure the picture. Since we are interested in distinguishing policies which are undertaken for ideological motives from those which have their political origins elsewhere, we shall, for the sake of clarity, focus our inquiry on the privatization of state assets and services. Moreover, we try to avoid the trap of treating all forms of state intervention (or withdrawal) as broadly equivalent. Since we are concerned with "who benefits," both on its own terms and as an indicator of likely constituencies, we distinguish the diverse forms of safety or public health regulation for example, from those which merely protect and allocate private shares of a market. This more finely conceived, cross-national exploration of privatization helps discriminate the politics behind the policy.

Privatization as discrete techniques

The list of specific techniques frequently associated with privatization can be a lengthy one. Privatization of services can include *management reforms* – incremental efforts to make government agencies operate in a more business-like and market-oriented manner. Americans have recently been exposed to this view in a host of reforms inspired by Osborne and Gabler's influential *Reinventing Government,* while the British have adopted the similar "Next Steps."[15] Management reforms can be quite incremental in their effect on the structure and form of government, but other modes of privatization can be much more radical. *Load-shedding,* for example, entails the complete withdrawal of government from certain services, usually with the stated expectation that the eliminated services can be provided through voluntary institutions, charity, or self-help. Usually more moderate in their initial impact are such other varieties of privatization as *asset sales,* in which government sells all or part of state-owned enterprises or property; *contracting out,* in which public officials act as service arrangers, deciding on what needs to be done and soliciting

---

[14] These neo-liberal policies are linked by their reliance on similar ideological justifications and political constituencies. The particular form of privatization they champion can be selective and opportunistic.

[15] David Osborne and Ted Gabler, *Reinventing Government: How the Entrepreneurial Spirit is Transforming the Public Sector* (Reading, MA: Addison-Wesley, 1992). As discussed in chapter 3, this book helped to shape the thinking of the Clinton administration, and was especially likely to be cited by Vice President Gore. For a comparative view of similar management reforms in Britain, France and Australia, see Sylvie Trosia, "The Uniqueness of the Australian Service Quality Experience," *Evaluation Journal of Australia,* 6, 2 (1994), 17–34.

bids from private firms that are willing and able to perform the specified task; *user fees*, through which governments institute charges to citizen–consumers for the use of public facilities or services that might otherwise be supported through general tax revenues; *voucher systems*, in which governments provide citizens with coupons redeemable for the purchase of specified goods or services in the private sector, as an alternative to providing those goods and services directly through governmental grants or service agencies; and *public–private partnerships*, in which government works directly with private firms, in formal or informal relationships, to jointly pursue common goals.

These different approaches to privatization can be intertwined and openly pursued as part of a comprehensive effort to redefine the role of the state. In chapter 2 we introduce the term "systemic privatization" to account for such occurrences, and to differentiate them from privatization initiatives that are more modest in aspiration and consequence. Systemic privatization better accounts for the thrust of policies initiated by the Thatcher regime in Great Britain, but in the USA, in contrast, privatization has more typically been portrayed as equivalent to a grab-bag of institutional mechanisms that can be tried out and selected according to the dictates of the situation. Treating privatization as one among many politically neutral policy options to be considered by public officials obscures the underlying political dimension that has given the privatization movement much of its vigor and controversy. This underlying dimension has to do with deep-seated disagreements about the proper scope of public versus private spheres, and grappling with it requires a more sophisticated understanding of how those spheres interrelate.

Dimensions of the public–private continuum

What links the various forms of privatization is less their substantive similarities than the fact that they stand in common juxtaposition to the implicit alternative: the direct governmental model. Under the direct governmental model, public sector institutions fund and provide key services, and do so in response to political, rather than market, incentives. Implicit in this is what Martin Rein labels the "dualist" perspective, which assumes "that the government is different from the rest of the world and that a sharp demarcation between government and the rest of society can be systematically drawn."[16] Also implicit is a belief that the growth of the modern welfare state has been characterized by a growing reliance on government as opposed to the private sector.

Such a dualist perspective suits conventional discourse – academic as

---

[16] Martin Rein, "The Social Structure of Institutions: Neither Public nor Private," in Kamerman and Kahn, eds., *Privatization and the Welfare State*, p. 50.

well as popular. We typically talk about the public and private "spheres" or "arenas" as if they are distinct, bounded, and mutually exclusive.[17] The public sphere is presumed to be the realm of the state and collective institutions; the private arena concerns firms, individuals and personal responsibility. In reality, though, the relationship between public and private is much more complex than this: "the modern institutions of social protection are neither public nor private in any unambiguous meanings of those terms."[18] Even the seemingly most private of interactions directly or indirectly comprise a public component; for example, a barter exchange among neighbors is ultimately constrained by legal definitions of property, strictures regarding who may undertake contracts, and available recourse to governmental sanction in the event of misrepresentation or fraud. By the same token, even the seemingly most authoritative exercise of governmental intent directly or indirectly relies on the cooperation or contribution of individuals or private firms; enforcement of criminal laws, for example, depends upon citizens' readiness to report violations and serve as witnesses.

Treating privatization as any technique that combines public and private elements obscures that fact that most governmental undertakings already assume such complex forms. And failure to consider the direction of change obscures the fact that mixed forms can represent an increase as well as a decrease in governmental responsibility. It is useful to think of four distinct dimensions that intertwine to define the distinction between public and private. These involve financing, delivery, responsibility, and decisionmaking (see figure 1.1). Privatization may involve a decreased role for government along any or all of these dimensions. Privatization in this sense is relative and directional rather than absolute; a formidable state that sheds some functions can be said to be privatizing even though it continues to play a much more substantial role than does the more limited state in another nation that has historically eschewed state ownership or other obvious forms of intervention.

Movement along one dimension often can spark parallel movement along another; e.g. a shift from public toward private provision of health services might also entail a shift toward greater reliance on a fee-for-service financing mechanism. But the dimensions are sufficiently independent that such complementary shifts need not necessarily occur. Indeed, one of the characteristics of privatization initiatives that often goes unnoticed is the tendency for shifts along one dimension sometimes to generate compensatory shifts toward a greater public sector role on other dimensions. For example, a reduction in the role of government in

---

[17] For a discussion of this, see Arnaud Sales, "The Private, the Public and Civil Society: Social Realms and Power Structure," *International Political Science Review*, 12, 4 (1991).

[18] Rein, "The Social Structure of Institutions," p. 49.

Public   **Private**

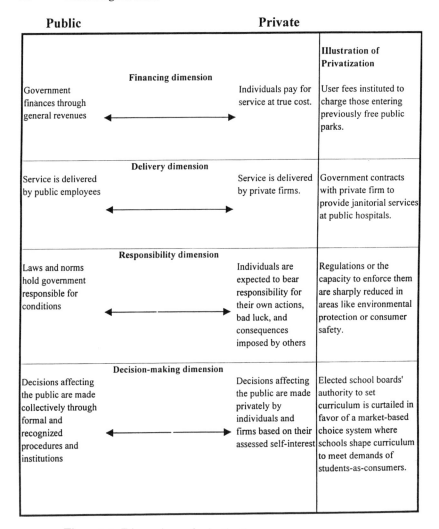

Figure 1.1 Dimensions of privatization

the direct provision of a service such as electrical power (as when a nation sells state-owned utilities to private firms) may be coupled with an increase in the regulatory responsibility; due to the greater visibility and sensitivity of the issue following such privatization, it is possible that citizens could hold public officials even more accountable for rising prices or declining services than they had previously. Thus, in addition to being relative, we argue that privatization should be judged in terms of aggregate shifts; a nation that fully compensates shifts away from the public sector along one dimension with corresponding increases in public sector involvement on other dimensions cannot be said to be privatizing in aggregate terms.

In defining privatization this broadly, we are self-consciously taking sides in an issue subject to dispute. Many authors limit the concept only to sales of nationalized firms and other state assets. We, however, locate the idea in the broader trend of policy advocacy whose various forms emphasize a return to concepts associated with economic liberalism.[19] These broader movements are linked by their reliance on similar ideological justifications and political constituencies. The particular form of privatization they champion can be selective and opportunistic. As we argue throughout this book, overemphasis on the distinctions among specific forms of privatization can obscure critically important political underpinnings. It is thus worth repeating that privatization need not shrink the state. But it is equally true that sometimes it does. What, then, are the conditions which lead to a shrinking of the state? To answer this question, it is necessary to understand why states grew in the first place.

Privatization as theoretical anomaly

The eruption of a worldwide privatization movement challenges many of the ideas about government and society that had begun to crystallize into conventional wisdom by the end of the 1960s. During the three decades following the Great Depression, state intervention in national economies had become a fixed element in Western industrial countries, and social scientists had devised a series of explanations of why this could not have been otherwise. The privatization movement has shaken the foundations of those explanations, but their reformulation has not proceeded apace. Moreover, the seeming simultaneity of the movement in nations of very different political, economic, and cultural institutions flies in the face of much conventional thinking about why countries select the policies they do.

In the remainder of this chapter, we seek to situate the contemporary privatization movement within the broader considerations of the nature of government that accompanied the growth and expansion of the state. We have two purposes for doing so. First, we believe that intellectually integrating the recent privatization movement leads to a more subtle and sophisticated understanding of how the interventionist state came about in the first place; the overly deterministic caste of much of the theorizing about governmental expansion obscured the many ways in which it was contingent upon political forces that are neither uniform nor predictable

---

[19] Henig, Hamnett, and Feigenbaum, "The Politics of Privatization": Suleiman and Waterbury, eds., *The Political Economy*; Kamerman and Kahn, eds. *Privatization and the Welfare State*; Starr, "The Meaning of Privatization"; Swann, *The Retreat of the State*.

in outcome. Secondly, we believe that reflecting on the contemporary privatization movement through a longer lens properly encourages a more considered assessment of the extent of the change that so far has taken place; it is not yet determined whether the loudly trumpeted initiatives of the 1980s will prove themselves to be harbingers of radical redirection or mid-course correction.

Broadly, there seem to have been two major trends in modern state development. These involved two distinct, but occasionally overlapping constituencies, each with a stake in separate state functions. One constituency favored redistribution while the second favored capital accumulation. The redistributive function is most closely associated with the Welfare State, while the second is associated with the "Developmental State."[20]

The seemingly inexorable growth of the welfare state

If Noah had collected a pair of social scientists, by the thirty-ninth day they would have developed a definitive explanation of why the rain would never end. By the middle of the 1960s, the welfare state was on the march throughout most Western industrialized nations. Extensions of governmental involvement in the economy – initially tolerated as short-time responses to a critical emergency – had come to be regarded as permanent, necessary, and, for the most part, welcome, even by constituencies previously inclined toward a laissez-faire perspective. And, as governments accepted responsibility for reducing poverty, they also quickly found themselves being pulled into further involvement in matters of family, child-rearing, and social service delivery that had less to do with economics than with social policy. President Lyndon Johnson's proclamation of the Great Society signaled that even the United States, by culture and tradition more skeptical of government than most nations, had signed on to the welfare state. In Europe these social innovations were added to other institutions which had been developed to correct the failings of the market. Public enterprises flourished in fields as diverse as trucking (Britain) and advertising (France). Figure 1.2 illustrates the size of the public sector in OECD countries.[21]

Noting this seemingly inexorable trend, analysts seeking to understand the factors that set the boundaries of public versus private responsibility

---

[20] We borrow the term "developmental state" from Chalmers Johnson, *MITI and the Japanese Miracle* (Stanford, CA: Stanford University Press, 1982).

[21] This is not, however, a clear indicator of the *relative size* of the welfare state in each country because of the distorting effect of defense expenditures. Figure 1.3 takes these expenditures into account.

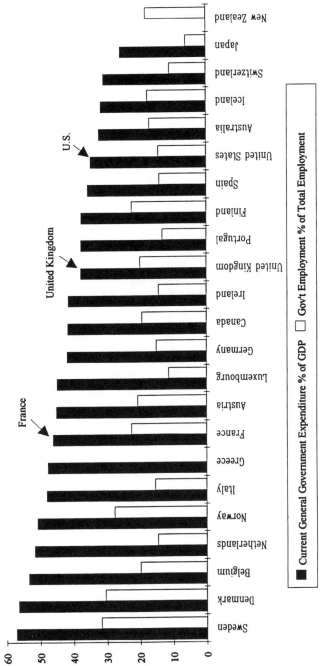

Figure 1.2 Size of public sector, OECD member nations: general expenditure and employment

■ Current General Government Expenditure % of GDP ☐ Gov't Employment % of Total Employment

fashioned explanations that presumed a steady and reinforcing pressure for governmental expansion. Although there are many theories about the sources of governmental growth that differ in their specifics, they can be broadly characterized as falling into three types, depending upon whether they explain governmental growth as resulting from environmental demands, domestic political pressures, or organizational dynamics internal to the state itself.

Environmentally imposed demands

Some social analysts such as Olson have suggested that the development of human institutions can be likened to the evolution of plant and animal species. Just as species adapt to the environment around them, governmental institutions might adapt in response to demographic shifts, technological innovations, and the changes in economic systems. Based on this perspective, Olson has argued that the growth of the welfare state was an inevitable consequence of an increasingly complex environment.

Demographic changes (population growth, urbanization, heterogeneity), it has been argued, create pressures for governmental growth by increasing the number of claimants, by undermining traditional primary groups like tribe and family that served as alternate providers of security, by increasing the need to regulate external spillovers from individual actions,[22] and by generating a greater need for institutions of social control such as policing. Technological innovation (growing complexity, speeding rate of change, public health and medical advances, the deadliness and sophistication of weaponry), it is argued, creates pressures for governmental growth by increasing the need for – and the power that accrues to – public investment in knowledge and expertise.[23] The

---

[22] Mancur Olson writes that

> The types of collective goods and externalities with which governments have to deal are not only diverse in their scope and locale, but are presumably also becoming more numerous and important over time. As population, urbanization, and congestion increase, external diseconomies almost certainly increase too. For example, the farmer in a sparsely settled area who is careless about disposing of his garbage, or who has a noisy household, or who decides to go off to work just when everybody else does, creates no problems for anybody else, whereas the same behavior in a crowded city imposes costs upon others.
> *The Logic of Collective Action* (Cambridge, MA: Harvard University Press, 1971), Appendix p. 172.

[23] "As economic development proceeds and technology becomes more advanced, it is probably also true that education and research become relatively more important, and many types of education and research appear to provide significant benefits to the society in addition to those for which the educated person or researcher is rewarded financially." Olson, *The Logic of Collective Action*, p. 172.

development of modern industrial techniques, it is further suggested, generated economies of scale that have favored larger units in both private and public sector, increased the geographic range of spillover effects from private transactions, sustained classes of physically dependent citizens, and finally made spiraling capital and R&D expenditures a necessary component of national defense. The evolution of economic systems (concentration of corporate power, increased mobility of capital, inter-twining of national economies, dependence of business upon a public infrastructure and regulated monetary and financial environment), it is asserted, has made a larger state apparatus necessary lest the public sector be out-muscled or outmaneuvered by private actors pursuing narrower interests at the expense of national goals.

Flora and Heidenheimer's *The Development of Welfare States in Europe and America* (1981) provides a good illustration of this functionalist –environmentalist perspective. They argue against linking the basic definition of the welfare state to a particular collection of policies or a par-ticular national model such as Great Britain. Rather, the welfare state should be understood "as an answer to basic and long-term develop-mental processes and the problems created by them" and "as an answer to the growing needs and demands for socioeconomic security in the context of an increasing division of labor, the expansion of markets, and the loss of 'security functions' by families and other communities."[24]

Marxists and neo-marxists such as Castells, Gough and O'Connor argue that the state intervenes to ensure continued capital accumulation, the conditions which enable the reproduction of labor power and for reasons of social and political legitimation.[25] In some ways, they see state intervention as response to market failures which threaten to undermine continued capital accumulation as a result of a failure to ensure the repro-duction of labor power. Thus, poor housing conditions, poor health and poor education provision for the working class eventually necessitate state intervention. The extent to which the state intervenes, and the timing of such intervention is, however, seen as a result of the balance of class forces at a particular time. Most social policy analysts from this perspective, tend to argue, however, that in most European countries there was a

[24] Peter Flora and Arnold J. Heidenheimer, eds., *The Development of Welfare States in Europe and America* (1981; New Brunswick: Transaction, 1984), p. 8.

[25] C. Offe, "The Theory of the Capitalist State and the Problem of Policy Formation," in L. Lindberg, et al., eds., *Stress and Contradiction in Modern Capitalism* (London: Lexington Books, 1975), pp. 125–144; M. Castells, "Advanced Capitalism, Collective Consumption and Urban Contradictions," in ibid.; B. Fine and L. Harris, "State Expenditure in Advanced Capitalism, a Critique," *New Left Review*, 98 (1976), 97–112; I. Gough, *The Political Economy of the Welfare State* (London: Macmillan, 1979); J. O'Connor, *The Fiscal Crisis of the State* (New York: St Martins Press, 1973).

strong pressure for greater state intervention in welfare provision after both World Wars.

Domestic political pressures

Without denying the importance of broad environmental shifts, some analysts argue that the growth of the welfare state must ultimately be explained by reference to internal political pressures. Some of these analysts emphasize the role of political culture and changing conceptions of the legitimacy of state action. Others emphasize changes in political processes and the way interests come to be mobilized into organized, demand-making groups.

Political culture approaches point to broad shifts in those societal values and habits of perception that influence the manner in which citizens set the boundaries between the public and private spheres. Political culture may account for the growth of the state if citizens have become gradually more accepting of a shared communal responsibility or if they have become gradually inured to the cramping of their individual prerogatives by an expanding governmental apparatus. Such shifts are sometimes explained as the result of the natural hierarchy of basic human needs. As industrial societies succeed in meeting the immediate physiological and safety needs of their citizens, they bring to the fore higher order needs relating to belongingness, esteem, and self-actualization.[26] These "post-materialist" values help define a constituency for the "helping" and "collective" dimensions of the welfare state.[27] James Q. Wilson and Edward Banfield, for example, suggest that some subcultures among voters "are more disposed than others to rest their choices on some conception of 'the public interest' or the 'welfare of the community'."[28] They turn to this notion of a public-regarding culture to account for their finding that some groups are willing to support government initiatives (such as bond referenda to construct hospitals and expand sewer facilities) even when they are unlikely directly to benefit from those initiatives and their tax contribution is likely to provide disproportionate support for them. To the extent that additional groups may gradually be acculturated into such a public–regarding perspective – something

---

[26] Such perspectives build on the theories of A. H. Maslow, *Motivation and Personality* (New York: Harper, 1954). See also Christian Bay, *The Structure of Freedom* (Stanford, CA: Stanford University Press, 1958).

[27] Ronald Ingelhart, *Culture Shift in Advanced Industrial Society* (Princeton: Princeton University Press, 1990).

[28] "Public-Regardedness as a Value Premise in Voting Behavior," *American Political Science Review*, 58 (December 1964), 876.

Wilson and Banfield expect to be a concomitant of growing affluence[29] – gradually spiraling support for governmental spending can be anticipated.[30]

Peacock and Wiseman offer a version of the view that domestic values and expectations operate to create inexorable pressure for a larger state.[31] They emphasize the role of external disturbances (such as wars) as the stimulus for an expansion of government which then alters people's ideas about acceptable levels.

People will accept, in times of crisis, methods of raising revenue formerly thought intolerable, and the acceptance of new tax levels remains when the disturbance has disappeared . . . Expenditures which the government may have thought desirable before the disturbance, but which it did not then dare to implement, consequently become possible. At the same time, social upheavals impose new and continuing obligations on governments both as the aftermath of functions assumed in wartime . . . and as the result of changes in social ideas.[32]

Others explained the apparently inexorable growth of government by "laws" that seem to characterize the processes through which groups' interests are recognized, articulated, legitimated, responded to, and institutionalized. Political demand explanations tend to focus on changes in political culture and values, the dynamics of voter mobilization, or the role of organized interest groups.

Especially important for the last of these are the processes by which interests join together to influence how government establishes its priorities. Given the processes by which demands are generated and sustained in pluralistic, democratic societies, some argue that "there is a systematic political imbalance between those who desire more spending and those who desire less . . ."[33] The imbalance may exist in electoral and pressure group arenas. Elections are designed to respond to majorities, and, since the majority of citizens are likely to have lower than average incomes, elections may become a source of spiraling pressures for a stronger govern-

---

[29] The premise that there is general movement toward the values associated with public-regardedness is stated most clearly in Banfield's *The Unheavenly City Revisited* (Boston: Little, Brown, 1974). Banfield refers to "middle-class-ification" and worries that it may lead to an overly eager readiness to define minor social problems as major crises and to insist upon massive governmental interventions where (Banfield believes) such interventions are likely to fail (pp. 284–285).

[30] Moreover, the very existence of such groups makes government more effective and reinforce the positive view of government: Robert Putnam, *Making Democracy Work* (Princeton: Princeton University Press, 1993).

[31] Alan T. Peacock and Jack Wiseman, *The Growth of Public Expenditures in the United Kingdom*, 2nd edn (London: Allen and Unwin, 1967).   [32] *Ibid.*, p. xxiv.

[33] Stuart M. Butler, *Privatizing Federal Spending: A Strategy to Eliminate the Deficits* (New York: Universe Books, 1985), p. 2.

mental redistributory role. According to Melzer and Richard, this leads to a situation in which politicians "attract voters with incomes near the median by offering benefits . . . that impose a net cost upon those [fewer in number] with incomes above the median."[34]

When the benefits of governmental expenditures are concentrated on easily identifiable groups, and the costs of those expenditures spread broadly and obscured by a complex system of revenue raising, the beneficiaries presumably have a stronger incentive to invest their energies in collective action to protect and expand the programs in which they have a stake. Although public choice theorists have been the most shrill about this pattern, it was explicitly recognized by Schattschneider over fifty years ago. Schattschneider noted that industries favoring higher tariff duties were more likely to mobilize to influence policy deliberations than were the many other industries that did not stand to benefit and might be indirectly harmed.[35] Once organized, such interest groups are in a better position to institutionalize their presence, for example by establishing selective incentives to members,[36] by taking advantage of speedier access to information, and through readier access to policy makers. Pro-spending interests, moreover, may form coalitions of convenience with service providers and program administrators to protect or expand programs beyond the level justified by efficiency or needs.

Cameron, in a variation on the argument, sees a correlation of the growth of the public sector with increased openness of the economy, as groups vulnerable to the world market mobilize to achieve welfare state compensations for hardships brought by international trade.[37] Katzenstein takes this further, by arguing that vulnerability due to openness not only contributes to increased state intervention, but also, in tandem with some historical predispositions, transforms the interest group structure (corporatism), which in turn reinforces the tendency toward increased public sector interventions.[38] The result, some argue, is a "ratchet effect," in which governmental expenditures continually are nudged to higher levels by new and existing group demands but are prevented from contracting when needs and demands diminish.

---

[34] "Why Government Grows (and Grows) in a Democracy," *Public Interest* no. 52 (Summer 1978), 111–118. See also Samuel Brittan, "The Economic Contradictions of Democracy," *British Journal of Political Science*, 5 (1975), 129–159.

[35] *Politics, Pressures and the Tariff* (Englewood Cliffs, NJ: Prentice-Hall, 1935).

[36] Olson, *The Logic of Collective Action*.

[37] David R. Cameron, "The Expansion of the Public Economy: A Comparative Analysis," *American Political Science Review*, 72 (December 1978), 1243–1261.

[38] Peter J. Katzenstein, *Small States in World Markets* (Ithaca: Cornell University Press, 1985). Ronald Rogowski carries the idea even further where he attributes the development of party systems to degrees of openness: "Trade and the Variety of Democratic Institutions," *International Organization*, 41 (Spring 1987), 203–223.

The rise of the developmental state

It is a matter of observation that most developed countries have significant redistributional mechanisms, which collectively have come to be known as the welfare state. While this is, for all practical purposes, a universal phenomenon of the industrial world, many countries have state institutions which developed as mechanisms of capital accumulation. Most famously, the economic historian, Alexander Gerschenkron, recognized that countries that industrialized after Great Britain tended to have larger public sectors and that the later a country industrialized, the larger and more obtrusive its state institutions.[39] He reasoned that the later a country industrialized, the greater the gap between the developing country and the already developed ones with which it intended to compete. With surplus capital a rare and highly dispersed commodity in agricultural societies, those countries which had, or could create, institutions for gathering and centralizing capital were more likely to develop competitive industries. Thus, Germany and France had greater public sectors than Britain or the USA, Japan more so than Germany or France, and Russia the largest and most repressive of all.

In a sense this is an argument about macroeconomic market failure. Markets left to their own devices will not necessarily lead agricultural producers to shift to industry and economies will remain in a low-income macroeconomic equilibrium without state intervention. While neoclassical economists have debated this conclusion, it is the received wisdom in comparative political economy.[40] Moreover, the consequences of state intervention have been not only economic development but the creation of a stratum of new economic actors with a stake in that intervention. Guizot's invitation to his supporters, "*Enrichissez-vous*," is suggestive: new state undertakings were differential in their benefits. Of course, while the most visible to benefit were the new public sector employees, the more important beneficiaries were in the private sector. Some strata benefited from subsidies, some from protection and some from cheap inputs produced by nationalized firms. In short, the developmental state created its own constituency.

---

[39] Alexander Gerschenkron, "Economic Backwardness in Historical Perspective," the title essay in his collection *Economic Backwardness in Historical Perspective* (Cambridge, MA: Harvard University Press, 1962), pp. 1–30.

[40] See for example, Peter J. Katzenstein, "Conclusion", in Katzenstein, ed., *Between Power and Plenty* (Madison: Wisconsin University Press, 1978); Peter Gourevitch, "The Second Image Reversed," *International Organization*, 32 (Autumn 1978), 881–912; James R. Kurth, "The Political Consequences of the Product Cycle: Industrial History and Political Outcomes," *International Organization*, 33 (Winter 1979), 1–34; John Zysman, *Governments, Markets and Growth* (Ithaca: Cornell University Press, 1983).

Internal dynamics: bureaucratic imperialism and theories of public choice

The notion that government might nurture the seeds of its own expansion is not novel. For many years, the battle between personal liberty and a seemingly unquenchable governmental thirst for power and control was an overriding concern of Western democratic theorists such as John Stuart Mill and Alexis de Tocqueville. The establishment of a legal framework for protecting citizens' rights and the bureaucratization of government during the nineteenth and twentieth centuries somewhat diminished the intensity of these concerns. The formal apparatus of democracy encouraged an image of government as a mechanism for registering citizens' preferences, instead of shaping and constraining them. And the institution of a hierarchical, professionalized civil service encouraged an image of governmental apparatus as a neutral tool for implementing publicly defined goals.[41] Thus, governmental growth came to be seen in many countries as an extension of the popular will, rather than as an independent force standing in opposition to personal liberty.

Over the past twenty-five years, however, there have emerged several theoretical perspectives that once again give life to the notion of government as an independent actor capable of sustaining momentum toward its own expansion. Some of the relevant groundwork for this perspective was laid by sociologists and others with an interest in organizational theory. But the more controversial formulations are identified with public choice theories and theories about the autonomous state.

"Prior to the twentieth century," writes William T. Gormley, Jr., "neither bureaucratic discretion nor bureaucratic authority was much of an issue in the United States."[42] The Progressive Movement of the early 1900s began to change that, through its successful promotion of institutional reforms intended to insulate bureaucrats from political pressures. The New Deal, during the 1930s and 1940s, took matters further. Whereas the Progressives sought bureaucratic autonomy, Gormley suggests that the New Dealers sought bureaucratic empowerment. Federal agencies were provided strong staffs and delegated presidential authority in order better to serve Franklin Roosevelt's goals of instituting aggressive reforms; when Roosevelt's death and the end of World War II left the

---

[41] See the discussion in Joel Aberbach, Robert Putnam, and Bert Rockman, *Bureaucrats and Politicians in Western Democracies* (Cambridge, MA: Harvard University Press, 1981), ch. 1, and Colin Campbell, *Managing the Presidency* (Pittsburgh: University of Pittsburgh Press, 1986), ch. 1.

[42] *Taming the Bureaucracy* (Princeton, NJ: Princeton University Press, 1989), p. 7.

White House less capable of exerting strong leadership, the bureaucratic agencies were freed to ally themselves with others to form powerful "sub-governments."

Reflecting this growing autonomy and power of public agencies, analytic theories in public administration and the social sciences began to reconsider bureaucracy as an independent actor which could exert pressure as well as record it, pursue its own values as well as carry out programs in the name of others.[43] James Q. Wilson credits Chester I Barnard as being the first to draw attention to the importance of organizational maintenance.[44] Early organizational theorists like Barnard focused primarily on business organizations. Later, sociologists like Amitai Etzioni extended the perspective to account for the behavior of voluntary organizations. Still later attention switched to government itself. Wilson, along with Edward Banfield, found it useful to look at political parties – and particularly the partisan underpinnings of urban machines – as having distinct interests in retaining power and as using the prerogatives of authority to further that narrow aim.[45] Others extended the perspective to bureaucracies' budgetary battles.[46] Symbolic of a gradual reorientation in the way bureaucracies came to be perceived is the shift from an emphasis on "agency capture" (in which governmental units are perceived to be manipulated by the stronger and more purposeful private organizations they are intended to regulate) to those of "iron triangles"(defined by mutual interests among key legislators, bureaucratic regulators, and powerful private interests) and "regime" (which sees governmental units as equal partners in governing coalitions

---

[43] We will argue later that theories and ideas sometimes *lead* events. Aggressive new initiatives were limited, but built-in pressures from entitlement programs and the expansion of key beneficiary groups (especially the elderly) made inaction tantamount to the continuation of expansion. That governmental expansion continued even in the face of economic slowdown seemed to validate claims that growth was irresistible and self-sustaining. At the same time, however, it fed a sense of an impending day of reckoning in some quarters. Intense disappointment in the Reagan presidency was expressed by many conservatives in spite of Reagan's substantial legislative successes during his first term. Reagan's early popularity and legislative momentum represented a rare opportunity to undertake structural reforms that would permanently unravel the welfare state coalition, but this opportunity was squandered in the minds of some (for more, see chapter 4). It was not until after the 1979 election that the Thatcher administration really began putting privatization into practice.

[44] Wilson credits Barnard's *The Functions of the Executive* (Cambridge, MA: Harvard University Press, 1938), in his *Political Organizations* (New York: Basic Books, 1973), p. 30. [45] *City Politics* (Cambridge, MA: Harvard University Press, 1963).

[46] Aaron Wildavsky, *The Politics of the Budgetary Process* (Boston: Little, Brown, 1984); Francis E. Rourke, *Bureaucracy, Politics, and Public Policy* (Boston: Little, Brown, 1969), and Matthew Holden Jr. " 'Imperialism' in Bureaucracy," *American Political Science Review*, 60 (Dec. 1968).

that protect their shared interest while proclaiming allegiance to a public good).[47]

The European tradition, manifested in figures as diverse as Napoleon Bonaparte and Max Weber, has mostly been noted for its advocacy of strong and professional bureaucracy. However, there is also a skeptical European current that goes at least as far back as Robert Michels' 1915 work *Political Parties*. While noting the tendency toward an "iron rule of oligarchy" in which the bureaucracy raises itself above the public from which it derives its mandate, Michels' did not believe that genuine popular control was a realistic alternative. Efforts to rein in bureaucracy through rules and regulation would, in the final analysis, only serve to increase the leverage and discretion of the bureaucrats who are the true masters of such an environment.

Thinking of governmental agencies as organizations with their own goals of maintenance and expansion seemingly helped to explain the phenomenon of steady, incremental growth in public budgets. By assuming that bureaucracies are interested in nonmaterial incentives such as power, status and control, organizational theorists could extend their explanations to account for regulatory expansion as well.

Because organization theory drew its conceptual orientation from sociology, it found it natural to think of social units, like bureaucracies, as having interests of their own, distinct from those of the individuals whom they comprised. Public choice theory, based in economics, rested its explanation of governmental expansion on individuals' pursuit of self-interests but, like organization theory, the public choice perspective traced the impetus toward governmental growth to internal factors.[48]

Public choice theorists argue that the activities of politicians, governmental bureaucrats, and voters can be understood in much the same way as economists try to understand the behavior of business firms and consumers. Like business firms, politicians have a product to sell. For the most part, that product consists of material favors distributed by government to the areas and groups that make up the politician's constituency.

---

[47] For an early elucidation of the agency capture thesis, see Marver H. Bernstein, *Regulating Business by Independent Commission* (Princeton: Princeton University Press, 1955). On iron triangles and subgovernments, see for example, Arthur Maas, *Muddy Waters: The Army Engineers and the Nation's Rivers* (Cambridge, MA: Harvard University Press, 1951) and Douglas Cater, *Power in Washington* (New York: Random House, 1964). On regimes, see Stephen L. Elkin, *City and Regime in the American Republic* (Chicago: University of Chicago Press, 1987).

[48] Among the relevant works are: James M. Buchanan and Gordon Tullock, *The Calculus of Consent* (Ann Arbor: University of Michigan Press, 1962); William A. Niskanen, *Bureaucracy and Representative Government* (Chicago: Aldine-Atherton, 1971); E. S. Savas, *Privatizing the Public Sector* (Chatham, NJ: Chatham House, 1982).

To be elected, in other words, politicians must promise new governmental expenditures; to remain in office, they must deliver on those promises. Bureaucrats, for their part, seek to maximize "salary, perquisites of the office, public reputation, power, patronage, output of the bureau, ease of making changes and ease in managing the bureau,"[49] and these for the most part tend to expand along with the agency's budget. Although public choice theory, in the final analysis, makes much the same predictions about governmental behavior as organization theory, its impact has been greater. This can be attributed in part to the greater stature currently accorded by many to economics over sociology, and in part to its readier adaptation to mathematical and modeling techniques that seem to lend an air of objectivity and sophistication to its otherwise straightforward accounts.

In addition, public choice theory adds an appreciation of the concept of "public monopoly." Corporate monopolies, because they dominate the market in the goods they provide, are under little pressure to be efficient or responsive to consumer demands. Where government is the dominant provider – e.g. elementary and secondary education, utilities, urban services – the situation is even worse. The consumer who is unhappy with a private monopoly has the option at least to boycott the offending service, but the citizen who is unhappy with a public monopoly is forced by law to continue paying (through taxes) even for those services he or she does not use. In addition, while the cost of services provided by private monopolies may be inflated, they are, at least, known: consumers are billed for products they receive.[50] Because citizens cannot readily trace the links between the taxes they pay and the particular services the government provides, public monopolies can mask their wastefulness more easily.

The semi-autonomous state

Public choice theory is an outgrowth from classical liberalism, its advocates sharing with their predecessors the assumption that politics can be understood in terms of individuals' rational self-interest. Moreover, it assumes personal aggrandizement to be an inherent goal of human nature, requiring no explanation. These assumptions have yielded the anti-statist conclusions noted above.

Marxists and "neo-institutionalists" have also looked at the state crit-

---

[49] Niskanen, *Bureaucracy and Representative Government*, p. 103.
[50] Buchanan, in Borcherding, cites finding by W. C. Stubblebine (research for The Foundation for Research in Economics and Education) found citizens underestimate the true costs of state-local programs by a factor as high as 2/3.(11)

ically, although in the case of latter, not necessarily with hostility.[51] These scholars responding to Marxist thought elaborated a perspective with three central components: (1) while economic elites retain disproportionate influence over governmental operations, that influence is attenuated; (2) the state has institutional interests distinct from those of external supporters and distinct from the personal ambitions of members of its bureaucracy; and (3) the state possesses resources of power of its own.[52]

The influence of economic elites is attenuated by uncertainty regarding what constitutes the interest of capital in concrete instances, by divisions of interest within the capitalist class, and by the fact that working class and other noneconomic interests under certain conditions represent a powerful counterbalance. It is one thing to presume that owners of capital have a common interest in preserving the legal, political, and economic institutions that permit them to prosper. But to move from such an abstract common interest to concerted elite or class action on specific initiatives is highly problematic in our uncertain world. Will making a progressive income tax moderately less regressive benefit capital by stimulating aggregate demand or will it spark a political backlash? The capacity of elites to foretell the consequences of alternative political courses is limited, making them as vulnerable as the masses – or at least nearly so – to hesitation, disagreement, and miscalculation. Mobile capital, moreover, may have fundamentally different interests than capital that is spatially constrained by market, labor, or natural resource requirements. Economic elites who benefit from the value of land – landlords, mortgage lenders, realtors, and the like – may often find their interests at odds with other economic elites whose commitments to particular locations are wholly contingent.[53] Declining industries do not have the same objective interests as growing ones.

When the institutional interests of the state do diverge from those of other powerful actors, the "autonomous state" literature suggests that the state has sufficient resources of its own to ensure that it can pursue those interests with some effectiveness. Some of the state's resources are traced to its formal status. As John Mollenkopf puts it, "However constrained, states are sovereign, exercise a monopoly on the legitimate use of force,

---

[51] For a review of some of this literature, see especially Martin Carnoy, *The State and Political Theory* (Princeton, NJ: Princeton University Press, 1984) For a critique of the neo-institutionalists, see Paul Commack, "Review Article: Bringing the State Back In?" *British Journal of Political Science*, 19 (April 1989), 261–290.

[52] For a review of the debates on this last point, see G. William Domhoff, *The Power Elite and the State* (New York: William De Gruyter, 1990), ch. 1.

[53] Harvey L. Molotch "The City as Growth Machine," *American Journal of Sociology*, 82 (September 1976), 309–330; John R. Logan and Harvey L. Molotch, *Urban Fortunes: The Political Economy of Place* (Berkeley: University of California Press, 1987).

establish the juridical basis for private property, and shape economic development in myriad ways."[54] Beyond these formal powers, state managers may have monopoly of certain types of information, benefit from a reputation for expertise, are able to wield in their favor various symbols of authority, and in many instances may be insulated from external forces by civil service protections and earmarked sources of revenue.

Like the public choice perspective, theories about the semi-autonomous state see the internal needs of the state as a principal engine of its growth. But, unlike the public choice perspective, this approach also sees state growth as responding to pressures from business interests and even sporadically mobilized working class groups. It is the conflict between capitalists and the working class, combined with divisions among elites, that allow state managers strategically to get maximal effect out of their own distinct resources, despite the fact that the State – as traditional Marxists emphasize – is ultimately dependent upon the continued productivity of the economic sphere.[55]

Rethinking theories of the state

For all of their differences, most major theories of state growth spoke in a language of universalism and determinism. While recognizing that some nations had developed more extensive and modern governmental social programs and governmental institutions to support them, the tendency was to think of this as a matter of timing: some nations simply were ahead of others in making the transition.

The emergence of privatization as an apparently viable counter-force challenges this imagery. As we suggest in the next section, coming to grips with privatization can lead us to a better understanding of the ways in which the growth of the state may be conditional, rather than determined, and how its shape may shift and diverge, rather than being universal. We argue against jettisoning the insights of these earlier theories, however. It is our sense that one of the clearest failings of the contemporary literature on privatization is its overeagerness to construct its understandings *de nova* – as if the phenomenon of privatization represents so sharp a break with the past that we must wipe clean our cognitive slates and unhinge our speculations of the future of the state from our previous understandings of its growth. A more appropriate respect for the insights pro-

---

[54] "Who (or What) Runs Cities, and How?" *Sociological Forum*, 4, 1 (1989), 119–137.
[55] Fred Block, "The Ruling Class does not Rule: Notes on the Marxist Theory of the State," *Socialist Review*, 33 (1977); Theda Skocpol, "Political Responses to Capitalist Crisis: Neo-Marxist Theories of the State and the New Deal," *Politics and Society*, 10, 2 (1981), 155–201.

vided by theories about the growth of the state, we also argue, can lead to a better understanding of the potential bounds to privatization.

Using privatization to better understand the growth of the state

From determinism to conditionalism

"Conditional" explanations represent a broad theoretical alternative to deterministic theories that narrow the range for strategic intervention. Conditional explanations portray the current scope of governmental authority as the result of prior and continuing battles, compromises, and concessions among competing interests. Because the relative power of the competing interests depends on variable factors – shifting resources, evolving institutions, changing ideas – the outcome of future battles cannot readily be predicted. And, because many of the key factors potentially are manipulable through concerted action, there is a substantial role to be played by group strategy and governmental policy.

Conditionalism is premised on the belief that governments make choices, that these choices matter, and that – while they may be constrained by environmental conditions, economic elites, relative class power, and institutional rules and habits – these choices are substantially influenced by situational and short-term forces including shifting resources, group tactics, leadership, ideology, evidence, and ideas. Ultimately, moreover, even structural parameters are subject to purposeful change. To argue that governments make choices requires rejecting any structural-functional perspective that implies that there is only one "solution" to the confluence of opportunities and constraints that the environment presents. Some statistical analyses of policy outputs seem to account for much of the variation across jurisdictions using independent variables relating primarily to economic and demographic factors.[56] But these studies tend to define policy in fairly crude budgetary terms. When redistributive aspects of policies, and issues of the timing and scope of social welfare measures are taken into account, it appears that jurisdictions facing similar environments have considerable leeway to shape their own specific responses.

To argue that governmental choices matter means to establish that the existing range of policy outputs generates some substantial differences in policy outcomes. In addition to recognizing the open-ended nature of the

[56] E.g., Harold L. Wilensky *The Welfare State and Equality* (Berkeley: University of California Press, 1974) for cross national evidence; Thomas R. Dye, *Politics, Economics and the Public* (Chicago: Rand McNally, 1966) for evidence across the fifty US states.

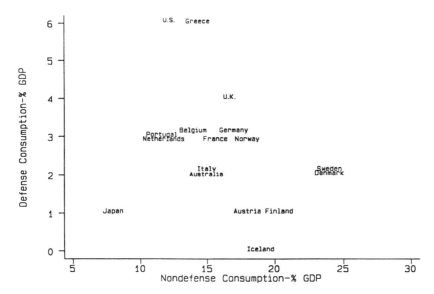

Figure 1.3 Defense vs nondefense consumption as a percentage of GDP

battle to define the public sector's role, a conditional approach acknowledges that states can take different *forms*, as well as different sizes. In figure 1.3 we illustrate this by separating defense spending from other parts of the public sector. The resulting scattergram suggests why it can be misleading to think of state growth as the culmination of a single trend or a product of universal pressures; states of equal size may allocate their energies and resources differently, and these qualitative distinctions may be at least as important as those attended to when one simply looks at expenditures, or tax burdens, or number of public sector employees. Industrial advance meets with international conflict, ideological predisposition and group interest in a variety of ways. Among other things, this opens to us the possibility that differences in the particular *shape* of the state encountered across counties may represent meaningful alternatives, not simply national eccentricities.

To argue that situational and short-term political forces make a difference means to claim that neither the array of external groups nor the internal pressures for expansion are sufficient in and of themselves to account for the options that governments chose. And, to argue that structural constraints are themselves subject to manipulation through purposive action is to insist that the definition, production, and distribution of resources, information, and access can be the result of public policies as well as the shapers of those policies.

*Privatization as policy reversal: toward a more sophisticated
understanding of the relationships among institutions, interests,
and ideas*

Many observers of public policy in industrialized nations have noted a
strong tendency toward incrementalism, or gradualism. Policy typically
changes in small steps, and change is often restricted within a relatively
narrow range. This incrementalism is sometimes attributed to the
dynamic interplay among interest groups in pluralistic societies; the
mobilization of one set of interests seems often to spark the mobilization
of countervailing forces.[57] Institutions are also seen to play a role. By frag-
menting authority, institutional separations among levels of government,
branches of government, and functionally organized bureaucracies seem
to multiply potential veto points, making it easier to derail new initiatives
than to get them off the ground. Institutions and interests reinforce one
another, too, as when existing programs develop tight constituencies that
are dedicated to their maintenance – "iron triangles," comprising elected
officials who rely on the programs as a source of patronage and a symbol
of their efficacy, governmental bureaucrats who rely on them for their jobs
and sense of purpose, and interest groups that rely on them for access to
public resources, valued points of access, and a buffer against incursions
by competing groups.[58]

The rather sudden emergence of privatization on the international
agenda appears to challenge such images of gradualism, resembling more
closely the pattern that Baumgartner and Jones refer to as "punctuated
equilibrium."[59] Although stability and incrementalism may characterize
polities for sustained periods, Baumgartner and Jones point out that sharp
and substantial changes often do take place. Such sharp reversals are not
readily accounted for by pluralistic models of interest groups; such models
presume that policy reflects a relative equilibrium among interests, and
typically rely on some sharp external shock (war, economic depression) to
account for new interests or sudden shifts in resources among long-standing combatants. Elitist, or stratified, models – which presume a dominant
interest rooted in class, race, or control over the instruments of government – are even less equipped to explain why the deck of power might be
suddenly reshuffled in a way that allows previously subordinate interests
to challenge tradition and the status quo. And models that emphasize the
constraining effects of institutions are no help at all.

[57] David Truman, *The Governmental Process* (New York : Alfred A. Knopf, 1951).
[58] Theodore Lowi, *The End of Liberalism* (New York: Norton, 1979).
[59] Frank R. Baumgartner and Bryan D. Jones, *Agendas and Instability in American Politics* (Chicago: University of Chicago Press, 1993).

Largely in response to the limited utility of traditional interest-based and institution-based explanations in accounting for sharp policy reversals, scholars have more recently increased their attention to the role of theory and ideas in altering the political landscape.[60] By changing the way that groups define problems and evaluate their own interests, new theories and ideas have the potential to rapidly shift political battle lines.

On the face of it, the "privatization revolution" provides further support for this growing interest in ideas as meaningful independent variables. Certainly, some of the proponents of privatization have attributed its rapid diffusion to broad social learning and power of the ideas; they argue that the economic theories behind privatization have helped policymakers and citizens to shed a kind of false consciousness that made them overly reliant on government, too quick to see social spending as the avenue to prosperity, and blinded them to the waste, and oppression that the modern welfare-state had come to represent.[61]

Like others who have found them to be a potent explanation for policy reversals, we find that shifting ideas and emergent theories play a key role in the case studies of the politics of privatization that we will present. But relying on the sweep of new ideas to account for political change can be overly seductive. What are presented as new ideas are often old notions that have been suddenly given new voice; in such cases, it is not the ideas, but altered conditions, that account for subsequent change.[62] Much of the theoretical infrastructure for privatization predated the current boom by decades. Many of the key themes were sharply articulated by Milton Friedman over twenty-five years ago.[63] Some see the roots running deeper, to the writings of Ludvig von Mises and Friedrich von Hayek in the 1920s and 1930s.[64] Still others push the quest back two centuries to Adam Smith;[65] undoubtedly, some would excavate deeper still. As Kingdon warns, there is a danger of infinite regress whenever one sets out to seek intellectual origins of contemporary policies: "When one starts to

---

[60] In addition to Baumgartner and Jones, *Agendas and Instability*, see: John W. Kingdon, "Ideas, Politics, and Public Policies," paper prepared for delivery at the 1988 Annual Meeting of the American Political Science Association, Washington, D.C., September 1–4, 1988; Peter A. Hall, ed., *The Political Power of Economic Ideas: Keynsianism Across Nations* (Princeton: Princeton University Press, 1989); David A. Rochefort and Roger W, Cobb, *The Politics of Problem Definition: Shaping the Policy Agenda* (Lawrence, KS: University of Kansas Press, 1994).

[61] E.g. Young, "Privatization Around the World."

[62] John N. Kingdon, *Agendas, Alternatives, and Public Policies* (Boston: Little, Brown, 1984).

[63] Milton Friedman, *Capitalism, Freedom and Democracy* (Chicago: University of Chicago Press, 1962).

[64] For example, Steve H. Hanke, "Privatization: Theory, Evidence, and Implementation," in C. Lowell Harriss, ed., *Control of Federal Spending* (New York: The Academy of Political Science, 1985).   [65] Linowes, *Privatization*, p. 234.

trace the history of a proposal or concern back through time, there is no logical place to stop the process."[66] The interesting question, then, is not "where did the idea come from?" but "why did it fail to gain currency until it did?"

Ideas have power only when they are rooted in constituencies that give them articulation and that mobilize behind them. Rather than pose ideas as *an alternative* to interests and institutions, we seek in this book a more sophisticated understanding of the ways in which ideas, interests, and institutions interact.

Using the growth of the state to better understand the constraints on privatization: explanatory variables and "state shrinkage"

To see the future of the state as open-ended and subject to purposive intervention and variable manifestations of power should not mean abandoning the insight that broad and powerful forces can structure the terrain on which the battles will be fought. While we will argue that differences among nations can be important, we suggest that both the growth of the state and the emergence of the privatization movement highlight the need for better understanding of the role of extra-national forces upon internal political dynamics. And, while we credit the notion that the coalitions that gave birth to the welfare state, as well as those which were the consequence of the developmental state, have weakened and fragmented in many ways, we are not so quick as others to presume that they cannot be refashioned and revived.

An hypothesis that flows from the foregoing analysis is that the size of the state is a consequence of which constituency has gained access to policy-making. If those benefiting from redistribution have lost power, a shrinking of the welfare state is a likely consequence.

Alternatively, a second hypothesis argues that states may be victims of their own success: developmental states, having successfully incubated new economic forces, become obsolete as the costs of administration and the dangers (to a privileged stratum) of redistribution begin to outweigh the advantages of state protection.

Theories about why nations behave as they do, of course, often give great weight to additional factors that vary from country to country. Among these factors are culture, national experience, indigenous institutions, economic resources, and political leadership. Clusters of nations –

---

[66] Kingdon, *Agendas*, p. 77.

defined by shared region or shared stages of development – may exhibit broadly similar patterns of behavior, but even within such clusters nation-specific variations in the key independent variables are expected to result in non-trivial differences of politics and policy. Note the tremendous differences in policies from such culturally similar countries as France, Italy and Spain; or equally the disparities in policy choices of the USA and Canada.[67]

A third hypothesis would suggest that state shrinkage is rooted in external factors. If variable domestic factors determine policy, explaining the emergence of privatization on the agenda of so many different nations at roughly the same time poses a theoretical puzzle – just as it does to theories that presented governmental growth as inexorable. One possibility, of course, is that the appearance of an international movement is misleading. Upon closer examination, some of the loudly heralded privatization initiatives prove to be less substantial and less definitive than initially presumed. As we will demonstrate, leaders' publicly stated intentions to privatize have not always resulted in approved privatization programs. Approved privatization programs have not always been implemented as envisioned. And the implementation of privatization programs has sometimes sparked political backlashes that result in the reassertion of the governmental role.

While the breadth, success, and permanence of the international privatization movement may have been exaggerated, however, the international scope of the politics of privatization is more than a mirage. While the specific manifestations and ultimate consequences vary from country to country, the movement to scale back the state is an important strain in the domestic politics of many countries of various types. The intellectual challenge to explanations rooted primarily in country-specific explanations remains.

The growing interdependence of the world economy raises the possibility that the independent causal power of domestic variables is gradually being attenuated. International organizations (like the World Bank and the IMF) and multinational interests (highly mobile corporations and international banking and investment concerns) may be taking

---

[67] On the first group of countries, see Colin Campbell, Harvey Feigenbaum, Ronald Linden, and Helmut Norpoth, *Politics and Government in Europe Today*, 2nd edn (Boston: Houghton Mifflin, 1995), ch. 37; on the North American cases, see, for example, Harvey Feigenbaum, Richard Samuels, and Kent Weaver, "Innovation, Coordination and Implementation in Energy Policy," in R. Kent Weaver and Bert A. Rockman, *Do Institutions Matter?* (Washington: The Brookings Institution, 1993), pp. 42–109.

their place, carrying policy ideas from one place to another with little sensitivity to national boundaries or local context. These international forces currently appear to be structurally undermining some of the political forces that once gave powerful support to the expansion of the state. Labor, environmental interests, and organizations representing the elderly and disadvantaged are weakened by the possibility that mobile capital will use its threat to relocate to bully and punish those nations that seek to tax them and regulate them in the name of equity, social justice, or redistribution. Conversely, the roots of the developmental state, anchored in a notion of capital shortage, are also obviated by the presence of international capital which flows easily from one development opportunity to the next.[68]

Acknowledging the substantial import of extra-national forces, however, does not mean that there are no countervailing forces worth taking into account. We see evidence in the case studies we will be presenting for a fourth hypothesis, that privatization may lose momentum, stir the resurgence of the pro-state coalition, or even generate new political forces that will successfully demand a sustained and substantial – albeit reconfigured – welfare state. Some of the countervailing factors are domestically generated; indeed, one of the strongest forces sparking resistance to privatization in some places is old-fashioned nationalism that rears up defiantly against the prospect of foreign investment. Some of the countervailing factors may be international as well. We summarize our guiding hypotheses in figure 1.4.

Why theories about governmental growth and retrenchment matter

Most debates among social scientists percolate quietly with little notice by the broader community. But others burst out of the confines of academic journals, accompanied by a level of passion that seems inconsistent with the traditional norms of scholarly discourse. Such has been the case with debates about the causes of the growth of the state, and – although the debate has not yet fully been joined – such is likely to be the case with discussions about the nature of privatization. Even when the researchers and analysts focus on the narrow empirical dimensions, these debates

---

[68] This is Ellen Commisso's fundamental explanation for the collapse of socialism. See her "Crisis in Socialism or Crisis of Socialism?" *World Politics,* 52 (July 1990), 563–607. However, such arguments can't have it both ways: Raymond Vernon argues that privatization policies were adopted in so many countries at the same time because of an international *shortage of capital.* Vernon, "Introduction," in Vernon, ed., *The Promise of Privatization* (New York: Council on Foreign Relations, 1988), p. 19.

Cause of State Growth	State Function	Cause of State Shrinkage
Industrialization	Developmental	Beneficiaries of State become competitors. Costs of State outweigh benefits
Technology & environmental pressure	Developmental	Changes in technology make possible market solutions
Growth of political power of labor, minorities, and other beneficiaries of state intervention	Welfare State Redistribution	Multinationalization weakens labor and other geographically immobile interests. International organizations encourage austerity

Figure 1.4 Hypothetical causes of state growth and shrinkage

unavoidably have implications that draw their findings onto a broader field.

The way we understand government growth and retrenchment matters, first of all, because it helps to shape the way we come to terms with the normative status of government – the question of whether the expansion of state responsibility is something to be desired or something to be regretted. When explanations of the growth of the welfare state are framed as necessary adaptations to environmental change, or as responses to democratically expressed citizen demands, or as the realization of efforts by public administrators and managers to bring about professionalization and administrative reform in the pursuit of a commonly acknowledged public good, the clear and nearly unmistakable corollary message is that governmental expansion is something to be appreciated, even celebrated.

If governmental expansion erodes societal capacity for innovation and adaptation, or if it represents responsiveness to the particular needs of a political elite at the expense of the broad masses, or if it results from the unrestrained self-interest of governmental employees in the growth of their privileges and power, the explanations carry the opposite normative punch. Theories about government growth and retraction are important, therefore, because of their relationship to evaluations of the desirability of government. Just as important as their normative consequences are their implications for assessing the prospects for reasoned, collective intervention. The way we understand government growth and retrenchment helps to shape our understanding of the extent to which the conditions that affect us are manipulable through deliberate, collectively organized action – the question of whether citizens can hope to reshape government to more effectively meet a broad range of human needs or whether its scope of potential intervention is sharply limited by external economic constraints.

The dominant explanations of governmental growth have been deterministic; by emphasizing forces outside of direct human control they allow for little likelihood that patterns of governmental expansion can be altered. Most of these deterministic explanations are linked to a projection of continued growth, although some suggest the pattern may be cyclical or self-limiting. Albert O. Hirschman, for example, argues that societies move through alternating patterns of commitment to public and private values. Periods of collective pursuit of public values stimulate expansion of the social welfare functions of government, but these periods ultimately lead to periods of disappointment and exhaustion and the consequent return to a preoccupation with personal interests and material desires.[69] Yet, these too ultimately disappoint, Hirschman suggests, resulting in a cyclical pattern of governmental expansion and contraction. Other explanations, while seeing growth as rooted in powerful forces and well-entrenched institutions, hold out the possibility for reversal through extraordinary intervention, such as might follow severe fiscal crisis or radical constitutional and administrative reform.

We do not set out, in this book, to answer the thorny question of whether government is good or bad. Indeed, the political perspective that we develop ultimately rejects the premise that government necessarily must be one or the other. The normative status of the state depends upon the procedures it adopts and the uses to which they are put – and these, in turn, are not predetermined but are defined by open-ended and contingent battles among competing interests. But the manner in which theories about the growth of government interweave with normative perspectives about the legitimacy of the state makes it unlikely that any extended treatment of privatization can remain aloof from such controversial issues. Accommodating theories of the state to take the privatization movement into account almost certainly requires – at least, eventually – normative conclusions.

We do, however, hope to provide some insights into the nature of the factors accounting for state growth and decline, and in doing so we are animated by a desire to better understand both the possibilities and the limits upon purposeful political action. In considering the politics of privatization, we are led to a greater appreciation of the open-ended and contingent nature of the collective enterprise through which we define and pursue societal interests. In place of a vision of privatization as an inexorable and universal phenomenon that reflects the truth of economic

[69] Albert O. Hirschman, *Shifting Involvement* (Princeton: Princeton University Press, 1982).

laws and their power of revelation, we offer a view of privatization as a political battleground, where outcomes remain uncertain, where victories and losses may depend on local terrain, and where ideas play an important role but not an independent one.

2   The political underpinnings of privatization

In chapter I we noted that literature in political science of the 1960s and 1970s would not have predicted the privatization movement of the 1980s and 1990s. Most analysts were struck by the growth of the welfare state and focused on theories that would explain its rise. While writers anchored in the disciplines of political science, public administration and public choice economics were not uncritical of the highly interventionist states that grew up in virtually all developed countries, there was little in their explanations that would have predicted a turnabout in the 1980s. In this chapter we return to these theoretical perspectives to capture their respective views and consequent advocacy of the privatization movement. Because policies are not always what they seem, and because all policies affect citizens unevenly, with some benefiting and others losing, we think it is useful to look at how privatization reaches the agenda of different political actors.

Essentially, it is our contention that the very mixed bag of policies which broadly fit under the rubric of privatization can best be categorized in terms of the motives of their advocates. The extensiveness and diversity of privatization policies, found in countries as different as United States and Uzbekistan, can be understood by relating the policy outcomes to a variety of political agendas. For this reason we offer a typology of privatizations based on the politics which underpin them. Moreover, because policies can have unforeseen results, we also consider at the end of this chapter alternative scenarios by which privatizations have unintended political consequences.

Privatization, defined broadly in chapter I as "the shifting of a function, either in whole or in part, from the public sector to the private sector,"[1] involves the increased reliance on private actors and market forces to pursue social goals. We argue that in shifting responsibilities from government to market, privatization alters the institutional framework through which citizens, companies and organizations articulate, mediate, and promote their individual and shared interests. While the specific conse-

---

[1] Stuart Butler, "Privatization for Public Purposes," in William T. Gormley, Jr., ed., *Privatization and Its Alternatives* (Madison: University of Wisconsin Press, 1991), p. 17.

quences of such an institutional restructuring are uncertain, few could doubt that major consequences would ensue. In a more privatized arena, some groups would find their interests more clearly defined and more readily promoted. Other groups would find the opposite. This conflict of goals and interests is, of course, the essence of politics. Yet most of the literature which purports to analyze, but often advocates, privatization policies sees these as either pragmatic adjustments emerging out of a process of apolitical problem solving, or as the necessary result of economic logic. We label these the Administrative and Economic perspectives on privatization, and we examine them first.

The administrative and economic perspectives

The administrative perspective

The administrative perspective presents privatization as a series of options available to public officials seeking to make government work better. In the United States, particularly, discussion of privatization has frequently reflected this "good government" orientation. This orientation presumes the existence of a relatively well-specified set of public goals. Such public goals are broadly accepted as legitimate, because they have emerged from democratic processes, deliberation by acknowledged experts, or assertion by recognized authorities. With public goals clear and accepted, the central task for public officials is to pursue rationally the most efficient and effective means to those ends.

Privatization, from the administrative perspective, represents a "toolbox" of techniques, from which officials may draw the most appropriate to meet the tasks at hand. Among the tools available are contracting out, user fees, vouchers, asset sales, and load-shedding. The administrative perspective presumes that government officials seek to serve public interests to the best of their ability, recognizing the limitations posed by imperfect information and the intrusion of personal biases and self-concerns. It also acknowledges that the efficiency and effectiveness of specific initiatives may depend upon the organizational and economic context.

Proponents of the administrative perspective seek to specify the conditions under which different privatization tools (or combinations of tools) are likely to work best.[2] They argue that there is no single and universal

---

[2] See Marc Bendick, Jr., "Privatizing the Delivery of Social Welfare Services: An Idea to be Taken Seriously," in *Privatization and the Welfare State*, Sheila B. Kamerman and Alfred J. Kahn, eds. (Princeton: Princeton University Press, 1989), pp. 97–120; John Donahue, *The Privatization Decision* (New York: Basic Books, 1989); William T. Gormley, Jr., "Two Cheers for Privatization," in Gormley, ed., *Privatization and Its Alternatives,* pp. 307–318; and Lester Salamon, *Beyond Privatization: The Tools of Government Action* (Washington: The Urban Institute, 1989).

best way for government to pursue the social good. Under some circumstances, it may be appropriate for government to fully finance and directly provide a good or service. Under different circumstances, it may be best for government to subsidize beneficiaries who then obtain the desired services from private producers. Factors such as the tangibility and divisibility of the service, the degree of competition within the private provider community, the availability of information, and the organizational capacity of government must be weighed in considering which technique, or mixture of techniques, to pursue.

The economic perspective

The economic perspective presents privatization as the inevitable consequence of neoclassical truths that dictate the retraction of a bulky, intrusive, and parasitic state. There are both macro and micro elements to this perspective. The macro argument suggests that there are structural limitations to the relative size and intrusiveness of the public sector, that movement beyond those limits is sustainable only for short periods, and that efforts to challenge this economic reality inevitably result in stagnation and decline.[3]

This reasoning resonates in the arguments of both the Left and Right. The Right, of course, has always argued that the expenses of the welfare state lead to predatory taxation, which reduces profit margins and discourages private investment. On the Left, observers argue that the Keynesian welfare policies of the post-war period, necessary both for the legitimation of capitalist regime and as a spur to productive investment, suffer from political processes that allocate capital irrationally, in response to power rather than need.[4] As Thompson points out,

During the post-war period, up until the late 1970s, "market failure" arguments were widely deployed to justify the interventionist stance taken by successive governments. However, the disappointing performance of the economy, and in particular some of those enterprises under the direct control of government, led to a reaction. Such a reaction pointed now not to the issue of *market failure* but perhaps more importantly to that of *government failure*.[5]

While sharing the macroeconomic assumptions of the Right, public choice theory relies on microeconomic principles to explain the apparent irrationality of the state's capital allocations. The theory locates the

[3] See, e.g., Gary S. Becker, "Surprises in a World According to Adam Smith," *Business Week*, August 17, 1992, p. 18.
[4] James O'Connor, *The Fiscal Crisis of the State* (New York: St. Martins Press, 1973), p. 10; Joel Krieger, *Reagan, Thatcher and the Politics of Decline* (New York: Oxford University Press, 1986), p. 27; G. Thompson, *The Political Economy of the New Right* (London, Pinter Publishers, 1990).   [5] Thompson, *The Political Economy of the New Right,* p. 11.

source of state expansion in the self-interested behavior of politicians, bureaucrats, and interest groups (like governmental contractors and beneficiaries of social welfare programs) that gain more in their role as beneficiaries than they lose in their role as taxpayers.[6] This approach characterizes the state sector as composed of individuals rationally pursuing personal material gain, the sum of whose actions lead to macro-level inefficiency. Privatization is thus portrayed as a mechanism that takes resources out of the hands of bureaucrats and entrusts those resources to the more efficient invisible hand of the market.

The economic perspective tends to categorize privatization initiatives in relation to three major values: ownership, competition, and the alignment of benefit to price. Sale of state assets implicitly is treated as the most extreme (and in this sense "best") form of privatization, since it simultaneously reduces the public sector deficit, reduces the size of the governmental apparatus, shifts decisions into the hands of private actors presumably more attuned to market signals, and gives more people a direct and material stake in promoting economic growth. Increasing reliance on competitive forces without changing ownership – as when governments contract out for public services – leaves responsibility for setting and enforcing goals in the public sector, but is seen to have the advantages of promoting efficiency and reducing the bureaucracy. Alignment of price with benefit – as when services are funded by user fees rather than general tax revenues – is presumed to indirectly retard governmental growth, by reducing the tendency of governments to oversupply certain services relative to their true market value to those who consume them.

Limitations of the two perspectives

Our dissatisfaction with these two perspectives stems from three sources. First, although presentations about privatization often borrow concepts and terminology from both, the key premises of the administrative and economic perspectives are inconsistent with one another. Whereas the administrative perspective presumes public officials to be relatively informed, motivated by a conception of broader interests, and operating with a degree of independence and discretion, the economic perspective sees public officials as unequipped to assess market signals, motivated by

---

[6] See Thomas Borcherding, ed., *Budgets and Bureaucrats: The Source of Government Growth* (Durham: Duke University Press, 1977); James M. Buchanan, "Why Does Government Grow?" in Borcherding, ed., *Budgets and Bureaucrats*; William A. Niskanen, *Bureaucracy and Representative Government* (Chicago: Aldine-Atherton, 1971); and Gordon Tullock, "Why Politicians Won't Cut Taxes," *Taxing and Spending* (October/November 1978), 12–14.

a desire to appropriate a greater proportion of the public wealth for themselves, and ultimately constrained by fiscal and monetary forces that
operate on a logic of their own.

Secondly, both perspectives obscure important distinctions. The adoption of a particular form of privatization can be less significant than distinctions in the way privatization is formulated and implemented. It is one
thing, for example, to contract out a service to a private provider when
public officials can precisely specify the desired goal and intermediate
steps, when they have independent sources of information, and when they
have the manpower and commitment to oversee providers and terminate
those whose performance is unsatisfactory. It is quite thing another to
contract out an ill-defined project, when officials are dependent upon the
contractee for performance data, or when the absence of viable competing providers or the existence of political pressures gives the private provider a *de facto* monopoly. Similarly, it is one thing to sell a state-owned
industry that is demonstrably inefficient, that has been reconfigured to
promote greater competition in the private sector, and that will be
effectively overseen by an appropriate regulatory apparatus;[7] it is another
to sell off valuable public assets simply to close a short-term budget gap,
to transfer a public monopoly into a private monopoly, or to provide an
almost guaranteed profit to valued supporters.

Finally, both perspectives de-emphasize the political dimensions of
privatization rooted in the conflict of interests among competing classes
and groups. Characterization of privatization as economic adjustment is
too restricted and overly deterministic; it understates the actual variety in
behavior of states and citizens facing similar objective conditions; it
downplays the motivating power of non-economic forces such as nationalism, ideology, ethnicity, and race; and it fails to acknowledge the fluidity
and indeterminacy of the demarcation between public and private in
modern societies.[8] While the characterization of privatization as prag-

[7] The economics literature includes both advocates and critics of the notion that ownership
affects performance. However, more recent work by orthodox economists makes it quite
clear that ownership means little, compared to the degree of competition in a firm's
market, in determining the efficiency of an enterprise. See especially Douglas W. Caves
and Laurits R. Christensen, "The Relative Efficiency of Public and Private Firms in a
Competitive Environment: The Case of Canadian Railroads," *Journal of Political Economy*,
88, 5 (October 1980).

[8] See Desmond S. King, *The New Right: Politics, Markets and Citizenship* (Chicago: Dorsey
Press, 1987); Martin Rein, "The Social Structure of Institutions: Neither Public Nor
Private," in Kamerman and Kahn, eds., *Privatization and the Welfare State*, pp. 49–71;
Paul Starr, "The Meaning of Privatization," in Kamerman and Kahn, eds., *Privatization
and the Welfare State*, pp. 15–48; and Todd Swanstrom, "Beyond Economism: Urban
Political Economy and the Postmodern Challenge," Paper prepared for the American
Political Science Association Annual Meeting, Washington, D.C., August 28–September
1, 1991.

	Administrative	Economic	Political
Emphasized Goal	achievement of socially defined goals	maximization of individual's utilities	redistribution of power and control
Unit of Analysis	discrete societal problem	individual/firm	group/class
Concept of Privatization	tool box	preferred mechanism	weapon

Figure 2.1 Three contrasting approaches

matic adjustment recognizes privatization as an option that may be chosen or rejected, it overstates the degree of social consensus on goals and priorities. In addition, by focusing on aggregate benefits and costs, the administrative perspective does not give due consideration to how those costs and benefits are distributed among occupational, racial, and class-based groups; it ignores the potential for privatization initiatives to alter the landscape of political interests; and it fails to confront the broader ideological claims being advanced in the name of privatization.[9]

A political perspective

Our principal argument is that the broad privatization movement is, in most of its manifestations, better understood as a political phenomenon than as a technical adjustment to changing conditions or as a consequence of economic laws.[10] Rather than treating privatizations as a choice among *means* to achieve recognized and broadly social goals, we argue that privatization often takes the form of a strategy to realign institutions and decision-making processes so as to privilege the goals of some groups over the competing aspirations of other groups. As figure 2.1 indicates, this political perspective differs from the administrative and economic approaches in the primary motivation ascribed to political actors, the

---

[9] See Timothy Barnekov, Robin Boyle, and Daniel Rich, *Privatism and Urban Policy in Britain and the United States* (New York: Oxford University Press, 1989); Harvey B. Feigenbaum, "France: From Pragmatic to Tactical Privatization," *Business in the Contemporary World*, 5, 1 (Winter 1993), 67–85; Jeffrey Henig, "Privatization in the United States: Theory and Practice," *Political Science Quarterly* 104, 4 (Winter 1990), 649–670; and Starr, "The Meaning of Privatization."

[10] Political choices are not the result of infinite options. Not every policy will work and reality is an ultimate constraint for decision makers who subscribe to even the most resilient ideologies. There are, therefore, outer limits, that is, technical limits, which constrain choice. However, within those technical parameters there lies room for political discretion.

central unit of analysis employed, and the basic conception of privatization engendered.

The typology introduced

We anchor our typology initially in the motivations of key actors responsible for promoting privatization in the public arena. There are, we suggest, at least three types of privatization strategies: pragmatic, tactical and systemic.[11] Pragmatic privatization reflects most of the characteristics associated with the administrative perspective, although with one important difference. Whereas the administrative perspective presents this set of characteristics as if it is universally applicable, the political perspective considers such pragmatic privatizations to be discrete and context-dependent episodes. Pragmatic privatizations generally are carried out by bureaucratic units somewhat insulated from the push and pull of normal political pressures. American municipal contracts for private provision of public services provide a good illustration. They are frequently introduced as technical solutions to meet an immediate social problem. The key actors perceive privatization simply as one among several alternative "tools" through which recognized priorities of the society might be furthered. In deciding whether and when to privatize, they focus on the specific characteristics of the problem and its context, and give little thought to considerations of ideological consistency or political consequences.

Tactical privatizations, in contrast, are advocated to achieve the short-term political goals of particular parties, politicians, or interest groups. They seek either to alter the balance of power by attracting allies and rewarding supporters or to achieve specific short-term objectives such as reducing the budget deficit. In some cases, privatization appeals tactically as a form of "political product differentiation." For example, the program of asset sales by 1986–88 Chirac government in France seems to have primarily been aimed at winning election by promoting a distinctive program that differed from the otherwise conservative policies of the Socialists.

Systemic privatization strategies, such as those pursued in Britain and New Zealand in the 1980s, and now being pursued in Eastern Europe, are intended to reshape the entire society by fundamentally altering economic and political institutions and by transforming economic and polit-

[11] A similar typology is developed by Ben Ross Schneider in "Privatization in Brazil and Mexico: Variations on a Statist Theme," in Ezra N. Suleiman and John Waterbury, eds., *The Political Economy of Public Sector Reform and Privatization* (Boulder, CO: Westview, 1990). Schneider, however, focuses primarily on decision makers and their motivations in Brazil and Mexico. We are grateful to an anonymous reviewer for signaling this reference.

ical interests. Systemic privatization seeks to lower people's expectations of what government can and should be held responsible for, reduce the public sector's oversight and enforcement infrastructure, and transform the interest group landscape to make it less supportive of governmental growth.

In the best Weberian tradition, our typology is an analytic construct intended to sharpen and focus understanding by abstracting key underlying dimensions of social behavior. As such, it inevitably shares some of the disadvantages that are typical of the genre. First, by posing certain categories as "pure" types, it tends to understate the complexity of the phenomenon under review. Policies often have multiple authors who have different agendas, so specific privatization initiatives rarely constitute pure examples of one type or another. Some may be attracted to a policy because of its long-term implications, such as Margaret Thatcher's advocacy of privatization as a means of transforming Britain into a "people's capitalism," while others have their eyes on the short-term electoral benefits, such as selling profitable state-owned enterprises in order to reduce a politically embarrassing deficit.[12] Nonpartisan city managers may privatize city services as a way of dealing with restricted budgets, but they may get the idea from position papers churned out from highly politicized "think tanks,"[13] and some with ambitions for higher office may favor privatization as a way to build a reputation for innovation. Indeed, multiple justifications are a source of broad appeal. Policies come about because they attract coalitions of complementary, though hardly identical, interests. Privatizations are no exception.

Like most other typologies, too, ours risks freezing events into a static framework that belies the dynamism of political life. Strategies can evolve, and privatization initiatives undertaken in pursuit of one set of objectives might change in type as different constituencies mobilize to gain influence or as key actors reinterpret their interests in the light of changing events. Indeed, one of the findings that we will emphasize is that the politics of privatization does shift gears at various times within the nations we consider.

Finally, in anchoring our typology in the motivations of key actors, we are focusing attention on one key dimension – intended effects – to the possible exclusion of another key dimension, namely actual effects. There

---

[12] Categorization of policies may also be a function of timing: French tactical privatizations might have become systemic had the Conservatives not lost the 1988 elections. We are grateful to Mark Kesselman on this point.

[13] On the importance of think tanks, see, for example, Henry Nau, *The Myth of the American Decline* (New York: Oxford University Press, 1991), chapter 1. On the evolution of think tanks, see R. Kent Weaver, "The Changing World of Think Tanks," *PS: Political Science and Politics*, 22, 3 (September 1989), 563–578.

is many a slip between cup and lip, and we do not mean to imply that all privatization efforts which are promoted in the hopes of inducing systemic change will – even if fully implemented – have more than an incremental effect. Our decision to focus on motivation is prompted in part by our sense that it is still premature to determine empirically the effects of relatively recent privatization initiatives. It is not, however, premature to examine the forms of privatization enacted, their stated rationales, and the coalitions promoting them in an effort to infer the political objectives which underpin them.

Whether such limitations outweigh the contributions of a typology depend on the particulars of its formulation and the ways in which it is employed. They are most likely to do harm when typologies reify the unimportant, or when the typologies are presented as ends in themselves, rather than as conceptual tools with which to initiate an empirical probing of important phenomena. In the discussion which follows, we attempt to highlight the illustrative value of the typology without losing sensitivity to some of the more complex and dynamic aspects of the cases involved. In addition, we begin to build upon our initial typology by expanding from the dimension of motivations to that of actual effects. With these caveats in mind, what follows is an analysis of the political underpinnings of each kind of privatization strategy.

Pragmatic privatizations

Struck by the appearance of so many privatization projects that were initiated around the world at almost the same time, Raymond Vernon noted a pragmatic reason to explain the international phenomenon. He argued that there had not been a basic ideological shift, even though much policy learning about the virtues and disadvantages of state intervention had taken place. The simple explanation for the diverse privatizations of the early 1980s was that these policies were a "reflection largely of the drying up of cash in that period . . ."[14] This reflects the views put forward by O'Connor, Gough and others regarding the "fiscal crisis of the state."

Pragmatic privatizations are short-term solutions to immediate problems. There is an *ad hoc* element to them. The immediate need for cash can account for many privatizations. The Italian conglomerate, IRI sold off a number of its affiliates for that reason.[15] So did St. Gobain in France, despite official policy to the contrary.[16] The Italian nationalized railway, FS, introduced market-oriented reforms largely to reduce possibilities for

---

[14] Raymond Vernon, ed., *The Promise of Privatization: A Challenge for US Policy* (New York: Council on Foreign Relations, 1988), p. 19.   [15] Ibid., p. 16.

[16] Vivian Schmidt, "Industrial Management under the Socialists in France: Decentralized *Dirigisme* at the National and Local Levels," *Comparative Politics* 21, 1 (October 1988), 61.

corruption and the Labour government in Britain sold some of its shares in BP in 1978 to raise money for the Treasury.[17]

The home of pragmatic privatization may well be the United States. This is especially true at the municipal level where pragmatic privatizations considerably predated the policy fashion of the 1980s. Many privatizations of city services, as well as user fees, began as early as 1932. Henig argues that: "These diverse governmental arrangements did *not* represent a broad but heretofore unacknowledged privatization movement, but a series of pragmatic adjustments, more often undertaken in the context of an expanding public sector rather than in a deliberate effort to shrink the governmental realm."[18]

The American experience in privatizing public services suggests an apolitical conception, which, in its more sophisticated form, can be expressed as a contrast between the goals of the public and private sectors. The public sector in this sense is conceived of as essentially the civil service or state bureaucracy, while the private sector is viewed as the world of hierarchically organized firms. Thus the former organization emphasizes due process, administrative fairness, and protection of citizens' rights while the latter emphasizes flexibility, adaptation to changing technologies, and overall economic efficiency.[19] Privatization, in this view, becomes an administrative solution to a functional problem. That is, it is a change in organization to achieve goals for which private firms are deemed better suited.

This separation of public and private spheres is, of course, a kind of ideology.[20] It is frequently expressed in a superficially apolitical form. This is especially true of the technocratic outlook inherent in the city manager form of local government in the USA, an inheritance of the Progressive era in the late nineteenth to early twentieth centuries, and in the "nonpartisan" good government slates in French municipal elections occurring since the 1960s.[21] Thus, privatizations were more likely to appear pragmatic at the local level in these two countries than in Britain, where partisan politics remained out in the open and led in fact to systematic efforts (under Margaret Thatcher) to draw authority away from Labour-dominated councils.

---

[17] Haig Simonian, "Little Push from the Market will Speed Italy's Trains," *Financial Times*, June 12, 1991, p. 4. Of course, as any accountant will note, the market alone offers no guarantees against profit skimming and less-than-above-board behavior by managers.

[18] Henig, "Privatization in the United States," p. 657.

[19] Donahue, *Privatization Decision*, p. 216.

[20] Arnaud Sales, "The Private, the Public and Civil Society: Social Realms and Power Structure," *International Political Science Review*, 12, 4 (1991).

[21] Of course the French national administration has based its power on the notion that technocratic solutions are apolitical. See Ezra N. Suleiman, *Politics, Power and Bureaucracy in France* (Princeton: Princeton University Press, 1974).

The examples of pragmatic privatization cited above are suggestive of some of the political characteristics of the genre. They are not only projects undertaken with little thought to ideology, they occur in an environment that is not *highly politicized*. That is, they tend to occur in policy arenas that do not encourage, or have been insulated from, in Schattschneider's[22] famous expression, "the mobilization of bias." Rather than actually being *apolitical*, pragmatic privatizations tend to turn up in areas that already have been successfully *de*politicized, and they reinforce that depoliticization: "A long list of ideas concerning individualism, free private enterprise, localism, privacy and economy in government, seems to be designed to privatize conflict or to restrict its scope or to limit the use of public authority to enlarge the scope of conflict. A tremendous amount of conflict is controlled by keeping it so private that it is almost invisible."[23]

This is not to say that the apolitical intent of pragmatic privatizers is insincere. By and large they see their actions as serving the general interests of their constituents, or at least of the majority of them. Thus, for example, city managers may be well aware that privatizing garbage collection hurts the interest of public sector unions (where private firms would pay lower wages), but they may believe that by saving money at the expense of a fairly small group, they make funds available for other worthy purposes, such as education.

The depoliticized nature of pragmatic privatizations is apparent, too, where carried out by managers of public firms, who see the issuance of stock to private shareholders, or the sale of subsidiaries, as merely instrumental techniques to assure their firm's short term profitability or long term strategy.[24] The obverse, however, may be entirely political, as when, in 1988, France's President Mitterrand specifically precluded additional sale of public firms to conform to his "ni . . . ni . . . [neither . . . nor . . .]" electoral promise of neither new nationalizations nor new privatizations.[25]

On the other hand, some forms of pragmatic privatization may be crisis

---

[22] E. E. Schattschneider, *The Semi-Sovereign People* (New York: Holt, Rinehart and Winston, 1975).   [23] Ibid., p. 7.

[24] See, e.g., William Dawkins, "France's Restive State Sector Senses Freedom," *Financial Times*, April 11, 1991, p. 3.

[25] See, for example, the *Financial Times* editorial, "Dilemmas of Dirigisme," April 8, 1991, p. 14. For an example of the gymnastics the state exercised to work within the ban, see Eric Le Boucher "L'Etat actionnaire à la recherche des moyens pour soutenir l'aeronautique et l'électronique," *Le Monde*, February 22, 1991, reprinted in the *Selection Hebdomadaire du Journal "Le Monde,"* February 27, 1991, p. 11. In some instances, the political *naiveté* of pragmatic privatizers may have unintended political effects on constituencies of the ruling political coalition: thus the privatization in Mexico injured the labor unions supporting the PRI. See Schneider, "Privitization in Brazil and mexico."

driven. That is, they may be inaugurated to solve an internal budgetary crisis or external balance of payments deficit in conjunction with an austerity plan. This appears to be frequently the case in Third World countries. Mexico and Ghana represent, according to some interpretations, examples of this form of pragmatic privatization.[26] Motives here, however, are not always pure, nor are decisions taken in a vacuum. Whether, or not decision makers choose to privatize may be as much a function of coercion (or at least suasion) from external financial authorities, as a function of objective financial conditions or non-privatizing alternatives.[27]

Tactical privatizations

Pragmatic privatizations occur, for the most part, in depoliticized and restricted arenas, but tactical privatizations occur in situations that are directly, if not necessarily overtly, political. These privatizations are intended for the short-term political benefit of those backing the policy, although other impacts of the privatization may be long term. Privatization policies may be intended to appeal to specific groups of voters or to reward one's political friends. Evidence of both of these are easily found in the recent histories of Britain and France.

The French case offers, perhaps, the clearest illustration. Privatization of nationalized companies initiated by the Chirac government of 1986–88 came about for tactical reasons. The usual justifications that the state companies were poorly run were belied by profit and loss statements that were increasingly positive under state management.[28] The tactical reasons for the privatizations were first, that the Conservative parties needed a platform that distinguished themselves from the Socialists. Since 1983 the Socialists had slowly deregulated the economy, reduced taxes, and liberalized capital markets.[29] While they had deregulated for

[26] See, especially, Rod Alence, "Moments of Truth: The State, Economic Institutions, and the Political Economy of Export Instability in Gold Coast/Ghana," *1937–1984*, PhD dissertation, Department of Political Science, Stanford University.

[27] See Don Babai, "The World Bank and the IMF: Rolling Back the State or Backing its Role?" in Vernon, ed., *The Promise of Privatization*, pp. 254–275. See also discussion below.

[28] Harvey Feigenbaum, "Democracy at the Margins: The International System and Policy Change in France," in Richard E. Foglesong and Joel D. Wolfe, eds., *The Politics of Economic Adjustment* (New York: Greenwood, 1989), pp. 92–3. More recently, some industries, especially Bull and Thomsen, the state electronics groups fell on harder times (Le Boucher, "L'Etat actionnaire," p. 11); however, the problems of the enterprises had more to do with their respective sectors, rather than their ownership. This calls to mind a similar analysis of British industries by Richard Pryke, *The Nationalised Industries: Policies and Performance Since 1968* (Oxford: Martin Robertson, 1981), p. 264.

[29] See Michael Loriaux, *France after Hegemony* (Ithaca: Cornell University Press, 1991).

pragmatic reasons, largely because they had no other ideas after the failure of their 1981 economic program,[30] this left the Conservatives with little to call their own. Thus, they blamed France's problems on the public sector, especially on the nationalizations of the Socialists.

The Thatcher government followed a similar electoral logic in adopting privatization. Privatization was not part of the government's initial economic agenda, but turned out to be a useful tactic in the run-up to the first re-election campaign:

Margaret Thatcher, Geoffrey Howe, and Keith Joseph recognized the need for a policy initiative that would revitalize their free-market ideology when monetarism lost its appeal due to its excessively deflationary consequences during 1981. Not only did privatization respond to the party's natural constituency by increasing profit opportunities, it also provided a new direction in the face of the rapid contraction of industrial production and the dramatic increase in unemployment.[31] Moreover, once safely returned to office, the Thatcher government was willing to risk crowding out private investment[32] by using privatization as a method of reducing the Public Sector Borrowing Requirement, as the rise or persistence of the PSBR would be politically embarrassing.[33]

Following the first rule of politics that one must punish one's enemies and reward one's friends, the second tactical advantage of privatizing public companies was that the shares in the newly privatized firms could be sold to friends of the Conservatives at a generous discount.[34] Indeed, the whole process of state asset sales had a ring of venality that might have made Mayor Daley's (Senior) Chicago seem pristine by comparison.[35] This tendency to reward one's friends was true in both the British and

[30] While the Socialists liberalized the French economy largely because they could think of no alternative after employing state interventionism *à l'outrance* in the first two years of their mandate, they suffered from the fact that they pursued pragmatic privatizations in an arena that was highly politicized (national politics) and suffered the consequences at the polls in 1986. Their traditional voters saw them as having abandoned socialism, while centrist voters simply reacted to the stagnation of the economy.

A similar case can be made for Mexico's abandoning its traditional *dirigisme* in the 1980s, i.e., there was nothing left to try (we are grateful to Eduardo Margain for this point). The Mexican government, on the other hand, with its idiosyncratic form of "democracy", did not have to worry about the losing at the polls.

[31] Joel Wolfe, "Reorganizing Interest Representation: A Political Analysis of Privatization in Britain," in Wolfe and Foglesong, eds., *The Politics of Economic Adjustment*, p. 19.

[32] That is, investors or banks who might provide funds for capital goods or expansion in already private companies would instead take their money and buy shares in privatized firms.

[33] Ezra N. Suleiman, "Privatization in Britain and France" in Suleiman and Waterbury, eds., pp. 114–15.

[34] See Michel Durupty, *Les Privatizations en France* (Paris: La Documentation Francaise, Notes et Etudes documentaires, No. 4857), pp. 117–20; *Le Monde*, September 17, 1988.

[35] See Michel Bauer, "State Directed Privatization: The Case of France," *West European Politics*, 11, 4 (October 1988), 49–60.

French cases. In Britain, where a number of motives supported various privatizations, tactical politics were occasionally covert, as in the case of private asset sales,[36] and often overt, as Peter Self points out:

> the Thatcherite strategy clearly shows that it is just as possible (and a lot quicker) to provide private profits out of running down the state as out of building it up. The beneficiaries of this strategy include not only those groups, such as public industry management and employees . . . who must be bribed into compliance, but City institutions making a fortune from the privatization boom and the top quintile of households who are the main gainers from the tax reliefs financed by the sale of public assets.[37]

Tactical privatizations, as the label suggests, are not ends in themselves. Where pragmatic privatization selects its targets based on pressing problems or indications of poor performance, tactical privatization is guided more by political opportunism and the amount of "booty" potentially at stake. Thus, privatizations may in some instances be targets of opportunity where strong allies are at hand or where resistance is weak. An example of the former might be the sale of a national airline supported by private transportation interests. An example of the latter might be Bush administration initiatives intended to sell public housing; such initiatives benefit from the political weakness of the lower income and minority residents of public housing and from fragmentation, disarray, and dispirit-edness among the organizations that historically have taken up their cause.

Part of the strategy is to neutralize short-term opposition to a long-term project. Thus, privatizations may be sweetened by offering discount shares to managers and employees.[38] As Self puts it, "The necessary tactics, however, are not a frontal attack upon the system (which would be doomed to failure because of the political accumulation of vested interests), but piecemeal changes which offer transitional or new political benefits to groups disadvantaged by each step of the process."[39] Or, as Stuart Butler notes about the British strategy to break down the coalition normally likely to oppose the sale of British Telecom: "This was accomplished by offering key constituents free or discounted stock, together with below-market pricing of the issue, so that the stockholders could be sure of an immediate benefit through appreciation of their holdings."[40]

---

[36] Cosmo Graham and Tony Prosser, *Privatizing Public Enterprises* (Oxford: Clarendon Press, 1991), pp. 105–29.
[37] Self, "What's Wrong With Government? The Problem of Public Choice," *Political Quarterly* 61, (January–March 1990), 23-35.
[38] See Oliver Letwin, *Privatising the World* (London: Cassell Educational, 1988).
[39] Self, "What's Wrong With Government?", p. 26 n. 41.
[40] Butler, "Changing the Political Dynamic of Government," in Steve H. Hanke, ed., *Prospects for Privatization* (New York: The Academy of Political Science, 1987), pp. 10–11.

Third World countries may exercise a different kind of tactical privatization. The World Bank and International Monetary Fund frequently demand privatization plans as a prerequisite to receiving funds.[41] While international lending institutions may be satisfied if a country merely introduces market principles into the public sector, rather than full scale sale of assets, liberalization is the price of the loan.[42] In thirty-eight structural adjustment loans to developing countries from 1980 to 1986, the World Bank recommended liquidation or divestiture of state-assets in twenty-five of them. In addition, they recommended increased market orientation of state firms in thirty-six of the thirty-eight loans.[43] When the international financial community is in a position to provide Third World leaders with immediate injections of funds, in-kind services, and a degree of legitimacy, local governments may be induced to liberalize for tactical reasons, even if their leaders are not convinced of the long-term advantages of free markets for the majority of their citizens.[44]

Tactical privatizations can also explain some of the inconsistencies of privatization programs. For instance, the Thatcher government privatized the national gas utility as a single monopoly despite the commitment of the government to competitive market principles because the sale of the monopoly intact offered the possibility of the quickest sale, giving the privatization program the appearance of dynamism after the stock market disaster of October 1987. The French conservatives sold companies at discounts, limiting the impact on budget deficits, to political friends who could have afforded more. The ironies may reach their apogee in the Third World, however: the principal purchaser of public enterprises in Morocco is the king.[45]

Systemic privatizations

Systemic privatizations are the most ideological in their origins, and the most widespread in their intended impact. Rather than being the techno-

---

[41] See Babai, "The World Bank and the IMF."   [42] Ibid.

[43] Compiled from ibid., Annex 1, pp. 276–281 (The Annex was in turn compiled from World Bank internal documents.) Loans were made to the following countries (some more than once): Bolivia, Burundi, Chile, Costa Rica, Cote d'Ivoire, Guinea, Guyana, Jamaica, Kenya Malawi, Mauritius, Niger, Pakistan, Panama, Philippines, Senegal, South Korea, Thailand, Togo, Turkey, and Yugoslavia.

[44] As mentioned in the discussion above, tactical motives may be reinforced by pragmatic ones if the country in question is experiencing a balance of payments or budgetary crisis. Politicians who are unconvinced by neoclassical logic may nevertheless find their hands forced by the lack of alternatives. Here tactical and pragmatic privatizations merge empirically, even if we may *analytically* distinguish the sets of motives for such privatizations.   [45] We are grateful to Charles-Albert Michalet for pointing this out.

cratic solution to a discrete number of specific problems, systemic privatization aims at permanently changing class relations. Referring to our discussion in chapter 1, systemic privatizations are both initially intended and ultimately likely to shrink the state.

Systemic privatization may take any of three forms. The first involves a nontransient change in the capacity of already mobilized interests to pursue their agendas as currently conceived. Systemic privatization of this form describes a situation where the withdrawal of the state results in a substantial and not readily reversible decrease in the power of working classes relative to that of economic elites. This may be the case when privatization efforts primarily function to undermine the power of organized labor, for example by relocating jobs from a unionized public sector to a nonunionized private sector.[46] This form of systemic privatization constitutes a "Power Shift."

The second form of systemic privatization involves a nontransient change in the values, culture, and expectations of the active public, resulting in a broadening of the sphere of activities regarded as personal and private and a shrinking of the sphere of activities considered to constitute legitimate areas for public scrutiny and intervention. The effect of privatization in this sense is to delegitimize the public sector. That is, the intent of the policy is subtly to imbue broader constituencies with the ideological perspective already shared by the advocates of privatization. In Britain the intent of some key actors was to permanently transform the way citizens related to each other, especially to break down class bonds. The idea was to change British society from a Marxian world of class conflict to a Hobbesian world of atomized individuals. As Margaret Thatcher once infamously declared: "There is no such thing as society, only individuals and their families." A similar agenda prevailed in New Zealand, where the degree of privatization parallels, if not exceeds, that in Britain.[47] In Hall's words,

[Privatization] displaces an existing structure of oppositions – "them" versus "us." It sets in its place an alternative set of equivalents: "them and us equals we." Then it positions we "the people" – in a particular relation to capital: behind it, dominated by its imperatives (profitability, accumulation): yet at the same time yoked to it, identified with it.[48]

---

[46] For a study of the dramatic changes in New Zealand, see A. Bollard and R. Buckle, eds., *Economic Liberalisation in New Zealand* (Auckland: Allen and Unwin), and Ian Duncan and Alan Bollard, *Corporatization and Privatization: Lessons from New Zealand* (Auckland: Oxford University Press, 1992).

[47] Wolfe, "Reorganizing Interest Representation," p. 20.

[48] Stuart Hall, "The Great Moving Right Show," in Stuart Hall and Martin Jacques, eds., *The Politics of Thatcherism* (London: Lawrence and Wishart, 1983); quoted in Wolfe, "Reorganizing Interest Representation," p. 18.

Paradoxically, privatization policies become a mechanism by which the state delegitimizes certain functions, though never the central role of the executive, and through which the privileged strata extend their cultural hegemony.[49] This form of systemic privatization constitutes what we call a "Perceptual Shift."

The third form of systemic privatization involves a nontransient restructuring of the institutional arrangements of the society (legal, political, economic) in such a way that the array of incentives presented to individuals and groups encourages a greater reliance on private and market oriented solutions. The intended effect is to rearrange the institutional assignment of responsibilities, shifting basic decision processes from a public to a private realm. As Madsen Pirie, an influential British advocate of such systemic privatization, argues, "The transfer of public undertakings to the private sector takes away their status as political entities and transforms them instead into economic entities. Once they are free of the state, most of the decisions made about them will become economic ones."[50] This form of systemic privatization constitutes an "Institutional Shift." The impact of the institutional shift is to change the mechanism of social control from overt bureaucratic and political structures to the less accountable and more subtle forces of the market.[51] It is, of course, possible for all three types of shift to occur more or less simultaneously.

The importance of changes in systems of institutionalized accountability obliges us to draw a distinction between democratic and nondemocratic countries. While the nature of control changes with privatization in all countries, the degree of accountability may change in different directions, depending on the pre-existing form of bureaucratic

---

[49] Antonio Gramsci, *Selections from Prison Notebooks* (New York: International Publishers, 1971), p. 260; Martin Carnoy, *The State and Political Theory* (Princeton: Princeton University Press, 1984), pp. 75–76.

[50] M. Pirie, *Privatization* (Hants: Wildwood Press, 1988), 53.

[51] Wolfe, "Reorganizing Interest Representation," p. 17. This escape from accountability may be initiated for ideological reasons, but it also may dovetail with more tactical concerns of self-interested politicians. Political behavior in democracies is often explained by the desire of elected officials to avoid blame, rather than by more positive intentions of achieving results. See R. Kent Weaver, "The Politics of Blame Avoidance," *Journal of Public Policy*, 6, 4 (1986), 371–398. Thus, by privatizing a national railroad, for instance, members of parliament are absolved from complaints about poor or disappearing service. By privatizing a nationalized corporation, the government sheds responsibility for layoffs. Former French Prime Minister Raymond Barre told the authors that one of his reasons for not wanting to nationalize French industries that were in trouble was to avoid taking responsibility for layoffs. Personal communication with Harvey Feigenbaum, George Washington University, Spring 1983. See also Thompson, *The Political Economy of the New Right*.

control and on the kind of regulatory apparatus put in place after privatization. Thus, privatization in formerly nondemocratic countries may lead to greater accountability if the previous bureaucracies were not accountable at all. On the other hand, the loss of direct accountability when democratic countries privatize may be compensated, or even improved upon, if states put in place a regulatory apparatus that can obviate potential abuses by private companies.[52]

The accountability issue may also help explain the motives of privatizers in newly democratic countries. In Spain, public ownership was associated with Franco's rule, so that privatization was not only offered as a pragmatic solution to the country's problems by neoclassically trained technocrats, but could be championed by the Socialists as an advance in democratization.[53] Whether motivated by neoclassical economic thought, or by democratic ideology, the effect of such privatizations remains systemic.

Sometimes institutional restructuring changes class relationships by creating new interests, perhaps even *new classes*. This is what appears to be happening in Eastern Europe, at least to the extent that privatized firms are being turned over to citizens, rather than foreign investors.[54] Private firms have their own interests and state firms, once privatized, can be expected to have preferences which diverge from that of government. It can also be assumed, if the Western experience is a guide, that the newly

---

[52] Alec Nove in *Efficiency Criteria for Nationalised Industries* (Toronto: University of Toronto Press, 1973) has argued, for example, that public monopoly that is not subjected to a regulatory authority may be more prone to abuse its position than a private monopoly which is held rigorously accountable for its actions by a Public Utilities Commission. If government shifts from state ownership to a regulatory form of oversight *with the intent of increasing its effectiveness* as a protector of public interests, however, we would argue that this constitutes pragmatic rather than systemic privatization. The reason that this becomes an instance of pragmatic privatization is that the state would not be less interventionist, but would only have changed the form of intervention. See Harvey Feigenbaum, *The Politics of Public Enterprise* (Princeton: Princeton University Press, 1985), ch. 1. Whether the overall impact is, indeed, to increase the role of the state is, of course, important. Such examples highlight the need to pay attention to consequence as well as motivation, as we do below.

[53] See Nancy Bermeo, "The Politics of Public Enterprise in Portugal, Spain and Greece," in Suleiman and Waterbury, eds., *The Political Economy of Public Sector Reform and Privitization*; and Sofia Perez, "The Politics of Financial Liberalization in Spain," in Michael Loriaux, et al., *Capital Ungoverned* (Ithaca: Cornell University Press, 1997), ch. 6.

[54] In fact the very uncertainty generated by the transition to a market system seems to have resulted in a particularly resilient form of interest group found in market societies: the Mafia. To be fair to the proponents of privatization, however, this latter phenomenon must be viewed as an unintended consequence of policy. For a systematic analysis of the changing class structure of Eastern Europe under privatization see Selenzyi et al (1997).

	Pragmatic	Tactical	Systemic
Key Motives	*public sector "triage'* * reduce budget drain * adjust to changing circumstances	*short-term shift in party or interest group clout* * attract voters * reward supporters * product differentiation	*long-term shift in balance of power* * lower expectations of government * reduce government capacity *transform political stakes
Illustrations of Conventional Privatization Techniques: **Asset sales**	shedding costly public enterprise where private provision has become a viable alternative	selling profitable public assets at discounted prices as a form of patronage	selling public housing in order to convert tenants to a (more conservative) homeowner's mentality
Contracting out	competitive bidding among private firm to provide services where contracting agency has enforcement capacity	awarding "sweetheart" contract to campaign contributor	shifting governmentally provided services to private providers to build new interest group that will lobby for further privatization
Deregulation	deregulating sectors that are not natural monopolies, coupled with protection consumer interests	reduced enforcement of regulations that fall heavily on political supporters	across-the-board delegitimization of regulatory intervention and governmental capacity to oversee and enforce
User fees	raising new revenues and diversifying revenue alternatives	making it possible for the governing party to cut (or avoid raising) an unpopular tax	reducing the net progressively of public policies

Figure 2.2 The political dimensions of privatization

private firms will try to influence public policy in directions beneficial to their own interest.[55]

Conceptualizing political interests

Administrative and economic perspectives leave much of the story of privatization unaccounted for. Both the administrative and economic perspectives are based on the assumption that the most relevant interests are relatively stable, unified, and apparent. They differ in the nature of the interests they consider most relevant; the administrative perspective builds on a conception of a politically defined public interest, and the economic perspective builds on a conception of privately defined individual interests. A political perspective, in contrast, takes for granted that interests are divided and in conflict. Not surprisingly, the political perspective is better suited to understanding the intensity of the battles that privatization initiatives frequently spark, and the resistance by mobilized political forces to delegating privatization decisions to institutionally depoliticized units and technical criteria.

Figure 2.2 illustrates how our political typology draws attention to differences among privatization initiatives that are obscured when too much attention is paid to the distinctions among specific conventional privatization techniques. Both the administrative and economic perspectives direct attention to the choices governments make along the vertical dimension of the figure. We believe that within each of the three columns the differences among privatization techniques such as asset sales, contracting out, deregulation, and user fees – while potentially quite important[56] – are less significant than the differences encountered when one moves along the horizontal dimension. An asset sale of the pragmatic type can be understood in similar terms as a pragmatic deregulation initiative, and its implications are likely to be similar as well. But a pragmatically motivated asset sale differs sharply in origin and implications from one determined by tactical or systemic concerns.

Some of the added dimension that we wish to highlight can be brought into focus by traditional pluralist and class-based analyses. In particular, those familiar paradigms are well suited to investigating tactical

---

[55] One way systemic privatizations can be identified empirically is by the time horizon of the privatizers. Where pragmatic privatizations attack an immediate *practical* problem and tactical privatizations are aimed at an immediate *political* problem, systemic privatizations are in for the long term. As a Czech official put it when he went to London in search of foreign investors in the newly privatized Czech economy, "So we seek partners for the rest of our lives, not just for one night" (Glenn Frankel, "Czechs Head West to Pitch Privatization of Industries," *Washington Post*, June 14, 1991, p. A-24).

[56] As Salamon notes, "each instrument has its own distinctive procedures, its own organizational relationships, its own skill requirements – in short, its own political economy" (*Beyond Privitization*, p. 8).

privatization and the variant of systemic privatization that has to do with what we have called "power shifts." Understanding the potential for systemic change due to perceptual and institutional shifts calls for a more sophisticated approach – one quicker to recognize the senses in which political interests can be malleable and the institutional biases that make some types of interests more likely to be articulated and acted upon.

Broad shifts of the type we label systemic privatization alter the fundamental rules of the game under which political actors assess their interests and weigh their strategic alternatives. By fundamentally altering the basic premises by which people assess what is a public or private responsibility, by dramatically reconfiguring the array of opportunities for private advantage, and by undermining the institutional capacity of the public sector to respond to citizens' needs, systemic privatization promises to some groups the possibility of operating in an environment in which the "mobilization of bias"[57] is in their favor, although their interests may not universally or automatically prevail.

In addition to broadly shifting the evaluative lenses through which political actors assess their political interests, systemic privatization has the potential to create new interests. It not only creates new private corporations or privatized conglomerates, but privatization, through sales of stock to institutional or atomized investors, creates agglomerations of private actors, who are linked by ownership networks that create newly shared interests.[58] These new interest groups may try to influence political institutions when public policy threatens them or when political influence may generate new occasions for gain. A good example of this is the lobbying undertaken by the new Regional Electricity companies in Britain to oppose the proposed Labour windfall tax on privatized companies. Many REC's are now American owned as a result of take-overs and President Clinton was lobbied to try to get him to pressure Tony Blair the Labour leader. In the event, the windfall tax amounting to £5 bn was imposed in the 1997 Labour budget but privatization permanently affects the interest group environment within which governments must work.[59] Moreover, these nonincremental changes in both state and society create new opportunities around which political entrepreneurs may mobilize new nodes of collective action. Privatization allows the state to free itself from some constituencies while creating new ones. The successful

---

[57] Schattschneider, *The Semi-Sovereign People.*

[58] Groups of privatized firms in France were clustered together around various financial institutions which became core stockholders, remolding French industry into something resembling Japanese *keiretsu.*

[59] See Harvey Feigenbaum, "Privatization and Interest Groups in France," Paper presented to the SOG Conference on Government and Organized Interests, University of Zurich, Switzerland, September 27–30, 1989.

achievement of public policy in one period creates obstacles to public policy in the future.

Conclusions

Most models of political behavior presume a relatively stable institutional environment, and most of the time that is a safe assumption to make. But sharp changes – whether they are found in the rapid assembly of the New Deal programs and agencies in the United States, the wholesale dismantling of the public enterprise sector in Britain, or the collapse of Communist regimes in Eastern Europe – alter the landscape so sharply that normal assumptions about political rationality, motivation, and strategy no longer apply. Changing the balance between public and private in such dramatic ways profoundly reorients political actions. It is this change in balance that is the political expression of shrinking the state.

We are led to several conclusions about how consideration of systemic privatization mandates a different set of presumptions about political behavior and policy change. These relate to political rationality, governmental responsibility and capacity, and the stickiness of systemic change.

First, when opportunities to achieve systemic privatization exist, conventional assumptions about political rationality become problematic. For its instigators, the pursuit of systemic privatization is like betting on a long-shot or buying speculative stocks on margin. Probabilities of failure are high, but so are the rewards of success. Information needed to calculate those probabilities is in short supply. Assessing rationality in this context is difficult. As often as not, strategies predicated on achieving a systemic shift will appear irrational. The Reagan administration's early proposals to sell large tracts of federally owned park land despite widespread popular misgivings are an example; so are Margaret Thatcher's proposals to privatize elements of the National Health Service. Political backlash against these efforts was substantial and costly. But Thatcher's sale of a large slice of public housing (over 20 per cent or 1.5 million units) demonstrates the potential payoffs – a sizable boost to the treasury, shedding of a long-term governmental obligation, and transformation of working-class renters into homeowners who were considered to be more susceptible to Tory appeals.

Secondly, structural shifts in governmental capacity and responsibility – not simply variations in financing, ownership, regulation and service provision – should be the central focus in distinguishing among types of privatization. The administrative and economic perspectives identify privatization by shifts in financing (from general taxes to user fees), ownership (sale of public assets), regulation (reduction in rules and oversight), and service provision (contracting out to private providers). Whether such shifts decrease or increase the role of private versus public sector forces, however, depends upon the specific details of form and implementation.

Thirdly, the most important political criteria for evaluating privatization alternatives is whether they represent substantial and not easily reversible reductions in state responsibility and capacity. By state responsibility we mean *de facto* assignment of responsibility as determined by public values and expectations as well as formal legal definition.[60] By state capacity we mean the *de facto* ability of public institutions to mount resourceful, targeted, comprehensive, informed, and sustained efforts to fulfill their responsibilities. Revenues raised and number of employees are two ready indicators of capacity, but they hardly tell the whole story. Large state apparatuses can be flabby and lack direction. Lean ones can make up for lack of size through efficiency, strong leadership, good information systems, and public support. Distinguishing among privatization efforts by their long-term impact on governmental responsibility and capacity acknowledges the sharp qualitative distinction between privatization as a tool for improving government performance and privatization as a mechanism for shrinking the state.

Finally, some policy decisions are less readily reversible than others. Not only do the interests of constituencies often change with the advent of privatizations, but the policies, once in place, may engender new groups as well as behavior, groups endowed with powers that become hard or impossible to remove. Whether this takes the form of the creation of a new class, as some of the privatizations in Eastern Europe seem to indicate, the selling of a nation's assets to foreigners (as is the case of many privatizations in the Third World or Europe), or simply improving the competitive position of some groups with regard to others in the same society, the results of privatization may be permanent. This is, of course, what the opponents of privatization fear, and what the advocates of privatization are counting on.

What follows in the next three chapters is a more detailed look at how the politics of privatization plays out in three advanced industrial countries. We think that the diverse motives and variety of outcomes in Britain, France and the USA are illustrative of the phenomenon more generally, or at least in the societies which are home to advanced capitalism.

---

[60] Sometimes responsibility can be determined only by observation over time; for instance, we might consider government to be responsible for ensuring sufficient employment opportunities if a rise in unemployment level above some threshold mobilizes powerful political forces that induce governmental response.

3 The United Kingdom: from pragmatic to systemic privatization

Introduction

Privatization as a political movement is traced by most analysts to the United Kingdom, and was inaugurated under the stewardship of Margaret Thatcher. Certainly, disparate policies which fit the broad brush notion of "privatization" elaborated in chapter I took place earlier; in particular when the 1951 Conservative government retracted several of Labour's nationalizations. In scale, of course, the privatizations of the 1980s and 1990s dwarf all earlier asset sales. In addition to the sale of high-profile state owned corporations, other forms of privatization, including contracting out, were associated with the Thatcher governments.

However, the dominant legacy greeting the Conservative government of 1979 was a very large public sector which had been criticized for some time for its inefficiency, growing deficits, and troubled workforce.[1] It was, in the end, the rash of public sector strikes during the 1978/9 "Winter of Discontent" which ushered in the first Thatcher government. Thus the British case is distinguishable from the other two major cases in this book by several aspects of its policy legacy. Britain had a larger public sector than the United States, and thus had more to privatize. The French public sector, which more closely resembled the UK in size, did not mirror the latter's performance. French public firms by and large had the reputation of efficient operation and exemplary labor relations.[2]

In retrospect, it may seem natural that the birth and driving logic of privatization would be located in the British experience. This, however, is not the case. Although Thatcher was committed to "rolling back the frontiers of the state,"[3] privatization was not so much *conceived as accidentally discovered* in Britain. A systemic logic was applied after the fact, to a policy which had been initiated at first as a pragmatic response to cash shortages

---

[1] Richard Pryke, *The Nationalized Industries* (Oxford: Martin Robertson, 1981).

[2] Christian Stoffaes and Jacques Victorri, *Nationalisations* (Paris: Flammarion, 1977); Harvey B. Feigenbaum, *The Politics of Public Enterprise: Oil and the French State* (Princeton: Princeton University Press, 1985).

[3] Grahame Thompson, *The Political Economy of the New Right* (London: Pinter, 1990).

at the Treasury. Nevertheless, pragmatic and financially[4] driven as the policy may have been at its inception, it would not have been a choice at all, had the earliest steps of privatization not been compatible with the ideological convictions of Mrs. Thatcher and her associates.

Overview and background

The program of privatization introduced in Britain by Mrs. Thatcher's Conservative government from 1979 onwards is rightly seen as one of the most extensive anywhere in the world. However, there was no fully developed, coherent, and self-conscious plan for systemic privatization at the outset. Rather, Conservative policy evolved during the early 1980s until a full blown, ideologically driven, and systemic program emerged. The British case shows that governments do not necessarily have fixed or invariant privatization strategies. They can shift from one strategy to another over time, and it is possible to identify various phases. Over this period, under the leadership of Thatcher, and later of John Major, the great majority of Britain's existing state industrial sector was privatized. In terms of asset sales, the list includes the telephone system, electricity generation and distribution, coal, gas, water, British Steel and British Rail and part of the Nuclear Power generation industry. Rolls Royce, Jaguar, British Airways, the National Freight Corporation and British Ports have also been privatized, along with a number of other companies such as British Aerospace and the Trustee Savings Bank.

Individual tenants of publicly owned council houses were granted a "Right to Buy" their property in 1980 and this, together with the transfer by some local authorities of their entire public housing stock to housing associations, has meant that over 20 per cent of the total nationwide stock has been sold. In addition, the late 1980s witnessed the introduction of compulsory contracting out for several services previously provided by local governments (such as garbage collection), and in the early 1990s there has been a considerable degree of what is termed "market testing" and contracting out within public services such as the National Health Service and the Prison Service. A number of privately operated prisons have been built, and plans are well advanced for construction of privately operated hospitals for the National Health Service (NHS).[5] The scale and pace of privatization in Britain has been remarkable; as Veljanovski

---

[4] Peter Saunders and Colin Harris, *Privatization and Popular Capitalism* (Buckingham: Open University Press, 1994), pp. 14–16; Yair Aharoni, "The United Kingdom: Transforming Attitudes," in Raymond Vernon, ed., *The Promise of Privatization* (New York: Council on Foreign Relations, 1988), p. 37.

[5] Kate Ascher, *The Politics of Privatization: Contracting Out Public Services* (Basingstoke: Macmillan, 1987); title to follow *The Independent*, March 23, 1995.

comments, "privatization in Britain has been pushed further, faster, and into more controversial areas than elsewhere."[6] By early 1991, *over half* of the public sector had been transferred to private hands; 650,000 workers had changed sectors; a fifth of the British population now owned stock, compared to only 7 per cent in 1979; and nationalized industries accounted for less than 5 per cent of the UK output (down from 9 per cent in 1979). Nor was privatization limited to public corporations: 1.25 million council houses had been sold.[7]

The forms of privatization in Britain

Privatization in Britain has taken a wide variety of forms. These include: (1) asset sales, including the sale of public companies previously bought by the government, and the sale of state share holdings in private companies; (2) deregulation or the relaxation of state monopolies; (3) the contracting out of work previously done in house by central or local government, or other organizations such as the NHS; (4) increased reliance on the private provision of service, such as residential homes for older people; (5) the encouragement of private sector involvement in social policy; (6) reducing subsidies and increasing or introducing charges, particularly in welfare services; and (7) the sale of council houses.[8]

There is little doubt, however, that the most important, wide-ranging form of privatization in Britain has been asset sales. This chapter concentrates on these denationalizations, with additional attention to contracting-out and to council house sales, both major additional sources of income to government.[9] In terms of asset sales, the privatization program in the UK was by far the largest and most ambitious of any OECD country, with a value of £45 billion from 1980–91.[10] The total value of asset sales in Japan was slightly greater at £48 billion, but this was largely a result of the sale of Nippon Telegraph and Telecom (NTT) at vastly inflated share prices. Over the same period, the country with the next

---

[6] C. Veljanovski, *Selling the State: Privatisation in Britain* (London: Wiedenfeld Nicolson, 1987), p. xii.

[7] D. Marsh. "Privatisation Under Mrs.. Thatcher: A Review of the Literature." *Public Administration*, 69 (1991), 459–480.

[8] H. Young. *One of Us: A Biography of Margaret Thatcher* (Basingstoke, Macmillan, 1989); Marsh, "Privatization," p. 463.

[9] R. Forrest and A. Murie. "Fiscal Reorientation, Centralization, and the Privatisation of Council Housing." in W. van Vliet, ed., *Housing Markets and Policies Under Fiscal Austerity* (Westport, CN: Greenwood Press), pp. 15–31; R. Forrest and A. Murie, *Selling the State: The Privatization of Public Housing* (London, Routledge, 1991).

[10] B. Stephens, "Prospects for Privatisation in OECD Countries," *National Westminster Quarterly Bank Review* (May 1992), 2–22.

greatest value of asset sales was France, with £8.2 billion, and then Italy, at £6.5 billion. As a proportion of average annual GNP, Britain's sales were exceeded only by New Zealand (14 per cent) with Portugal (4 per cent) and Japan (3 per cent) far behind.[11]

Privatization, nationalization and shrinking the state

It is impossible to properly understand the objectives of privatization in Britain without some appreciation of the wider political background. In particular, it is important to note the significance of postwar nationalization, which, together with the growth of the welfare state set the context for the postwar consensus and its subsequent abandonment by Mrs. Thatcher. As we have pointed out in earlier chapters, large-scale privatization is partly dependent on the prior existence of large-scale state holdings or nationalized industries. This was clearly the case in Britain, where a very substantial nationalized industry sector had been built up over a 150-year period.[12] This expanding public sector was initially linked to Britain's imperial past and the development of state shipyards, the ordnance industry and radio-telephony as key elements of imperial power. Foreman-Peck points out that, prior to the First World War, substantial portions of gas, water and electricity were already owned by the state, along with most of telecommunications network, the postal service, and the naval dockyards. The proportion of total employment in state industry was still small, however, at about 7.4 per cent. Adding in the tightly regulated railway sector would roughly double the numbers employed in the state regulated sector.[13]

There were some relatively minor nationalizations carried out for strategic reasons during the inter-war period, but it was not until Labour came to power in 1945 that large-scale nationalization became a reality in Britain. Committed to a reformist program, and with a large parliamentary majority, the postwar Labour government carried out a number of key nationalizations. They were the British European Airways (1946), the National Coal Board (1947), British Transport Commission (1948), Electricity Generation and Distribution (1948), Gas Generation and distribution (1949), and Iron and Steel (1951). These mark what Foreman-Peck terms a "quantum jump"[14] in the nationalization process. As a whole, the 1940s settlement represented a genuine enlargement of the

---

[11] Ibid.
[12] J. Foreman-Peck, "The Privatization of Industry in Historical Perspective," *Journal of Law and Society*, 16, 1 (1989), 129–148. See also M. Beesley and S. Littlechild, "Privatization: Principles, Problems and Priorities," *Lloyds Bank Review*, July, 1983, 1–20.   [13] Foreman-Peck, "Privatization."   [14] Ibid.

functions and responsibilities of the state. The collective welfare was to be guaranteed through an expansion of the public sector, which now included utilities, social security, the National Health Service, and housing; while at the same time, the state increased its attention to economic planning and the environment.[15]

Although Labour was defeated in 1951, the return of the Conservatives did not mean that the collectivist advance of the 1940s was reversed.[16] Subsequent Conservative governments accepted the changes, although road haulage and iron and steel were denationalized. As Gamble points out in relation to Britain: "The prosperity and relative harmony of the 1950s made the 'mixed economy' and the Welfare state seem permanent fixtures of a modern capitalist economy."[17]

But during the 1970s, right-wing Conservative discontent with the postwar consensus, the growth of the state, and the power of the unions, was crystalized by two events. The first was the defeat in 1974 of Edward Heath's government over the question of "Who runs the country?" The second was the so-called "Winter of Discontent" in 1978–9, when the issue of trade union power was again center stage. There was also considerable Conservative disillusionment over what was seen to be a U-turn in policy by the Heath government which, after committing to reduced state intervention in 1971, none the less took over the ailing Rolls Royce and Upper Clyde Shipbuilders, which were both facing receivership. Despite promising the opposite during its electoral campaign, the Heath government left office in 1974 with a larger portfolio of state industrial assets than when it came to power four years earlier.[18] The right wing of the Conservative party saw the nationalized industries as a financial and political burden on the state and wanted rid of them. Simon Jenkins comments that:

They occupied extraordinary amounts of ministerial time and effort. The financial and industrial troubles of British Leyland, British Steel, and British Coal dominated the cabinet agenda. Their borrowing and subsidy requirements were a perpetual drain on public finances. In 1979, they were costing each taxpayer an average of £300 a year at 1995 prices.[19]

---

[15] A. Gamble. "Privatisation, Thatcherism and the British State," *Journal of Law and Society*, 19,1 (1989), 1–20.

[16] Samuel Beer, *British Politics in the Collectivist Age* (New York: Vintage, 1969), cp. 3. D. Heald, "The United Kingdom: Privatization and its Political Context," *West European Politics*, 11, 4 (1988), 31–48.   [17] Beer, *British Politics*.

[18] Foreman-Peck, "Privatization," p.129. Beesley and Littlechild note that in 1981 the nationalized industries in Britain employed 1.6 million people and had a turnover of £43bn.

[19] Simon Jenkins (1995) *Accountable to None: The Tory Nationalization of Britain* (London: Hamish Hamilton, 1995).

The role of ideas

At the same time, Keynesian ideas of economic management were falling into disrepute. These had dominated the macroeconomic policies of both Labour and the Tories since the war, but, following the oil crisis of 1973–74, the industrial world began to experience severe dislocations. Inflation and unemployment now rose in tandem, a development Keynesian theory and the Phillips Curve could not explain. Tinkering with the usual policy formulae failed to make much headway, despite innovations such as incomes policy and "cash limits." In a sense, the persistent economic problems of the 1970s seemed immune to treatment by the established policy doctrines, and Britain – as well as the rest of the world – became ripe for a dramatic shift in economic orthodoxy.[20]

Neo-liberal views, the most coherent alternative to Keynesianism,[21] became influential within the Conservative party. Their thinking was strongly influenced by a set of beliefs derived from Friedrich Hayek and other academic economists who had never been happy with the welfare state. The ideas were promulgated in the party by Keith Joseph and others associated with Margaret Thatcher. Nor was the call sounded merely among politicians and academics. Privatization found a strong champion in Samuel Brittan of the *Financial Times*,[22] while the more shrill conservative think tanks also joined the chorus. As Joel Wolfe notes, "privatization involved a small group of ideologically motivated leaders remolding the state itself . . . privatization realized the objectives of a neo-liberal ideology which had become ascendant in Britain through the efforts of Conservative Party politicians, media commentators, 'New Right' think tanks and academics."[23]

The result was a doctrine reminiscent of the famous dictum "Four legs good, two legs bad," of George Orwell's novel *Animal Farm*, with four legs embodying the virtues of a free market, consumer choice and private ownership, and two legs encompassing any form of state intervention and ownership. Thus, when Mrs. Thatcher took over control of the party in

---

[20] See especially, Peter A. Hall, "Policy Paradigms, Social Learning and the State: The Case of Economic Policy Making in Britain," *Comparative Politics*, 25, 3 (April 1993), 282–286. By using the notion of "paradigm shift," we, like Hall, do not mean to imply that the economic doctrines were "scientific" in the same sense as the "hard" sciences. Cf. Thomas Kuhn, *The Structure of Scientific Revolutions* (Chicago: University of Chicago Press, 1970).   [21] Hall, "Policy Paradigms," p. 286.

[22] Samuel Brittan, "The Politics and Economics of Privatization," *Political Quarterly*, 55, 2 (1984), 109–125.

[23] J. Wolfe. "State Power and Ideology in Britain: Mrs. Thatcher's Privatisation Programme," *Political Studies*, 34 (1991), 243. See David Heald, 'The United Kingdom: Privatization and its Political Context," in J. Vickers and V. Wright, eds., *The Politics of Privatization in Western Europe* (London: Frank Cass, 1989), pp. 31–48.

1975, the stage was set for a radical change of direction.[24] Thatcher's election in 1979 meant that the consensus politics of the previous thirty years were abandoned by a government intent on making a radical break with both Keynesianism and social democracy.[25] Indeed, the neoliberal ideas, which would eventually partly crystallize as privatization, had as their goal not just "rolling back the frontiers of the state, but the reorganization of both government institutions, and civil society, as well the border which separated them."[26] This new relationship involved a shift of control and responsibility from the state to individual producers and consumers who, it was hoped, would look to the market for services rather than to the state. Individuals were to be encouraged to stand on their own feet and not look to the state for provision. Thus, the neoliberal policy of shrinking the state was ideologically motivated, politically construed and economically implemented.

The development of Conservative privatization policy

All Conservative governments since the war have been committed to some degree of de-nationalization, and this commitment grew stronger during the 1970s culminating in the Ridley report in 1978 which advocated dismantling the nationalized industries and weakening the power of public sector trade unions. There is little evidence, however, of any Conservative commitment to widespread privatization prior to 1979. It is generally agreed[27] that Conservative privatization policy evolved from experimental origins as the Conservatives became increasingly more attracted to its perceived merits. The policy's evolution can be roughly divided into four phases, corresponding to the four administrations since 1979.

Thus, although Mrs. Thatcher declared in 1980 that "the two great problems of the British economy are the monopoly nationalized industries and the monopoly trade unions,"[28] the 1979 Conservative election manifesto did not use the term "privatization." It did, however, contain four specific proposals. These were: (1) to return to private ownership the recently nationalized aerospace and shipbuilding industries; (2) to sell shares in the National Freight Corporation; (3) to relax bus licensing

---

[24] P. Jenkins, *Mrs Thatcher's Revolution: The Ending of the Socialist Era* (Cambridge, MA: Harvard University Press, 1988); P. Ridell, *The Thatcher Government* (Oxford: Basil Blackwell, 1985); Young, *One of Us*; Jenkins, *Accountable to None*.

[25] Gamble. "Privatisation, Thatcherism and the British State." See also, Joel Wolfe, *Power and Privatization: Choice and Competition in the Remaking of British Democracy* (London: Macmillan, 1996), ch. 2.   [26] Ibid., p. 6.

[27] Marsh, "Privatisation;" Veljanovski, *Selling the State*; Wolfe, "State Power."

[28] Young, *One of Us*.

regulations, so as to encourage growth of private bus services; and (4) to grant council housing tenants a right to buy their homes at a discount on their market value. Such commitments hardly represented a coherent program, and they were dwarfed by the emphasis placed on monetarism, which had pride of place in the 1979 program.[29] Not only did privatization have a low priority in 1979, many Conservatives feared it would be extremely unpopular, both within the Party and electorally.[30] In the end, privatization unfolded in several phases.

The first, experimental, phase (1979–83) corresponded with the Conservatives first term of office. During this period the policy concentrated on selling what Wolfe terms "profitable firms at the periphery of the public sector."[31] The government privatized, or took steps to privatize, twenty-five enterprises, including five major state-owned undertakings which were converted into companies with just under 50 per cent private share holdings. These were British Aerospace (1981), Cable and Wireless (1981), Amersham International, the National Freight Corporation (1982) and Britoil (1982), of which only British Aerospace and the NFC had been mentioned in the election manifesto.

The government also began liberalization in the transport and telecommunications sectors, privatized Associated British Ports (in 1983), and sold a second, small, slice of its shares in BP, raising £565 million in the process. Interestingly, the first slice had been sold by Labour in 1976 to raise money to reduce the budget deficit and reassure the International Monetary Fund that its policies would be fiscally responsible. Since the most prevalent justification of state enterprise is in areas of perceived market failure – that is, areas of the economy where laissez-faire might allow monopoly rents, mean no service was provided, or result in other sub-optimal outcomes[32] – it is not surprising that the first phase involved "sales of firms with no real characteristics that would justify their retention in the public sector."[33] Nor is it surprising that, although some sales were outright sales of all equity, as in the case of Amersham International, most of British Rail Hotels, and some of the subsidiaries of the National Enterprise Board (especially Ferranti, International Computers Ltd. and Fairy Holdings), many sales involved only partial transfer of ownership. The usual approach of the government was a partial sale of assets, with the government retaining ownership of just less than 50 per cent.[34]

The first phase was also marked by the radical policy of selling council

[29] Marsh, "Privatisation," p. 460.   [30] Veljanovski, *Selling the State*, p. 3.
[31] Wolfe, "State Power"; Thompson, *The Political Economy of the New Right*.
[32] See especially, Feigenbaum, *The Politics of Public Enterprise*, ch. 1.
[33] Veljanovski, *Selling the State*.   [34] Ibid., pp. 3–4.

houses to sitting tenants. This policy, known as the "Right to Buy," gave tenants with over three years' residence a right to buy their home at a discount of 30 per cent of the market value, rising to 50 per cent for tenants of twenty years standing. This policy reflected a long-standing Conservative dislike of the extensive public housing sector in Britain, which accounted for almost a third of all units, and a desire to foster wider property ownership. In fact, the reduction of the size of the council sector has been the one constant in Conservative housing policy since 1979, and a variety of policies have been pursued to encourage this, including increasing the level of tenant discounts and permitting wholesale disposal of some local authority stocks to housing associations.

At the same time, central government funding for council house building has been considerably reduced to the point where, in 1995, it accounted for only a few thousand homes per year, mostly for special needs groups such as elderly people. New social rented building was placed in the hands of independent housing associations, which have also had the level of state funding cut in an attempt to bring in market finance. Rents for council houses were also forced up in an attempt to bring them nearer to market levels and, indirectly, to encourage tenants to buy. The scale of right-to-buy sales has been considerable, and by 1995 a total of 1.5 million homes had been sold. Government receipts from council house sales 1979–84 accounted for more than all other privatizations put together, including the sale of British Telecom.[35]

The date of the second phase of privatization is disputed. Wolfe suggests that it began as early as 1981 when the Conservatives "broadened an already viable program to include the major utilities."[36] He argues that in response to the 1981 economic crisis Mrs. Thatcher decided to deepen and broaden the privatization program setting targets for individual ministers. There were speeches by Cabinet ministers in 1982 which promised a major extension of privatization. Thus, for example, Geoffrey Howe stated, "that state ownership and control should be displaced or supplemented, wherever sensibly possible, by the discipline and pressure of the market place and by some degree of private ownership." Nigel Lawson asserted in 1982 that, "no industry should remain under state ownership unless there is a positive and overwhelming case for it so doing."[37] However, whatever the timing of the idea's germination, the resulting sales of major public corporations began in 1984, the year the Conservative's second administration effectively began.

Privatization accelerated rapidly during the second term of office. Sales

---

[35] Forrest and Murie, "Fiscal Reorientation" and Forrest and Murie, *Selling the State*.
[36] Wolfe, "State Power," p. 248.   [37] Quoted in Wolfe, "State Power," p. 248.

of Enterprise Oil, Sealink Ferries, Jaguar cars, and of British Telecom all took place in 1984. The latter, which yielded nearly £4 billion, at that time represented the biggest ever single equity issue in the world. This was followed by the sale in 1985 of the final slices of Cable and Wireless, British Aerospace and Britoil. In 1986, British Gas was privatized with receipts of £4.25 billion and in 1987 British Airways yielded £900 million. The privatization of British Telecom and British Gas were the government's first foray into the sale of public utilities and marked the beginning of systemic privatization.

By this time, the financial benefits from privatizations were considerable and formed an integral part of the government's financial calculations. In the autumn of 1985, the Chancellor set the government's target for receipts from the sale of state-owned companies at £4.7 billion per annum for the following three fiscal years – twice the sum for the two preceding years.[38]

The third phase of Conservative privatization began in 1987 when the government, confident after winning an unexpected third term of office, extended the privatization program to encompass most types of activity remaining in the public sector.[39] Major privatizations included the British Airports Authority (1987), Rolls Royce (1987), British Steel (1988) and the sale of a further slice of British Petroleum £7.2 Billion. This was followed by the controversial privatization of Rover Cars, which was taken over by British Aerospace with payment from government of almost £400m toward accumulated debts. British Aerospace subsequently sold off parts of Rover for substantial profits (primarily from property sales), which raised questions about the initial value put on the company by government, and the European Union subsequently made the company pay back a proportion of the grant it had received. A similar problem occurred over privatization of the Royal Ordnance factories, which again resulted in large profits from the sale of property and raised questions regarding under-valuation of the assets.

The major development in the privatization program, however, was the decision to privatize the water industry (1989), regional electricity distribution companies (1990) and the electricity generating companies (1991). Equally, the government attacked public sector services, with competitive tendering imposed on all local government services after 1989. In fact, market-oriented reforms had been introduced into the public service as early as the Financial Management Initiative (1982), "Next Steps" (1988), and the "Citizen's Charter" (1991), all of which aimed at making the public service more like a private corporation, and

[38] Veljanovski, *Selling the State*, p. 4.   [39] Wolfe, "State Power."

transforming *citizens* into *customers*.[40] By the 1990s little that had been previously public escaped. With most of state industry already sold, limited forms of privatization were proposed for education, and even the immensely popular National Health Service.[41] With an ideological commitment to systemic privatization emerging as the primary motivating force, the moderating effects of tactical and pragmatic considerations held less sway.

The changes in the NHS involved, among other things, the introduction of quasi-markets via self-governing hospital trusts. These have to sell their services to the general practitioners who hold their own budgets and buy in services. Such changes met fierce opposition from the British Medical Association and others who felt that the standards of service would be undermined. Other services in the NHS were also put out to competitive tender in an effort to reduce costs and increase efficiency. Councils were also forced to introduce competitive tendering for services, with their in-house providers bidding against external companies. This has led to a number of council services, such as rubbish collection and street cleaning, being privatized in many local authorities.[42]

Not surprisingly, this phase of privatization also saw the development of significant opposition to the process. Until the mid-late 1980s the Conservatives had clearly held the political initiative over privatization, and with the exception of criticisms regarding the undervaluation of assets, there had been little significant opposition to the privatization of industrial companies, not least because the power of the unions had been severely weakened. The opposition was mainly directed at the privatization of major utilities and the deregulation of bus services, where it was feared that privatization would replace public with private monopolies leading to a deterioration in service and rises in price. Opposition had begun with the sale of BT and British Gas where, as Veljanovski comments, privatization "moved into the area where the prospect of real competition was rather limited if not entirely absent."[43]

The sale of the water companies in 1989 generated fierce controversy, and this continued into the fourth phase in the 1990s, with the rundown and eventual privatization of what remained of British Coal after a major program of pit closures, the abandoned plan to privatize the Post Office, and the privatization of British Rail.[44] In all these cases there has been

[40] For an overview of British public service reform, see F. Leslie Seidle, *Rethinking the Delivery of Services to Citizens* (Montreal: IRPP, 1995), ch. 2; for a critique of the reforms, see Colin Campbell, "Does Reinvention need Reinvention," *Governance*, 8, 4 (1995), 479–504 and Ascher, *The Politics of Privatization*.
[41] Ascher, *The Politics of Privatization*, p. 249.   [42] Ibid.   [43] Veljanovski, *Selling the State*.
[44] Richard Bailey, "Coal – the Ultimate Privatization," *National Westminster Bank Quarterly Review*, August 1989, p. 2–17

concerted public and media opposition to what was seen as "privatization for the sake of privatization." By this stage, the Conservatives had got the privatization bit firmly between their teeth and what began as a pragmatic strategy had become a vision of systemic overhaul. The Conservatives were now seen, by many observers, to be pursuing a wholly ideological policy. Yet this seemed politically counter-productive as privatizations eventually generated increased opposition[45] and apparently undermined the Party's electoral support. The question, therefore, is why the Tories have pursued the strategy with such vigor, and what the major objectives of the strategy have been. We shall deal with each of these issues in turn.

Privatization: coherent strategy or gradual discovery?

There is considerable disagreement about the extent to which the Conservatives had a comprehensive privatization strategy from the start. On the one hand, there are those who argue that privatization was not a well-developed policy and had in fact been adopted almost by accident.[46] Gamble's comments are representative:

> The Government seems to have stumbled into the policy. Having successfully piloted the sale of a few small publicly owned industries and assets, ministers began to realize that the principle could be extended. It was not until 1983 and 1984 that ministers began to set out the principles behind privatization and to justify measures that had already been taken as part of a coherent program.[47]

The view that privatization had such humble origins is not, of course, universal. Young argues that there was a Conservative policy of privatization from the late 1970s (though it had an experimental element), on the grounds that "it was applied as a philosophy on a sustained and continuing basis."[48] He also claims that the "idea that there was an overall strategy is further shown by the way in which privatization policies were pursued even when they cut across other cherished government aims."[49] These include the promotion of competition and reduction of government expenditure.

How, if at all, can these two conflicting interpretations be reconciled? Our interpretation is that, although the Conservatives began in 1979 with a very strong antipathy to the state sector – reflected in their commitment to denationalize some companies, give council tenants a right to buy,

---

[45] See the conclusion to this chapter.

[46] Matthew Bishop and John Kay, "Privatization in the United Kingdom: Lessons from Experience," *World Development*, 17, 5 (1989), 643–57.

[47] Gamble, "Privatisation, Thatcherism and the British State."

[48] Young. *One of Us*, p. 245.   [49] Ibid., p. 247.

introduce greater competition, weaken the power of the public sector unions and roll back the frontiers of the state – they did not, at first, appreciate the potential of privatization as a systematic program. These initiatives gradually evolved into a policy of systemic privatization driven by an ideological compulsion to make what was public private, and a secondary goal to raise revenues by sales of public assets. We find little or no evidence of any systematic Conservative policy of privatization prior to 1979, and it was only in the second and third terms, with the rise of special asset sales, that privatization became a dominant theme of economic policy.[50] Jenkins argues:

> The new government's first steps towards the outright sale of assets were driven not by any manifesto commitment or sense of ideological excitement but by a fixation with cutting public borrowing . . . The cabinet never saw a white paper putting the public case for privatization . . . The money raising motive was pre-eminent for the cabinet through the first two Thatcher administrations.[51]

Geoffrey Howe, the then Chancellor of the Exchequer said: "The sensible disposal of public sector assets had grown in urgency, not least as a short-term way of helping reduce the PSBR. I set a target of £1 billion for 1979–80." And, as Samuel Brittan of the *Financial Times* pointed out, "selling public assets was politically much easier and more popular than cutting public expenditure."

Why did the privatization program grow so much during the Conservatives' second and third terms? One argument is that the Conservatives simply became more aware of the possibilities of privatization, and realized that what was previous regarded as unacceptable or impossible could be achieved without undue problems. In short, policy learning took place.[52] A second argument concerns the role of key individuals. Jenkins argues that the privatization debate received new impetus following the 1983 election and Nigel Lawson's appointment as Chancellor of the Exchequer. Jenkins states that Lawson "regarded tinkering with nationalized industries as fundamentally misguided and a distraction from the central task of privatizing them." Certainly, the 1983 manifesto was much more explicit, pledging to privatize shipbuilding, airways, cars, steel and airports. Additionally, privatization had political advantages. Monetarism decreed a reduction of the Public Sector Borrowing Requirement, but raising taxes to do so was politically unattractive. The government had begun to rely on privatization revenues to

---

[50] Marsh, "Privatisation," p. 461.   [51] Jenkins, *Accountable to None*, p. 25.
[52] Cf. John Ikenberry, "The International Spread of Privatization Policies: Inducements, Learning, and 'Policy Bandwagoning'," in Ezra N. Suleiman and John Waterbury, eds., *The Political Economy of Public Sector Reform and Privatization* (Boulder, CO: Westview Press, 1990), p. 103; Hall, "Policy Paradigms," pp. 281–283.

fund the PSBR (see figure 3.1). By 1985 the Chancellor was including receipts of £5 billion per annum in the budget estimates:[53]

selling public assets was politically much easier, and more popular, than cutting public expenditure. In addition, during its first term the government suffered a number of disappointments with its economic policy; unemployment rose rapidly, the recession deepened, inflation increased, manufacturing output declined and interest rates rose. Most embarrassingly, the money supply . . . grew consistently faster than the government's plans . . . It was not surprising that the government sized upon privatization as an alternative way to control the PSBR, given that the proceeds from such sales are treated as negative public expenditure and thus reduce the PSBR.[54]

The fact that privatization was a major government revenue earner does not undercut the ideological motive. Privatization was a way of killing several birds with one stone, cutting back the nationalized industries, reducing PSBR, and changing the structure of British society at the same time. As Jenkins comments, "Political enthusiasm for privatization now found itself riding in happy tandem with fiscal necessity."[55] While the Conservatives may not have had a policy of systematic privatization to begin with, the policy fulfilled many of their most cherished political objectives, not least that of fundamentally and irrevocably reshaping Britain. This brings us to the vexed question of competing objectives.

The objectives of privatization

What have been the objectives of privatization policy in Britain under the Conservatives and has there ever been a single underlying fundamental objective? The conventional answer to this question is that Conservative privatization policy has never had a single, overriding objective but has, instead, had a number of different and conflicting objectives, the balance of which has changed over time as policy evolved.[56] Importantly, these objectives have not necessarily been compatible, as they have included raising funds for the Treasury, widening share ownership to create a share-holding democracy, stimulating efficiency and depoliticizing economic decision making from the political process.[57]

While it is true at one level that the more specific objectives have changed over time, at a more fundamental level we argue that there has

[53] Marsh, "Privatisation."   [54] Ibid, p. 461.   [55] Jenkins, *Accountable to None*, p. 29.
[56] J. Vickers and G. Yarrow, *Privatisation: An Economic Analysis* (Cambridge, MA: MIT Press, 1988); L. A. Kay and D. J. Thompson, "Privatization: A Policy in Search of a Rationale," *The Economic Journal*, 96 (1986), 18–32; D. A. Heald and D. R. Steel, "Privatizing Public Enterprise: An Analysis of the Government's Case," *Political Quarterly*, 53 (1982), 333–349.
[57] P. G. Hare, "Eastern Europe: The Transition to a Market Economy," *Royal Bank of Scotland Review*, 169 (1981), p. 6. See also Henig, Hamnett and Feigenbaum, "Privatization in Comparative Perspective," *Governance*, October 1988, 442–468.

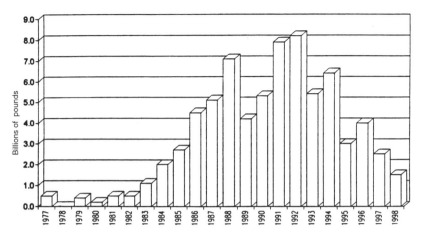

Figure 3.1 Privatization proceeds 1977–1998 (in billions of pounds).
Source: *Financial and Budget Report 1996–97* (London: HMSO, 1996),
p. 139. Figures for 1996 onwards are projections

been a single, overriding objective: the shift from public to private ownership, which is associated with a reshaping of the British economy and
society. Where more specific aims have shifted or been in conflict, this
goal has consistently underpinned policy, however implicitly.
Veljanovski, identifies at least eight different objectives that played a role
in motivating privatization policy. More or less chronologically they are:
(1) to reduce government involvement in the decision making of industry; (2) to permit industry to raise funds from the capital market on
commercial terms and without government guarantee; (3) to raise
revenue and reduce the public sector borrowing requirement (the
PSBR); (4) to promote wider share ownership; (5) to create an enterprise culture; (6) to encourage workers share ownership in their companies; (7) to increase competition and efficiency; and (8) to replace
ownership and financial controls with a more effective system of economic regulation designed to ensure that the benefits of greater
efficiency are passed on to consumers.[58]
    It is important to understand that these goals evolved gradually, that
the particular goals emphasized have varied from one privatization to
another, and that justifications were often articulated *ex post facto*.[59] It was
left to John Moore, financial secretary to the Treasury and principal
architect of privatizations, to "equip the de facto policy, after the event,
with a more or less consistent philosophy."[60] In Moore's own words,

[58] Veljanovski, *Selling the State*, p. 8.   [59] Ibid., pp. 7–8.
[60] Heidi Abromeit, "British Privatisation Policy," *Parliamentary Affairs*, 41 (1988), 72.

Privatization is a key element of the government's economic strategy. It will lead to a fundamental shift in the balance between public and private sectors. It is already bringing about a profound change in attitudes within state industries. And it opens up exciting possibilities for the consumer; better pay, conditions and employment opportunities for the employees, and new freedom for the managers of the industries concerned . . . Our policies have been specifically designed to further a number of objectives. They are designed to lead to greater efficiency . . . They reduce the role of the public sector and provide substantial sale receipts. They allow employees to take a direct stake in the companies in which they work and this leads to major changes in attitude. And importantly, they provide a major stimulus to wider share ownership.[61]

There is no doubt that popular share ownership in Britain widened considerably as a result of privatization. The proportion of the population owning shares rose from around 6 per cent in 1984 to 20 per cent in 1988, almost entirely as a result of privatization. But while this is a positive development, many shareholdings are small, and many share owners only own shares in one or two companies. Moreover, the distribution of privatized shareholdings is highly socially uneven, with a marked over-representation in the higher social classes and income groups, particularly in the South East of England.[62] To this extent, privatization benefited financially the constituency from which the Conservatives derived most support. The creation of a wider share-holding society occurred primarily within Conservative ranks and the policy had a clear material and electoral base.

But Moore's list of objectives does not mean that privatization policy was not driven by a deep, underlying political ideology in which private ownership was seen to be inherently superior and more socially beneficial than public ownership. It was simply assumed that a change in ownership would improve economic performance as well as having the political bonus (for Tories) of weakening public sector unions.[63] Privatization was thus the "proper and general solution"[64] based on the fundamental faith that market coordination was superior to the political or administrative varieties.[65]

Like all ideas that are intended to catch on, the policy was advertised to have benefits for Britain generally. Proponents argued that privatization would lead to a more entrepreneurial society. Orientations and attitudes in British society toward business and trade were seen by many of the policy's advocates as the source of British economic decline. Indeed, Veljanovski argues that this perception is "one which drives the privatization program." Not only was privatization rooted in such notions, but

[61] J. Moore, "The Success of Privatisation," HM Treasury. 1985.
[62] HM Treasury, Economic Progress Report, no. 195, April 1988.
[63] Saunders and Harris, *Privatization and Popular Capitalism*, pp. 19–24.
[64] Hare, "Eastern Europe," p. 6.
[65] Gamble, "Privatisation, Thatcherism and the British State."

implementation of the policy could *change ideas* along the length and breadth of British society. The power of policy to reorient attitudes toward economic behavior was itself an idea deeply seated within influential sections of the Conservative Party.[66] Thus, privatization was seen as a key element in a transformation of British society.

However, ideas do not exist in a vacuum. The transformation which the Conservatives wished to effect was the mirror image of the egalitarian goals which had justified the growth of the public sector. Welfare states everywhere have developed as a response to the inequities produced by the market. Likewise, the nationalizations inspired by the Labour Party's famous Clause IV were intended to reduce the inequalities generated by capitalist economies. The shrinking of the British state has consequently weakened the capacity to compensate for the inherent inequalities of capitalism. Policies intended to re-energize the individual have been at the expense of social solidarities. This was done intentionally. The breakdown of social solidarity was obscured by such slogans as "popular capitalism" and "share-owner democracy," but the contradictions became more apparent as the privatizations progressed, and especially as the public utilities raised their prices to the benefit of private investors and company directors. We will discuss this at greater length in the conclusion.

Privatization, competition and the consumer

The criticisms of the government's privatization program have been many and varied.[67] But one of the major ones has been that the government's desire to privatize led to them giving transfer of ownership to the private sector a much higher priority than greater efficiency or competition. Ironically, Beesley and Littlechild, both proponents of privatization, argued in 1983 that

> Privatization is not merely a matter of selling shares in a nationalized industry, the underlying context is to improve industry performance by including the role of market forces. Privatizations should be designed to maximise net consumer benefits measured primarily by lower prices and improved quality of service, rather than stock market proceeds. (p. 17)

At root, the argument is that the government consistently chose to create private monopolies rather than a system of competitive companies. These were ostensibly tolerated in order to attract the support of public company managers and employees, as well as to encourage wider share ownership in the name of "popular capitalism."[68]

---

[66] Veljanovski, *Selling the State*, p. 9.   [67] Ibid.
[68] Ibid.; see also Saunders and Harris, *Privatization and Popular Capitalism*, 21–26; Oliver Letwin, *Privatising the World* (London: Cassell, 1988), pp. 45–48.

Although this was not the case where British Steel, British Aerospace, Cable and Wireless, Rolls Royce and others were concerned, since they were industrial companies competing in competitive international markets, there was considerable degree of truth in this charge where the public utilities were concerned. British Gas was privatized as a monopoly supplier and the Water Industry and the Electricity Distributors were privatized in the form of regional monopolies.[69] British Telecom was not in quite the same league. Although the government privatized BT as one company, it also deregulated telecommunications and provided for the emergence of competitors. Simon Jenkins comments that, in the rush to get the utilities to market to relieve public borrowing, "Little thought was given to the philosophy of their regulation and even less to injecting into them competition or other market disciplines." John Kay concluded that "the conflict between privatization and liberalization is no longer a conflict but a rout,"[70] and Lawson himself admitted that "the most serious criticism is that the government concentrated too much on ownership and not enough on competition." [71]

As a result of this form of privatization, the privatized utility monopolies were apparently far more concerned to increase profits, dividends, and share prices than they were to reduce prices to the consumer. Although they may have been efficient in cutting costs (partly through large-scale redundancy programs), prices rose rapidly and some services declined sharply.[72] Consequently, the gains to consumers from the privatization of some utilities have been minimal if not negative. They are paying more for the same service, particularly in the case of water.[73]

A second criticism concerns the substantial premiums on shares earned by privatized companies immediately after trading commenced.

[69] For studies of electricity privatization, see Jane Roberts, David Elliott and Trevor Houghton, *Privatising Electricity: the Politics of Power* (London: Bellhaven, 1991); John Surrey, ed., *The British Electricity Experiment: Privatization, the Record, the Issues, the Lessons* (London: Earthscan, 1996).

[70] John Kay, *Privatization and Regulation* (Oxford: Oxford University Press, 1986).

[71] Nigel Lawson, *The View from No 11* (London: Bantam, 1992), p. 239.

[72] "Worst railway to cut rush-hour services," *The Independent*, March 14, 1997; "Profit and Loss: three privatized utilities – electricity, gas and water – are paying fat dividends but can barely deliver the goods to their customers. Is there a connection?" *Independent on Sunday*, February 4, 1997; "Rail passengers squeezed by cost cutting," *The Independent*, March 10, 1997.

[73] Veljanovski comments

> The critics argue that the use of privatisation as a revenue raising device for the government deters it from forcing a more competitive regime on industries such as BT and British Gas, because this would decrease the amount it could sell these utilities for. It has distracted the government from the real issues of market structure and how to foster greater efficiency in industry through competition. With few exceptions all the nationalised industries have been sold as one unit and important monopoly privileges have been preserved.
>
> Ibid., p.12. See also Surrey, *The British Electricity Experiment*.

Table 3.1. *Sales in Britain*

Company	Gross Proceeds (Lm)	Discount[a]
Offer for sale		
British Petroleum (1979)	290.4	3.0
British Aerospace (1981)	148.6	14.0
Cable and Wireless (1981)	223.9	17.0
Amersham International (1982)	71.0	32.0
Assn. British Ports (1983)	22.0	23.0
Jaguar (1984)	293.5	8.0
British Telecom (1984)	3915.6	92.0
British Aerospace (1985)	550.7	22.0
Britoil (1985)	448.8	22.0
Cable and Wireless (1985)	932.9	1.0
British Gas (1986)	5434.4	36.0
British Airways (1987)	900.3	70.0
Rolls Royce (1987)	1362.5	73.0
Brit. Airports Authority (1987)	918.8	46.0
British Petroleum (1987)	na[b]	na[b]
Tender Offers		
Britoil (1982)	548.8	−18.0
British Petroleum (1983)	565.5	3.0
Cable and Wireless (1983)	275.0	− 2.0
Assn. of British Ports (1984)	52.4	2.0
Enterprise Oil (1984)	392.2	0.0
Brit. Airports Authority (1987)	362.5	0.0

Notes:
[a] End of first day.
[b] Comparable information on the 1987 BP sale cannot be given. The Trustee Savings Bank sale has been omitted as a special case where proceeds went to the company itself rather than the government.

Table 3.1 demonstrates that government and their advisors underpriced the shares and thus the government receipts, either from ignorance or because of the desire to ensure a successful flotation. In many cases, immediate post-sale premiums exceeded 30 per cent and in some cases 70 per cent. In the case of the utilities, share prices have risen enormously since flotation, in many cases by several hundred percent.[74] Jenkins comments:

[74] Peter Curwen and David Holmes, "Returns to Small Shareholders from Privatization," *National Westminster Bank Quarterly Review,* February 1992, pp. 41–57; "Taxpayers are still short-changed in sell-offs," *The Independent,* September 26, 1996.

Thatcher's chief concern was to derive a political return from privatization. In meetings with the Treasury she stressed the need to sell fast, and if necessary cheap, to the widest number of shareholders. This led to many undervaluations which cost the taxpayers dear. British Ports was thirty four times oversubscribed, electricity ten times oversubscribed, Rolls Royce nine times and British Airways twenty three times. At the end of the decade the National Audit Office calculated that the manner of privatization cost the taxpayer £2.4 billion in expenses and asset values foregone, half of it on electricity and water.[75]

Investors have not been the only ones privileged by the sales of public firms. Directors' salaries have risen very significantly, while many have been awarded large share options despite undertaking effectively the same job as before. Thus, the *Independent on Sunday* ran the headline story, "Privatized power bosses give themselves £72m in shares."[76] *The Observer* ran a similar story, "'Share greed' exposed: the utility chief millionaires," with the sub-heading, "Special report into the power elites whose private greed is staining public life in Britain today."[77]

Viewed from the point of view of greater competition and benefits to the consumer, such a critique seems telling. Even these apparent miscarriages have their intellectual defenders, but to criticize privatization on the basis of the government's declared objectives about competition and the consumer may be naive. We find it reasonable to suggest that the government's objectives in privatization have been more fundamental, and that these criticisms are (in an intellectual if not a moral sense) misplaced. According to Madsen Pirie, one of the key advocates of privatization, government strategy embodied a stepbystep approach to privatization in which even "a private monopoly is better than a public one."[78] Thus, enhancing competition is only one (and not the most important) motivation. Privatization, rather than being an instrument of policy, became the goal. As another intellectual defender put it:

It could be argued that to privatize is itself an objective and one that has been achieved: further, that privatization is based on the government's belief that the state should not be involved in production but should provide the framework for private sector activity . . . In this view privatization is not a policy with static objectives but an approach to industrial policy.[79]

---

[75] Jenkins, *Accountable to None*, p. 32.

[76] "Privatized power bosses give themselves £72m in shares," *The Independent*, February 12, 1995.

[77] "'Share greed' exposed: the utility chief millionaires." *The Observer*, May 14, 1995; "Exposed: who gets what from Eversholt's great gravy train," *The Independent*, February 20, 1997; "In for a penny and out for a pound," *The Independent on Sunday*, February 23, 1997; "Rail chiefs to split £50m," *Independent on Sunday*, February 16, 1997; "Former BR managers to share in £40m sale bonanza," *The Independent*, June 20, 1997; "BT bonus limit doubles to 100% of pay," *The Independent*, June 5, 1997.

[78] Madsen Pirie, *Privatisation: Theory, Practice & Choice* (Hants: Wildwood Press, 1988).

[79] Veljanovski, *Selling the State*, p. 18.

The problem for these advocates was to "orchestrate a radical change in the ownership of resources and institutions in a political setting."[80]

This, we would argue, is at the root of the Conservative privatization policy as it evolved. The major objective became privatization *per se*: the transfer of ownership from the public to the private sector, preferably with a substantial flow of funds to the Exchequer, and with an increase in popular share ownership thrown in for good measure. In this respect, privatization is not simply an idea nor a policy with static objectives but a strategy for reshaping British society as a whole.

Privatization and its aftermath: the rise of regulation

As we argued in chapter 2, privatization need not necessarily result in shrinking the state. State intervention in the economy and society may be transformed without being eliminated and one of the most fascinating consequences of privatization in Britain has been the emergence of regulatory agencies designed to control the power of privatized monopolies to exploit consumers. Indeed, Thompson has suggested that:

> One of the most remarkable features of the "conservative turn" experienced in the UK since 1980 is the paradoxical emergence of extensive *re*regulation of economic activity in a period supposedly typified by drastic *de*regulation. Under an official rhetoric of regulatory reform and competitive advance, supported by a deep ideological commitment to the virtues of market-led solutions to economic problems, the Conservative governments since 1979 have presided over what can only be characterized as a renaissance of intervention.[81]

Veljanovski also comments that the emergence of Oftel (Office of Telecommunications), Ofgas, Ofwat, OfRail and a host of other regulatory agencies has meant that Britain is "witnessing the rise of the regulatory agency as a potent force in public administration." The goal in all these cases has been to trade public monopolies for private ones, but this is justified as being a more effective and efficient form of regulation.[82] Indeed, Jenkins states that: "The argument for Thatcher's privatization of monopoly industries was that it brought regulation out into the open," and he argues that by exposing these matters to public scrutiny, "regulation has had the effect of increasing public interest and public control."[83] Nor have such arguments only resounded from the political Right. No less a figure than Alec Nove noted over two decades ago that ". . . a public monopoly if told to operate 'commercially' will tend to behave exactly the same way as a private monopoly . . . Indeed, it can be argued that it would

---

[80] Ibid.   [81] Thompson, "The Political Economy of the New Right," p. 135.
[82] Veljanovski, *Selling the State*, p. 7.   [83] Jenkins, *Accountable to None*, p. 32.

be worse . . . A private monopoly is generally supervised by some sort regulating body to prevent an abuse of its position."[84]

Regulation in Britain is no slipshod affair. The regulators not only set the framework within which the privatized utilities must operate, they also specify explicit supply criteria and set the pricing formulae. This has been a subject of considerable controversy with critics arguing that the regulators have been unduly generous in their formulae, which typically allow the utilities to recover costs of inflation and then some.[85] But, although Ferdinand Mount, a former head of Thatcher's policy unit, said in 1987 that "it has become clear that the regulators have no teeth and the operators no conscience," the regulators have gradually begun to tighten up their previously rather generous controls which allowed the privatized utilities to make large profits. This can have a dramatic impact on the utilities. In March 1995, the electricity regulator suddenly announced that he was to reconsider previously agreed electricity prices. Unfortunately for the government, his announcement came the day after the sale of the two electricity generating companies (Power Gen and National Power), knocking £3.5 billion off the value of electricity shares and generating widespread anger in the City. Similarly, in 1995, the rail regulator decided to change the basis on which Railtrack would charge for access to its infrastructure and Jenkins points out that "This transformed the value of Railtrack as a private company and the value of the railway operating franchises," and led to questions about the accountability and freedom of operation of the regulatory agencies.

The regulators possess considerable power over the operation, service standards and pricing structure of the privatized utilities. While the Labour government is unlikely to attempt to renationalize any of the privatized companies, not least because of the prohibitive costs involved, it is likely that they will seek to ensure that privatized utilities are tightly regulated for the benefit of consumers rather than their shareholders or managers. Indeed, the months after the election of the Labour government have seen some major victories for the regulators. In June 1997, in an article: "Gas bills to tumble as BG loses battle: Victory by Ofgas will slash revenues by £380m," The Independent stated that:

---

[84] Alec Nove, *Efficiency Criteria for Nationalized Industries* (Toronto: University of Toronto Press, 1973), p. 20.

[85] For amplification, see Letwin, *Privatizing the World*, Annex 4, pp. 130–141. Typical of the criticisms now being made of the regulators is an article in *The Observer*, March 16, 1996 entitled "Utilities' excess profits blamed on lenient regulators." The article stated: "A damning report by an all-party committee of Mps will this week blame lenient regulation for allowing privatized utilities to make huge excess profits . . . The report . . . will say that the regulators were too soft in the early days of privatization. It will also blame the excess profits on the knock-down prices for which the utilities were sold by the Government."

British Gas's high profile campaign against proposed cuts in its pipeline charges ended in a spectacular defeat after the Monopolies and Mergers Commission backed the industry regulator. The decision will slash the company's transportation charges by 21 per cent and knock an average of £29 off this year's bills to 19 million domestic consumers.[86]

Shortly afterwards, the water regulator, Ofwat, announced that the water company dividends had been far too high for a low risk industry and that they would have to come down. Additionally, in early July the Electricity regulator, announced a more stringent pricing policy would be imposed on the electricity. It would seem, therefore, that although share holders have benefited considerably from high prices and dividends since privatization, the new regulatory regimes being put in place could bring the era of excess profits in the privatized utilities to an end. Also, it appears that Labour is putting pressure on the rail regulator to impose tough sanctions on train operating companies that fail to provide their advertised services.[87] Finally, in early July 1997 Labour announced its long-heralded one-off £5.2 Billion "Windfall Tax" on the excess profits made by privatized companies during the first four years since privatization before firm regulation was put in place. This took place despite a concerted program of lobbying by privatized utilities both in Britain and in the USA (several American companies having bought up privatized utilities in Britain).

The growth of regulation in Britain raises some interesting issues regarding the long-term impact of privatization. While it is clear that, in the short term, the privatized utilities have made large profits, the long-term trend is to tighter control, and John Redwood, a former head of Thatcher's policy unit, wrote that "the more detailed regulation becomes, the more the other benefits of privatization in terms of management freedom and innovation are likely to be lost."[88] If this means loss of freedom to exploit the consumer, it will be no bad thing, but there are major unresolved issues about the accountability of the regulators, to parliament, public and the industry. Although the regulators are scrutinized by the National Audit Office, produce reports to parliament and are open to judicial review, they do not hold public hearings and reach their decisions in private. This can lead to charges that they are in the industry's pockets, or conversely, that they are acting unreasonably to hurt

---

[86] "Ofgas shows the way for other regulators," *The Independent*, June 19, 1997; "Gas bills to tumble as BG loses battle," *The Independent*, June 16, 1997; "Water regulator turns off the dividends tap," *The Independent*, June 27, 1997; "Electricity bills to drop by 12 per cent," *The Independent*, July 4, 1997.

[87] "Why what counts is what runs on time: private operators could find Labour acts swiftly to make life better for train users', *The Observer*, May 11, 1997.

[88] Quoted in Jenkins, *Accountable to None*, p. 35.

industry profitability and freedom of operation. Over the next few years, the issue of who regulates the regulators and to whom they are responsible, is likely to become increasingly important.

Conclusions: tactical costs of systemic policy

Veljanovski concludes his analysis of privatization by suggesting that it is necessary "to evaluate policy as it exists. Politicians are self-interested individuals . . . The political payoffs from privatization are the ones which will be the dominant influence."[89] This is a remarkably frank statement which boils down at root to justifying policy on the grounds of political pay-offs; if it offers political benefits, do it. The problem, however, as was indicated earlier, is that privatization in Britain was running into strong opposition from the electorate and media as well as the opposition parties. A front-page story in *The Independent* is illustrative: "Consumers lose in power bonanza: government accused of failing customers as electricity firms plan huge payouts to investors."[90]

Referring to the hypotheses advanced in chapter 1, the evidence in the British case supports the first hypothesis that privatization occurred in Britain when the groups benefiting from redistribution lost power. This flows from the rather straightforward fact that the Conservative party owes less of its support to voters at the lower end of the income scale than it does from middle and upper income voters. The evidence also seems to support our fourth hypothesis, that privatization often generates a backlash within the broad public which, while resentful of taxes and bureaucracy, often rediscovers the appeal of government when efforts to pare the fat from the system begin to cut near the bone.

This analysis suggests that systemic privatization in Great Britain may be an idea whose time has come and gone. The alleged economic advantages of privatization seem, at best, less alluring. More importantly, the political advantages seem to have passed from the positive to the negative side of the balance sheet. On this interpretation, the Conservatives should have been looking very hard at the scaling down or abandonment of privatization in the mid 1990s. But they did not; instead, they pursued the privatization of British Rail even though most commentators saw the project as highly problematic.[91] Jenkins, for example, states: "By the mid-

---

[89] Veljanovski, *Selling the State*, p. 19.

[90] "Consumers Lose in Power Bonanza: Government Accused of Failing Customers as Electricity Firms Plan Huge Payouts to Investors." *The Independent*, February 21, 1995.

[91] The track, stations, and signaling have been made over to Railtrack, the locomotives and rolling stock have been sold to three leasing companies, and the routes and services have been franchised to the train operating companies (TOCs). They have to lease the rolling stock and pay Railtrack to run services. Because it is assumed that all the TOCs will run

1990s the concept, if not the practice, had turned electorally sour. Less than a quarter of opinion poll samples felt utilities privatization had been a good thing. Two-thirds wanted water and electricity renationalized and there was overwhelming opposition to privatizing the Post Office and the railways."[92]

This underlines, we think, the ideological character of the policy, and notwithstanding the strong criticism of the impact of rail privatization, the Conservatives went into the 1997 election on a platform which included privatization of the London underground system. While we can only guess the impact of this on voting, it is appropriate to note that the swing to Labour in London and the South East (large parts of which are very dependent on commuter rail services) averaged nearly 15 percentage points: higher than any other region of Britain, notwithstanding the strong middle-class electorate in the region and its previous support for the Conservatives.

In terms of our threefold typology of privatization, Britain provides an example of a shift from pragmatic to systemic privatization. Although there were strong pragmatic and short-term elements, Britain provides an example of a privatization policy which was driven by a political ideology which had the objective of irrevocably converting Britain from a mixed to a neoliberal market economy. Financial considerations played a part, although it is argued that these were secondary to the goal of transferring publicly owned enterprises into private hands and fundamentally reshaping the economic and social structure of Britain in a way and on a scale that would make it impossible for the changes ever to be reversed. It was

at a loss, they receive subsidies from the franchising director to run services. Each TOC wants to have its own timetables and ticketing, and the current integrated national service with common timetables, ticketing and schedules may disappear. Campbell has termed this the "Balkanization" of the railways. Campbell, "A railway with no passengers," *The Independent*, June 21, 1994. Not surprisingly, the press have run numerous stories with headlines such as "Trains vanish from the timetables," *The Independent on Sunday*, November 13, 1995, and "Panic stations over Railtrack" *The Independent*, November 24, 1994. More recently, *The Independent*, March 27, 1997, ran a long article "Taxpayers foot £5bn bill for rail privatization," summarising the results of a study by a rail economics consultancy which attempted to assess the financial impact of rail privatization. The study put the cost of preparing the industry for privatization at £1.2 bn, and estimated that the £1.9 bn sale proceeds of Railtrack shortchanged the tax-payer by £2.4 bn based on the book value of the company at the time. Finally, it suggested that the biggest cost of privatization, put at £7.1 bn, are the 'interface costs' that result from the ninety-six separate train operators, leasing companies, suppliers, infrastructure companies, engineering and maintainence units having to deal with one another. Although the Conservatives challenged the view that the Railtrack sale was underpriced, it is worth noting that in the three months to July 11 the price of shares in Railtrack rose by over 65 per cent, *The Independent on Sunday*, July 13, 1997). Similarly, massive profits have been made by the sale of some rolling stock leasing companies subsequent to privatization. This suggests that they were greatly underpriced at privatization.

[92] Jenkins, *Accountable to None*, p. 23.

an attempt to change popular attitudes and expectations of the state by shrinking it. The idea was not simply providing sound budgetary management nor offering a more efficient economy, but as Norman Lamont, ex Chancellor of the Exchequer would put it, it was a way of "dishing socialism."

As we noted earlier, policies can have unintended consequences. Privatization aroused strong criticism and hostility in Britain in the late 1980s and early 1990s: some from within the Conservative party itself. Rather than an inevitable adjustment to deterministic economic forces, Britain's privatization policies may be stymied by repercussions that ultimately will establish a limit on radical change. Rather than benefiting the Conservatives politically, rising opposition to the policy has advantaged Labour.

Opposition emerged on three fronts. First, some major privatizations seem likely to have severe adverse effects on the level of service provision, and appear to be pursued largely for ideological reasons. This was the case with the planned privatization of the Post Office which was dropped in early 1995 after strong opposition from Conservative MPs worried about rural closures. In addition, railway privatization, originally scheduled for 1996, was also widely regarded as suspect. The second source of opposition stems from a combination of large profits made by many privatized utilities, sharp rises in prices and the large pay increases awarded to the chief executives and directors of the privatized utilities. The pay rises have generated an upsurge of media criticism at what is commonly seen as privatized corporate greed. Finally, the third source of criticism has focused on the development of "quasi-markets" such as Hospital Trusts in the National Health Service and a series of well-publicized incidents in which patients have been denied treatment or told that beds are unavailable because of cuts and closures. Until the 1997 election there was a widespread fear that the NHS was being privatized by stealth and that this would have an adverse affect on the availability and cost of health care. In a number of respects privatization has become a source of discontent and criticism amongst the British public and mass media.[93]

[93] For a dissenting view, see Jeremy Warner, "Why privatization has been a success story," *The Independent*, January 4, 1997. Warner notes that "The general perception, mostly accurate, is that of excess profits, excessive executive pay and options, excessive returns to shareholders, under-investment and a raw deal for customers," but he argues that there is a flip side to the coin and asks "Would the situation have been any better had these industries not been privatized?" His answer is firmly no. He admits that "there would, it is true, be no excessive profits or pay packets, or fabulous returns for shareholders," but argues that the companies would have remained bloated and inefficient. He also argues that while the regulators have perhaps not been as tough as they should have been during the periodic pricing reviews, if Labour attempts to remove "some of the more unpalatable effects of privatization, then Labour will be destroying the radical, reforming aspects of

The political downside to excessive privatizations became apparent to some members of the Conservative Party, and in November 1994 Michael Heseltine's attempt to privatize the Post Office was stopped by Conservative rebel MPs who said they would vote against the proposal. Some marked this as the end of an era for privatization in Britain. Martin Jacques, writing in *The Independent* in an article headlined "Time runs out for Mrs Thatcher's baby," argued that "as the rest of the world steams ahead, privatization has now come to a shuddering halt in its birthplace . . . there will be no more privatizations this side of a general election."[94] Jacques was too hasty. Despite political concerns, March 1995 saw the privatization of the electricity generating companies and the government privatized British Nuclear Power and British Rail in 1996.[95]

The fact that privatization has become a political liability is instructive from the point of view of the typology introduced in chapter 2. Thus, in the British case it appears that a systemic program can have tactical costs. In the name of tactical politics, a measured distancing from the policy would no doubt have helped the beleaguered Conservatives at the polls. But such was the Tory zeal for continued privatization that the policy may have been a key source of their demise. The radical program for reshaping Britain may have proven the right mechanism to undermine the Conservatives: ideology may have overtaken political judgment and, with it, political survival.

the process, to the ultimate detriment not just of shareholders, but of customers too." This seems to us a weak argument. It accepts that there have been and are major abuses which stem from privatization and weak regulation, and then suggests that it would be problematic to attempt to rectify them. See also McRae, "One day we will all love privatization," *The Independent*, May 17, 1997. Other Conservatives, however, accept the need for greater regulation and Simon Jenkins' "Monopoly game over," *The Times*, May 21, 1997, states that the windfall tax is justified: "From the moment that the monopoly utilities were sold without any profit clawback, a surtax was on the cards."

[94] Martin Jacques, "Time runs out for Mrs Thatcher's baby," *The Independent*, November 4, 1994. A similar argument was put forward in an editorial in *The Observer*, December 18, 1994. under the headline "Government running off the rails." It argued:

> For the past 15 years the Conservatives have run the country and kept themselves in power on the simple proposition that private gain equals public good. the pursuit of individualism has been held up not just as the foundation of democracy but as its only end . . . The mood is changing, however. As Ministers doggedly pursue the last items of privatization, and the behaviour of the management of previous sell-offs become more and more self-seeking, the voters and the Government are moving in different directions. Nowhere is this more evident that in the case of the railways. To the Cabinet, it is an essential means of keeping the privatization bandwagon rolling and ensuring that the coffers are filled for a pre-election tax cut. To the public, it seems that dogma is being pushed through at the expense of the traveller and to the detriment of the public.

[95] But, a controversial plan to privatize air traffic control was dropped in October 1994 and there is considerable debate over both the merits of continued privatization and forms of privatization.

Intriguingly, however, Labour's steadfast opposition to privatization while in opposition, appears to have weakened, faced as it is with demands for increased welfare spending on education and the NHS, and its pre-election promise to abide by the Conservatives expenditure limits. Thus, although Labour had previously declared its firm opposition to privatization of National Air Traffic Control Services, London Underground and the Post Office, in April 1997 Gordon Brown (then shadow Chancellor of the Exchequer) stated that: "We inherited Conservative plans on privatization proceeds. Once we had the chance to look at the Conservative public expenditure white paper, we decided we couldn't rule it out." Tony Blair said in April 1997 that "We have no dogmatic objection to services being run in the private sector. They should be judged on a case by case basis." Since the election, Post Office privatization has been ruled out by Labour – although it will be given more commercial freedom – and there are plans afoot to either sell London Underground or give control to the private sector in return for new investment. While Labour's experiment with privatization does not stem from ideological commitment, its self-imposed financial strait-jacket has meant that it is now having to look at privatization as a way of bringing in new investment into the public sector without breaching PSBR borrowing constraints.[96] Thus, Britain may have returned to pragmatic privatization driven by financial necessity. "Reluctant privatization" may be the best term. To this extent, Thatcherism may have succeeded in its long-term goal of fundamentally reshaping British society. Drawing the line against massive privatization may have helped Labour to achieve its initial goal of capturing government. Now it must manage to *govern* as well. And doing that successfully may require selective reconsideration of the vision of an expansive welfare state that once marked the core of the party's identity.

[96] "Privatization is exposed as Labour's Achilles heel," *The Independent*, April 10, 1997; "Beckett rules out move to Sell Post Office," *The Independent*, May 12, 1997; "Prescott plans to sell Tube," *The Independent*, June 16, 1997; "It's madness, a scandal . . . oh OK, if we need the cash," *The Observer*, April 13, 1997; "How Blair's blurring the Labour line on sell-offs," *The Observer*, March 16, 1997; "Labour expands scope of sell-off scheme," *The Independent*, April 7, 1997.

4 France: from pragmatic to tactical privatization

France was the exception, at least initially, to the world-wide fashion of privatization. It experimented with Keynesianism in 1981, just as its partners were abandoning the approach, and extended the state rather than retracted it. Nevertheless, after two short years of Socialist government, France too joined the privatization bandwagon. Both the Socialist and Conservative governments initiated privatization reforms, but they did so for different reasons. Briefly, we argue that the Socialist privatizations, essentially aimed at deregulating the economy, were pragmatic, motivated largely by the failures of the early nationalizations and Keynesian reflation to spur the French economy, while the Conservative privatizations – primarily, state asset sales – were tactical – aimed at providing voters with a political program distinguishable from the Socialists in the legislative elections of March 1986. Ultimately, privatization allowed the Conservative parties both to win the election and to reward their allies and friends with underpriced assets. The privatization program was put on hold when Mitterrand won reelection in 1988 by reaffirming that France would neither nationalize nor privatize more firms in the runup to increased European integration in 1992. When the Conservatives returned to power in 1993, they once again advocated the sale of nationalized industries, but their privatizations took on a more pragmatic coloration, as they used the proceeds of asset sales to finance employment programs. However, by the time the new Conservative presidency of Jacques Chirac got underway after the spring of 1995, privatization once again took on a tactical twist. This time, a backlash ensued. The backlash made itself felt in the early legislative elections of 1997. Lionel Jospin pronounced an end to privatization as one of the central planks to the Socialists' victorious platform. Privatizations, while not completely halted, were consequently scaled back to only modest and pragmatic proportions.

Background

The role of state intervention in the French economy has been sizable, if not venerable, since the time of Jean-Baptiste Colbert, Louis XIV's

aggressive minister of finance. Such intervention was not unusual for the time. Indeed, Adam Smith's *Wealth of Nations* (1776) was in many ways a diatribe aimed at the general practice of state economic intervention by virtually all European governments. What was unusual about France was the environment which made continued state involvement acceptable and appropriate. Indeed, not only was state intervention considered appropriate, it also was necessary by default. The hide-bound French private sector was traditionally inert. Curiously, the country that gave us the word *entrepreneur* had very few of them. French businessmen characteristically were risk-averse and rarely noted for commercial acumen.[1] Anything approximating modern capitalism was the province of the state. Even there, it was only with the arrival of "new men and new ideas"[2] after World War II that the French economy truly modernized.[3] While the ultimate aim after the war was to confront international market forces, it was taken for granted that such a confrontation should not take place without the guiding and very visible hand of the state. [4]

Unlike the situation in the United States or Britain, initial liberalization proposals originated with technocrats rather than with academic theorists of the Right.[5] Economic liberalism had never had a large following in France. The late industrialization had made state interventionism seem appropriate, and the Jacobin heritage supported the centralizing nationalism of the Right as it did the egalitarianism of the Left.[6] The Gaullists, by far the largest party on the Right, had seen the state as the incarnation of the Nation, while the welfare state was supported by years of tradition in Catholic social thought, going back at least to Pope Leo XIII's bulla, *Rerem novarum.*[7] Only the small, elitist Republic Party of Valéry Giscard d'Estaing championed neoliberalism.

The break with *étatisme* actually occurred with the election of Giscard d'Estaing to the presidency in 1974.[8] While the previous presidents had

[1] David Landes, "French Business and the Businessman," in Earl Meade, ed., *Modern France. Problems of the Third and Fourth Republics* (New York: Russell and Russell, 1964).

[2] Charles P. Kindleberger, "The Postwar Resurgence of the French Economy," in Stanley Hoffmann et al., *In Search of France* (New York: Harper Torchbooks, 1962).

[3] Andrew Shonfield, *Modern Capitalism* (New York: Oxford University Press, 1969), ch. 5; Ezra Suleiman, "Industrial Policy Formulation in France," in Stephen Warnecke and Ezra Suleiman, eds., *Industrial Policies in Western Europe* (New York: Praeger, 1975); John Zysman, "The French State in the International Economy," in Peter J. Katzenstein, ed., *Between Power and Plenty* (Madison: University of Wisconsin Press, 1978).

[4] Zysman, "The French State."

[5] Cf. Jeffrey Henig, Chris Hamnett and Harvey B. Feigenbaum, "The Politics of Privatization," *Governance*, 1, 4 (October 1988), 442–468.

[6] Suzanne Berger, *The French Political System* (New York: Random House, 1974), ch. 3.

[7] See Colin Campbell, Harvey Feigenbaum, Ronald Norpoth, and Ronald Linden, *Politics and Government in Europe Today* (San Diego: Harcourt, Brace Jovanovitch, 1990), p. 466.

[8] Volkmar Lauber, *The Politics of Economic Policy. France 1974–1982* (New York: Praeger, 1983).

been Conservatives, their Gaullist ideology was sympathetic to a powerful state, where public interest and national unity stood in stark contrast to an image of competing selfish interests that would leave France rudderless and vulnerable. Giscard, on the other hand, was trained in neoclassical economics and subscribed to the doctrinal truths of that discipline. The state, in Giscard's view, was lumbering and inefficient as an economic actor. He perceived his election as a mandate to limit its role.[9]

Despite Giscard's immense power, inherent in the French presidency with a (theoretically) friendly majority in the National Assembly, he found it difficult to impose his tastes in economic theory. Neither the fundamentally Gaullist administration, nor Giscard's coalition partners were especially attracted to rolling back the state apparatus that they in fact controlled. Not surprisingly, both interest groups and administrators favored retaining policies and programs set up for their protection.[10]

For a variety of reasons, including the failure of the Giscard-Barre[11] economic program, Giscard d'Estaing was turned out of office in 1981 and the Socialists took command for the first time since the founding of the Fifth Republic. Far from rolling back the state, the Socialists gave statism a shot in the arm. They nationalized five industrial corporations and almost the entire financial sector.[12] The first Maurois government also pursued a policy of Keynesian reflation at the same time, and the result was a foreign exchange crisis that ultimately forced retrenchment and austerity. While the nationalizations had very little to do with the hard times to follow – indeed, most had been brought back to profitability under Socialist management[13] – they formed a convenient focus for attacks by the conservative opposition.

Oddly enough, the Socialists, at this time, became the ones who made significant moves to shrink the state. While nationalization was part of an overall statist program, the experience of power forced modifications. The failure of the 1981 program to stimulate the French economy discredited the left wing of the party and opened opportunities for the centrists. Led by finance minister Jacques Delors, and later Laurent Fabius,

---

[9] Valery Giscard d'Estaing, *French Democracy*, trans. Vincent Cronin (New York: Doubleday, 1977).

[10] Cf. Ezra Suleiman, *Les Notaires* (Paris: Seuil, 1987); Harvey B. Feigenbaum, *The Politics of Public Enterprise. Oil and the French State* (Princeton: Princeton University Press, 1985).

[11] Raymond Barre, an economics professor, became Giscard's prime minister and minister of finance, after the latter fired Jacques Chirac for taking too independent a line on policy issues.

[12] Peter Hall, "Socialism in One Country: Mitterrand and the Struggle to Define a New Economic Policy for France," in Philip G. Cerny and Martin A. Schain, eds., *Socialism, the State and Public Policy in France* (New York: Methuen, 1985), pp. 81-107.

[13] *Wall Street Journal*, April 10, 1985.

the moderates urged a sharp revision of the government's budget cutting (the French deficit exceeded 3 per cent of GNP). Faced with a stagnant economy and a paucity of new ideas, they acted to dismantle much of the French regulatory apparatus, including price and credit controls, and regulations on French capital markets.[14]

Although not ideologically inspired, the need to provide aid to hard hit regions led to something resembling British or American "enterprise zones." These *pôles de conversion* were similar to enterprise zones in that areas experiencing high unemployment, *viz.* ship-building, steel and coal, were targeted for tax abatements and various methods for cutting red tape.[15] To be fair, the resemblance was a bit superficial in at least one respect. Whereas Reagan and Thatcher initially seemed to envision enterprise zones as areas of dismantled government intervention (including relaxed minimum wage and safety regulations), the Socialists planned, from the beginning, to include a host of subsidies for infrastructure and retraining, premiums for job creation, and reinforced power of the central authority in the form of an increased role for the Paris-appointed *Commissaire de la Republic* as local ombudsman.[16] It should be noted, however, that the French Conservatives introduced "*zones d'entreprise*" a much closer version of the "Anglo-Saxon" idea, when they returned to power in the second period of cohabitation (1993–1995).[17]

Round I: privatization as a campaign tactic

While the Conservatives introduced a number of social issues into their electoral campaign against the Socialists in 1986, promising law and order as well as new restrictions on immigration and naturalization, they made economic policy the centerpiece. This was something of an uncomfortable choice, as most of their intended neoliberal reforms

[14] Cf. Michael Loriaux, "State and Market: French Financial Interventionism in the Seventies," *Comparative Politics*, 20, 2 (January, 1988); John Zysman, *Governments, Markets and Growth*, (Ithaca: Cornell University Press, 1983).

[15] *Le Monde*, February 10, 1984; Vivien Schmidt, "Industrial Management under the Socialists in France: Decentralized *Dirigisme* at the National and Local Levels," *Comparative Politics*, 21, 1 (October, 1988), 53–72.

[16] On the regressive nature of enterprise zones, see William W. Goldsmith, "Bringing the Third World Home: Enterprise Zones for America," in Larry Sawyers and William K. Tabb, eds., *Sunbelt/Snowbelt* (New York: Oxford University Press, 1984, originally published in *Working Papers for a New Society*, March/April 1982). On the jungle of aids available to industry in France, see Jean-Pierre Robin, "La Jongle des aides à l'industries," *La Vie Française*, October 1–7, 1984. As Reagan administration proposals were reshaped to make them more politically feasible, they, too, began to deemphasize relief from major regulatory provisions and to add various incentives for state and local governments to provide infrastructure support.

[17] Nicole de Montricher, *L'Aménagement du Territoire* (Paris: Editions de la Découverte, 1995), p. 69.

already had been started (after 1982) under the chastened Socialists. Former prime minister Barre argued that the only workable employment plan was one that permitted a restoration of profitability, but his protestations only echoed those of Socialist prime minister Fabius.[18] Former Giscardian labor minister Stoléru dissented by saying that "to promise full employment now just by returning to growth is a shameful political lie," but concurred with Barre, as did the published Conservative coalition platform,[19] that most of the welfare state would remain intact when the Right regained power.[20]

Dramatic unemployment rates, which actually had risen as the Socialists allowed troubled nationalized industries to shed personnel, made the economy an attractive issue for Conservatives. The problem was one of product differentiation. How could the center-right parties distinguish themselves from the (now) very moderate Socialists, who had beaten them to the punch on issues of decentralization, deregulation, and modernization of industry? In essence, the post-1982 policies of the Socialists deprived the conservatives of offering voters a real alternative, save in one area: the nationalized industries.[21]

In some ways one can interpret the conservative adoption of privatization as part of a process of policy diffusion.[22] There is no question that the French Conservatives were influenced by British experiment as well as the seeming success of Ronald Reagan. Not only did memos on the British experience circulate abundantly in the Ministry of Finance [23] as well as elsewhere in the French government, but the rhetoric implied that the public sector borrowing requirement also was at the root of French troubles.[24] Also like Great Britain, the intent to create a "people's capitalism" was obvious in the incentives to small share holders built into the privatization offers that eventually appeared (see below). These considerations, however, were after-thoughts. Billboards promoting such a shareholder democracy appeared *after* the election.

It seems quite clear that the Gaullists and Giscardian's were more attracted to denationalization as an electoral strategy rather than as simply an economic reform. Not only were the public enterprises (for the

---

[18] Raymond Barre, *Réflexions pour Demain* (Paris: Livres de Poche, 1984); Denis Clerc, "Un Programme Pour la Droite?" *Le Monde Diplomatique*, June, 1985.

[19] *Le Quotidien de Paris*, January 17, 1985.

[20] Lionel Stoleru, *L'Alternance Tranquille* (Paris: Flammarion, 1985); Clerc, "Un Programme."

[21] The conservatives also advocated tougher immigration laws to attract votes destined for the National Front. We are grateful to Nicole de Montricher for emphasizing this to us.

[22] David Collier and R.E. Messick "Prerequisites versus Diffusions: Testing Alternative Explanations of Social Security Adoption," *American Political Science Review*, 69 (1975), 1299–1315.

[23] C. Pfaff, "The French state pulls into gear," *The Independent*, April 25, 1986.

[24] J. M. Levêque, "Reussir les denationalisations," *Le Monde*, June 25, 1985.

most part) profitable and efficiently run, but a key Conservative policy advisor admitted in public that there was no theoretical reason that the nature of ownership should affect the firms' management.[25]

The coalition of Gaullists and Giscardian parties (the RPR and UDF, respectively) came to power with a two-seat majority on March 16, 1986. After some stalling, legal wrangles, and assorted inter- and intra-party bickering, the National Assembly passed Law 86–793 on July 2, 1986 authorizing the denationalization of some sixty-six firms.[26] The Conservative hit list included not only the five industrial groups and myriad banks nationalized by the Socialists, but also aimed at privatizing older public firms. Nationalized insurance companies, advertising agencies, oil companies, glass factories, television networks, and steel mills all were to go on the block, albeit to different degrees, and at different times, intending the project completed by 1991, the end of the parliamentary term.[27] Ostensibly, the aim was to privatize all public sector firms where there existed the possibility for competitive markets. The French constitution forbade the privatization of public utilities.

While the plan for asset sales was significant by any standard and these alone put France among the leaders of the privatization movement, the Gallic project was significantly less ambitious at the local level. This distinguished France from not only Britain and the USA, but also from the more modest program of (then West) Germany.[28] Nevertheless, it should be noted that, while privatization of municipal services was not a major concern of the new government, they were certainly sympathetic to the idea. Prime Minister Chirac, as Mayor of Paris, had used the provisions under the Socialist Decentralization Law to privatize some Parisian municipal services.[29]

Justification

The justifications for denationalization were familiar. Public management was assumed to be inherently inefficient, although evidence for such assumptions, excepting, perhaps, for overmanning in the railway, steel

[25] Jean-Claude Casanova's remark at the conference on "Change and Continuity in Mitterrand's France." Harvard University, Cambridge, Massachusetts, December 17, 1985. Along with Renault, the least efficient nationalized firms were the banks, but it was not obvious that their inefficiencies, largely due to over-manning, were related to the legalities of ownership: *The Financial Times*, July 22, 1986. Casanova's opinion is, of course, not shared by many economists. See below.   [26] *Journal Officiel*, July 3, 1986.
[27] David Cameron, "The Nationalized Industries after March 16," *French Politics and Society*, 14, June 1986.
[28] Cf. Henig, Hamnett and Feigenbaum, "The Politics of Privatization"; and Christopher Allen, "Collective Privatization: Subnational Industrial Policies in the Federal Republic of Germany," paper prepared for presentation at the Annual Meeting of the International Studies Association, London, March 30–April 1, 1989.
[29] D. de la Martinière, "Privatisations," *Revue des Deux Mondes*, October 1986, 115–119.

and banking sectors, was scarce. Yet in part the argument for privatization was a pragmatic response to a government cash shortage. The most frequently cited reason for the privatization effort was the expected fiscal windfall from the sale of public assets.[30] Over 200 billion francs were estimated to accrue to the treasury from privatizing the nationalized firms. The windfall would serve the ends of industrial policy: it would allow the government to cut taxes, which would improve profit margins and therefore encourage investment.[31] In short, the main justification for the privatization program bears a striking similarity to the supply-side reasoning of the Reagan administration in the USA.

Privatization, however, was meant to solve more than the government's problems with cash flow. France has traditionally had narrow and shallow capital markets.[32] The new equity issues (along with deregulation begun under the Socialists) were expected to give France, for the first time, a real stock market. [33] Like Britain, the espoused purpose was to encourage small share-holders, creating a "people's capitalism." [34] The latter reason was the justification given for selling Saint-Gobain, the first company to go on the block, at a share price under market value. French small investors have a reputation for conservatism and reluctance to buy stocks.[35] Thus, small investors were given priority in case the issues were over-subscribed. Selling the stock cheaply also allowed Chirac and company to avoid the embarrassment Mrs. Thatcher suffered when British investors were reluctant to buy the shares of British Petroleum (initially floated in 1980) as well as other companies that were offered at market value.[36] (The BP privatization fiasco which succeeded the October 1987 world stock market crash was not anticipated by the French, but the episode underlined the potential fragility of depending on market prices to assure public purposes.) As with the case in Britain, small investors could be replaced by large investors by way of secondary trading. Many eventually were.

Some important divergences appeared between the USA and the UK on the one hand and France on the other. Because of France's shallow capital markets, Conservatives were especially vulnerable to the charge that the privatized firms would be bought by foreigners.[37] It was on this nationalistic basis that Mitterrand was able to credibly refuse signing the

---

[30] Ibid.   [31] Levêque, "Réussir."   [32] Zysman, *Governments, Markets and Growth.*
[33] De la Martinière, "Privatisations."   [34] Ibid.
[35] *Wall Street Journal*, November 5, 1986.
[36] *Wall Street Journal*, May 7, 1980; Harvey B. Feigenbaum, "Public Enterprise in Comparative Perspective," *Comparative Politics*, 15, 1 (October 1982), 101–122.
[37] This threat also appeared in Britain as demonstrated by the Westland PLC affair over the American bailout of a British helicopter firm, but the usual availability of British buyers made this aspect of privatization less politicized in the UK. Moreover, the issue that Westland politicized was the role of secrecy and the proper functioning of cabinet government, not the danger of British assets falling into foreign hands.

original privatization decree on the grounds of national interest. Under the French constitution, this forced the bill to be resubmitted to the National Assembly, which, in a slap at the President, weakened the "preference share" provisions. These allowed the state to control equity sales, by protecting a controlling bloc of stock from foreign purchase if the Minister of Finance so decided. (The "preference share" was thus similar to the British "golden share.") In addition, the National Assembly enabled foreigners to purchase a maximum of up to 20 per cent of any previously public corporation.

Paradoxically, foreign mergers were also touted as an advantage to privatization. European multinationals, with a continental scale, could be now formed, it was said, by merging the formerly nationalized firms with European, and especially Common Market, partners.[38]

Finally, it was argued, privatization would allow diversification.[39] This argument was also paradoxical because the Conservatives had used rationalization of industries as a principal argument for deregulating lay-off procedures. The Socialists had, in fact, rationalized much of France's industrial structures by nationalizing companies and shifting affiliates: e.g., shifting computers from St. Gobain, a glass maker, to CII-Bull; a computer firm.[40]

Nationalization versus privatization in practice

It must be reiterated that privatization, like the other elements of neo-liberalism, had in fact been inaugurated by the Socialists, who saw it as a pragmatic adaptation to economic reality. To Socialist purists, the policy was treason. Industry Minister (and later Prime Minister) Edith Cresson had created something of a furor (at least within her own party) by suggesting that partial de-nationalizations might be necessary to finance French public enterprises.[41] Since the policy contravened traditional ideology, the Socialist government was both more circumspect and more surreptitious about this particular aspect of its conversion to capitalism. While they did not advertise it, in fact, the Socialists had permitted the sale of non-voting shares in public enterprises since 1983 and they turned a blind eye to the blatantly illegal sales to the private sector of nationalized

---

[38] De la Martinière, "Privatisations."   [39] Ibid.

[40] Stephen Brooks, "The Mixed Ownership Corporation as an Instrument of Public Policy," *Comparative Politics*, 19, 2 (1987); Cameron, "The Nationalized Industries."

[41] *Libération*, March 30, 1985; David Wilsford, "The Private/Public Paradox: Privatization as an Instrument of State Control in France, 1983–1988," paper presented to the Annual Meeting of the Midwest Political Science Association, Chicago, April 14–17, 1989; Harvey B. Feigenbaum, "Democracy at the Margins: The International System and Policy Change in France," in Richard Foglesong and Joel Wolfe, eds., *Democracy and Economic Decline* (New York: Greenwood, 1989).

company subsidiaries.[42] These "occult privatizations"[43] had been carried out by public managers wishing to improve the overall profitability of their groups.[44] These were not marginal affairs. According to Schmidt,

Pechiney, by floating nonvoting shares as early as June 1985, was only the first of a number of nationalized concerns to contemplate bringing denationalization in through the back door in this way. In January 1986, Thomson CSF (the subsidiary which makes up two-thirds of the group and is 51 percent state-owned) was already waiting for the okay to raise equity from the markets and in this way to go private, and similar maneuvers were being undertaken by Alcatel (part of the CGE group), Pechiney (again), and the Credit Industriel et Commercial. By May 1986, moreover, [before the Conservatives gained power] Saint-Gobain was preparing to sell 8 million nonvoting shares (with 40 percent reserved for small investors) to raise 2.4 billion francs.[45]

The Conservatives did openly what the Socialists did almost secretly. Their selling of state assets was the fulfillment of an electoral promise rather than an admission of mistakes and a rejection of the Faith which the policy symbolized for the Socialists. The legal text of August 6, 1986 (the July law was modified after Mitterrand's objections had forced resubmission) aimed at selling off "66 firms comprising 27 independent groups, with a work-force of about 900,000. This involved a capital estimated at the time at 300 billion francs, a figure to compare with the total capitalization of the Paris Bourse at the same date: 1,200 billion francs."[46] In short, the French right eventually did more in two years than Margaret Thatcher had done in ten.

While some economic theory posits that the nature of ownership affects a firm's performance, this literature was largely ignored by French politicians.[47] Rather, privatization arguments were based on the notion that, *empirically*, nationalized firms were prone to incorporate externalities (political considerations) that detracted from profitability. However, empirical evidence did not justify privatization in France. Table 4.1 shows

---

[42] Vivien Schmidt, "Industrial Management under the Socialists in France: Decentralized *Dirigisme* at the National and Local Levels," *Comparative Politics*, 21, 1 (October, 1988), 61; Wilsford, "The Private/Public Paradox," p. 12.

[43] The Right had traditionally criticized French public enterprises for engaging in "occult nationalizations" when the latter purchased companies in the private sector. See Harvey B. Feigenbaum, *The Politics of Public Enterprise* (Princeton: Princeton University Press, 1985), ch. I.

[44] Schmidt, "Industrial Management," p. 61; Michel Bauer, "State Directed Privatization: The Case of France," *West European Politics*, 11, 4 (October, 1988), 50.

[45] Schmidt, "Industrial Management," p. 61.

[46] Bauer, "State Directed Privatization," p. 49.

[47] For a flavor of this theoretical debate, although not directly concerned with nationalized industry, compare Michael C. Jensen and William H. Meckling, "Rights and Production Functions: An Application to Labor-Managed Firms and Codetermination," *Journal of Business*, 52, 4 (1979); with Louis Putterman, "On Some Recent Explanations of Why Capital Hires Labor," *Economic Inquiry*, 22 (April 1984), 171–187. We are grateful to Stephen C. Smith for these references.

Table 4.1. *Profits of nationalized companies (in millions of francs)*

	1982		1983		1984		1985	
	Capital grants	Results	Capital grants	Results	Capital grants	Results	Capital grants	Results
Elf	0	+3,500	0	+3,700	0	+6,500	0	+5,300
Bull	0	−1,350	470	−625	1,170	−489	900	+110
EMC	430	−950	70	−159	170	0	230	+100
ORKEM (ex-CDF-Chimie)	570	−800	820	−2,200	1,050	−900	450	−1,000
Pechiney	500	−2,993	3,520	−463	2,150	+546	0	+732
Renault	1,020	−1,300	1,000	−1,600	1,900	−12,500	3,000	−10,900
Rhone-Poulenc	100	−844	400	+98	300	+1,989	0	+2,312
Thomson	200	−180	550	−2,200	1,180	−21	1,400	+126
Usinor-Sacilor[a]	4,500	−8,341	7,100	−11,066	7,900	−15,539	8,800	−9,233
Total	7,320	−13,258	13,430	−14,515	15,820	−20,414	14,780	−12,453

	1986			1987			1988		
	Capital grants	Results	Dividend[b]	Capital grants	Results	Dividend	Capital grants[c]	Results	Dividend
Elf	0	+4,300	870	0	+4,100	720	0	+7,000	800
Bull	1,030	+271	0	1,020	+225	0	1,000	+303	0
EMC	0	−2	0	300	−56	0	0	+200	0
ORKEM (ex-CDF-Chimie)	430	−2,600	0	2,970	+1,000	0	1,100	+3,000	0
Pechiney	220	−451	180	0	+729	10	0	+1,500	190
Renault	5,000	−5,500	0	0	+3,700	0	1,200	+6,500	0
Rhone-Poulenc	0	+2,008	390	0	+2,360	350	0	+3,500	420
Thomson	680	+882	0	500	+1,063	0	500	+1,330	160
Usinor-Sacilor[a]	10,000	−12,512	0	3,700	−5,600	0	9,000	+4,500	0
Total	17,360	−13,604	1,440	11,490	+7,521	1,080	23,600	+27,833	1,570

Notes:

[a] The figures for steel, especially for 1986, are uncertain because of the confusing effect of state costs on company accounts.

[b] The dividends are based on the previous year's profits.

[c] 1988 capital grants noted here are short term. The budgetary cost was only 1 billion for Renault and 1.3 billion for Usinor-Sacilor. On the other hand, forgiveness of Renault's debt (12 billion) required a 3 billion grant to Sodeva, a subsidiary created for the transaction.

Source: Le Monde March 16, 1989, p. 41.

Table 4.2 *Comparison of revenues of nationalized and private companies (gross revenues in millions of francs)*

	1976	1979	1982	1983	1984	1985
Seven nationalized cos.	24,441	42,027	68,622	83,129	109,314	130,481
% growth				21.1	31.5	19.4
Private companies (non-financial)	195,122	283,530	377,126	419,092	469,092	521,924
% growth				11.1	11.9	11.3
All companies (non-financial	219,562	325,557	445,748	502,157	578,406	652,405
% nationalized cos. of all cos.	11.1	12.9	15.4	16.5	18.9	20

Source: Centre Européen d'Entreprise Publique, Annales, 1987; Reprinted in Michel Durupty, *Les Privatisations en France*, Notes et Etudes Documentaires, no. 4857 (Paris: La Documentation Française, 1988), p. 16.

that the nationalized firms were in fact brought back to profitability by public ownership and table 4.2 demonstrates that those companies in fact did better than the private sector.

Moreover, as Bauer notes, underlining the electoral cynicism, the Conservatives' privatization in practice undercut the policy's principal rationale:

Privatization was not, as in some other countries, used to reinforce market forces or to undermine public monopolies. Traditional economic realities were not, from this point of view, changed. Finally, in spite of the ambitious nature of the program only healthy firms were to be sold off, thus explicitly underlining the two premises which were at the root of the nationalization of the Socialists: that nationalized firms can become economically viable; and that firms in difficulties cannot get out of trouble if they belong to the private sector.[48]

These tables suggest that the burden of public enterprise on the state treasury was not a serious justification for the privatization program. Capital grants could be amortized from profits. Economics did not justify privatization. Politics did.

"Noyaux durs" and economic nationalism

Nationalist fears had to be neutralized, however. The potential drain of public enterprise on the public purse did not outweigh the risk of foreign

---

[48] Bauer, "State Directed Privatization," p. 51.

take-over. The scale of the Conservatives' project and the historical risk aversion of French investors made foreign take-overs of much of French industry a real possibility. As mentioned above, under the new privatization law purchases of more than 20 per cent of a company's equity by any foreign investor at the time of privatization were prohibited. But the fact that the state could retain the right to create a 15 per cent "preference share," with an additional proviso that would permit the Minister of Finance to deny any potential investor, French or foreign, from acquiring more than 10 per cent of the privatized company's stock suggested the threshold for control was much lower than the 20 per cent obstacle to foreigners. In reality, then Finance Minister Baladur seemed unconcerned with the danger of foreign takeover and only rarely indulged in the preference share mechanism, as with the privatization of Havas, the communications company.[49]

This new-found relief from xenophobia seems to have two causes. First, although unanticipated, most privatizations were oversubscribed by Frenchmen, especially small investors. Second, the Conservative government relied on another mechanism to land control of privatized firms into the right hands.

As a practical matter, the government strategy was to use banks not yet denationalized to purchase enough shares in privatized firms to block possible foreign take-overs. But much more controversially, the Conservatives sold controlling blocs of stock (*noyaux durs*) to specific French investors, allegedly as a safeguard (or perhaps a preemptive strike) against foreign take-over. Not surprisingly, the lucky purchasers of these *noyaux durs* all had close links to the Conservative parties, especially Jacques Chirac's RPR.

Both the extensive demand for shares in the privatized industries and the good fortune of those selected as buyers of the *noyaux durs* had a common explanation: the government sold the shares at bargain prices. Shares were sold at 5 to 20 percent below market value.[50]

Popular capitalism?

The relative success of public enterprise in France and vulnerabilities of the French capital markets suggest that legitimacy of the privatization program depended on other considerations than economic efficiency. It might, of course, be argued that Conservatives intended to subsidize small investors so as to achieve the goal of a nation of share-holders. That is, in the language of chapter 2, the political goals might have been more

---

[49] Ibid., p. 56.   [50] Ibid., p. 58.

systemic than tactical. The country was indeed transformed from a nation of 1.6 million share-holders in 1981 to over 8 million after the initial wave of privatizations in 1987.[51] True, French law reserved sales to individuals in lots of up to ten shares each (St. Gobain was so popular that most only got four), but the figure of eight million new capitalists was no doubt misleading:

To take advantage of various bonuses associated with some flotations a household of two adults and two children would effectively quadruple their share allocation. Thus, although four individual applications would have been received, this probably effectively represented only one shareholder. Among the new shareholders there were many wives, children, grandchildren or parents of the shareholder of yesteryear. The press even carried stories of two-day old babies becoming shareholders in privatized companies.[52]

This analysis suggests, somewhat unkindly, that the French invested much like the citizens of Mayor Daley's Chicago voted: if not from beyond the grave, at least from the playpen. While dividing the eight-million shareholder figure by four, as Bauer does, to arrive at a truer notion of the country's ranks of popular capitalists may betray an exaggerated cynicism, he is certainly right to point out that a large part of the small investors' shares were resold quickly and more resembled a bet on a sure thing than an investment in the nation's future. By September 1, 1987 at least 20 per cent of the small investors resold their allocation, acting much as their British counterparts did.[53] Moreover a survey of who exactly bought in to the government sanctioned bet hardly reassured those interested in "popular capitalism" as a mechanism for spreading the wealth. Table 4.3 shows that only 6 per cent of the privatized companies' share holders were manual workers, only 2 per cent were farmers, and 2 per cent had a monthly salary of 6,000 francs (about $1,000) or less. On the other hand, 52 per cent of the new stockholders were supporters of the Conservative parties, a number which rose to 73 per cent if one included the far right National Front.

Other forms of privatization

While selling off the nationalized industries hardly created a popular capitalism in France, it might be argued that the asset sales at least provided significant revenues which would ultimately allow the state to ease the private sector tax burden and stimulate the economy. It might also be argued that the main thrust of the program was to increase the room to

[51] Ibid.   [52] Ibid.
[53] Ibid.; Henig, Hamnett and Feigenbaum, "The Politics of Privatization," p. 454.

Table 4.3 *Profiles of privatized companies' shareholders*

Category	Percent	Category	Percent
Gender		*Residence*	
Men	52	Rural	8
Women	48	Small town	30
		Small city	13
Age		Large city	26
18–24 years	10	Paris metro area	23
25–34 years	19		
35–44 years	21	*Monthly household income*	
45–59 years	28	Less than 6,000 Francs	2
60–69 years	11	6,000–12,000 Fr.	30
70 & above	11	12,000–18,000 Fr.	15
		Over 18,000 Fr.	27
Profession		Refuse to declare	7
Independent or			
upper mgt.	22	*Party preference*	
Other white collar	35	Communist	0
Blue collar	6	Socialist	7
Farmer	2	UDF	29
Inactive, retired	35	RPR	23
		National Front	21
		No response or no party	20

Source: IPSOS, *Le Monde*, August 5, 1987. Reprinted in Durupty, *Les privatisations en France*, p. 115.

maneuver for French industry. Sales of privatized shares under market value (see table 4.4) did not bolster a view of privatization as an effort to maximize state revenues; but, given the uncertainties of French capital markets, selling at bargain prices might be considered as satisficing behavior which did not, at least, inhibit the principal goal of creating a more "liberal" economy. Was the Conservative version of privatization, then, simply pragmatism at work?

This forces us to focus on other aspects of privatization beyond the sale of assets. Especially important, then, would be deregulation of labor and capital markets as a mechanism to improve the flexibility of the French economy to a changing market. This would allow French firms to more easily adapt to conditions, as well as avoiding the usual distortions attributed by conservative economists to state regulatory initiatives.[54] As noted above, much of the deregulation was accomplished by the Socialists,

[54] Richard Posner, "Theories of Economic Regulation," *Bell Journal of Economics and Management Science*, 5, 2 (1974).

Table 4.4 *Share discounts on asset sales in France*

Company	Gross Proceeds (FFrbn)	Discount end first day (%)
Elf-Acquitaine (Sept. 1986)	3.3	30.5
Saint Gobain (Nov. 1986)	13.5	19.0
Paribas (Jan. 1987)	17.5	24.2
SOGENAL (March 1987)	1.5	36.0
BTP (April 1987)	0.4	23.1
BIMP (April 1987)	0.4	21.4
TF-1 (April/June 1987)	3.5	7.9
Crédit Commercial (April 1987)	4.4	16.8
CGE (May 1987)	20.6	11.4
Agence Havas (May 1987)	6.4	8.0
Société Générale (June 1987)	22.3	6.1
Suez (Oct. 1987)	19.6	−18.0
Matra (Jan. 1988)	2.0	14.0

Source: T. Jenkinson and C. Mayer, "The Privatisation Process in France and the UK," *European Economic Review*, 32 (1988). Reprinted in Cosmo Graham and Tony Prosser, *Privatizing Public Enterprises* New York: Oxford University Press, 1991, p. 101.

especially in terms of the stock exchange and financial markets.[55] Indeed, the Socialists commitment to neoliberalism went as far as alienating their principal constituency, organized labor, as time after time they increasingly allowed lay-offs and averred the necessity of encouraging *la fléxibilité de l'emploi* (flexible labor markets).[56]

The Socialists not only applied the principles of privatization to these areas of traditional intervention, but, like their British and American counterparts, applied neoliberalism to the state itself. Acting on the earlier advice of the Conseil d'Etat, France's highest administrative court, the Socialists shifted from a PPBS-style system to one where, as the Court put it, "the aim was to increase efficiency and effectiveness, by relaxing administrative and budgetary rules . . ." with tasks set for the bureaucracy on a contractual basis.[57] Public sector unions, an important Socialist constituency, interpreted these reforms as an attack.[58]

[55] Cf. Michael Loriaux, "State and Market: French Financial Interventionism in the Seventies," *Comparative Politics*, 20, 2 (January 1988), 175–194.
[56] Wilsford, "The Private/Public Paradox," p. 12.
[57] Quoted in Yvonne Fortin, "Management Reforms and the Law: A Comparative Perspective," paper presented at the conference "The Executive at the Political Vortex," University of Canberra, Australia, August 1–3, 1996, p. 1. A series of cases leading to this recommendation had been decided by the Conseil d'Etat in the 1970s, but the reforms were implemented in the 1980s.   [58] Fortin, "Management Reforms," p. 15.

If the Socialists were willing to alienate their electoral clientele for the sake of a neo-liberal vision of the economy, the Conservatives were not. Far from abstaining from state intervention, there was not an issue that did not reach the Conservative Ministry of Finance for a decision.[59] The Ministry of Tourism made no effort to deregulate hotel prices, the Minister of Foreign Trade had no interest in curtailing export subsidies and the Ministry of Commerce vigorously enforced the *loi Royer* which protected small shopkeepers from the high volume competition of the *grandes surfaces*.[60] Alain Madelin, industry minister in 1986 and briefly finance minister in 1995, a Conservative apostle of *libéralisme* at election time, cynically dubbed the new Conservative regime "the political market."[61] Neoliberalism was more preached than practiced by its Conservative proponents.

The role of interest groups

Do the interventions of interest groups explain the disjointed implementation of privatization policies?[62] Were the Socialists and Conservatives merely responding to the needs and demands of different constituencies? Were the Conservatives simply more willing to translate the interests of their primary constituency into policy? At first glance, the role of interest groups seems obvious. Generally, organized labor has consistently supported an important state role in the economy and especially supported the Socialist nationalizations of 1982 in particular. Business groups supported the privatization policies of the Conservatives, but given France's history of protecting uncompetitive companies, it is not obvious that all of them should have been in favor of a wholesale withdrawal of the state from economic management. Some nuances are necessary.

Privatization, at least initially, was a selective affair. Early proposals aiming at privatizing a number of state functions occurred under Giscard d'Estaing's presidency (1974–1981), especially in the domain of privatizing radio and television service. Not surprisingly, a number of French consumer electronics and advertising firms lobbied for privatizing at least one television channel, although among the lobbyists was the then state-owned PR giant, Havas.[63] Moreover, the opposition to the project included strange bedfellows. Public sector and telecommunications

[59] Thierry Pfister, *Dans les Coulisses du Pouvoir* (Paris: Albin Michel, 1986), p. 212.
[60] Ibid.   [61] Ibid., p. 220.
[62] We use the term "interest group" with some caution, but, like Jack Hayward, we find it less value laden than "pressure group." See Jack Hayward, *The State and the Market Economy* (Sussex: Wheatsheaf Books, 1986), p. 42.
[63] Valerie C. Rubsamen, "Deregulation and the State: Mass Communications in France," Ph.D. diss., Princeton University, 1987, p. 109–113. Not the least of the privatization lobbyists was the President's brother Olivier Giscard d'Estaing.

unions opposed the program, fearing a loss of jobs, but Giscard's allies, the Gaullists, also opposed privatization because state-owned television had been a traditional mechanism for disseminating Gaullist propaganda.[64] The unions made their opposition known through a series of strikes. The Gaullists communicated their opposition in parliament and behind the closed doors of party negotiations.[65] Initially, it is reasonable to explain the defeat of privatization in a classically pluralist way: more, and more powerful, groups were opposed to privatization than were for it.

After the Communists and Socialists signed the Common Program of the Left in 1972, employers' groups mobilized predictably against the proposed nationalizations. Overtly, their role was essentially that of leading the public relations effort. Globally, the CNPF, the principal employers' federation, has rarely been more than a symbol of the interests of business.[66] As the late Henry Ehrmann remarked, noting the organization's reputation for being ineffectual, "if the CNPF did not exist, would anybody invent it?"[67] However, in the political battle over the Socialists' nationalization program, it did serve as an umbrella for the creation of more specific organizations. The most active of these was the Association des Grandes Entreprises Faisant Appel à l'Epargne (AGREF) under the leadership of Ambroise Roux, long time *éminence grise* of the Conservatives, and president at the time of Compagnie Générale Eléctrique.[68] AGREF led the campaign against nationalizations for France's largest private sector industries.

While smaller firms did not feel immediately threatened, AGREF defended its positions in ideological terms, touting the virtues of free enterprise and *libéralisme*, that is, the generic advantages of capitalism, so as to bring smaller businesses on board.[69] Another organization, "ETHIC," was created at the behest of the CNPF to bring medium-sized firms into the fray.[70] Once again the emphasis was on the virtues of the "free enterprise system."

Thus, in Gramscian terms, the CNPF did play something of an integrative role for the hegemonic fraction of the capitalist class, at least in the rhetoric of the electoral debate. Given that nationalizing the large firms might have reduced the cost of inputs for the smaller firms, for this had often been the role of such nationalized firms as SNCF (rail) and EDF

---

[64] Ibid.   [65] Ibid.

[66] Henry W. Ehrmann, *Organized Business in France* (Princeton: Princeton University Press, 1957); Henri Weber, *Le Parti des Patrons. Le CNPF (1946–1986)* (Paris: Seuil, 1986).

[67] Ehrmann's comment in a review of Weber's *Le Parti des Patrons*, in *French Politics and Society*, 5, 3 (June 1987), 46.

[68] Jean Magniadas, "Le CNPF dans la Lutte contre les Nationalisations," *Cahiers du Communisme*, 53, 11 (1977), 49. Roux was also vice-president of the CNPF.

[69] Ibid., p. 54.   [70] Ibid., p. 55.

(electricity),[71] casting the debate in terms of *libéralisme* produced a class unity that objective interests might have torn asunder.[72] *Libéralisme* became a kind of slogan summarizing opposition to socialism, rather than a blueprint for a genuine free-market economy. Indeed, as Michel Bauer has noted, nowhere was state interventionism more centralized than under the decision-making apparatus of Edouard Balladur, the Conservative finance minister from 1986 to 1988, who became prime minister in 1993.[73]

Union opposition to the Conservative project was rather limited, once the elections of 1986 were lost. Partially, this was due to disaffection with nationalizations, for the Socialist restructuring of the public sector had cost them more jobs than they had gained by the 1982 Keynesian stimulus. It was not only the Communists and their CGT labor confederation who recognized that simply changing the nature of ownership was insufficient to *"changer la vie."* Partially, union interest tended to focus on the health of individual companies as implementation of the *loi Auroux* (the Socialist's industrial relations reform) reoriented worker concerns to company-level negotiations.[74] Since "contracting out" was not a major part of the Conservative program, public sector unions did not perceive as significant a threat to government service employment as did their counterparts in Britain, Canada and the USA.[75] Once again, pluralists could explain the success of privatization in a classic manner. Privatization succeeded because the potential opposing coalition was weak.[76]

"Noyaux durs" and the new political landscape

The initial focus of opposition to privatization,[77] and the key to the argument we make below, concerns the mechanism by which firms were pri-

---

[71] For a discussion of public enterprises' subsidizing inputs, see Harvey B. Feigenbaum, *The Politics of Public Enterprise* (Princeton: Princeton University Press, 1985), chs. 1 and 5.

[72] The Conservative political parties, of course, played the same kind of integrative role and cemented their coalition by injecting xenophobic social issues, viz. North African immigration, to bring marginalized groups into the Conservative camp, groups that in an earlier epoch might have voted for Pierre Poujade. This latter strategy proved to be dysfunctional when Mitterrand introduced proportional representation into the 1986 election, buoying the results of the National Front, and consequently reducing the "Civilized Right's" parliamentary majority to a two-seat margin.

[73] Michel Bauer, "State Directed Privatization."

[74] Guy Groux, "Organized Labor and Industrial Relations," paper presented to the panel, "Changing Patterns of French Political Economy: an End to French Exceptionalism?", Sixth International Conference of Europeanists, Washington, DC, October 30–November 1, 1987.

[75] Cf. "Why Unions Oppose Privatization," *The Worklife Report*, 6, 3 (1988), 2–3.

[76] On the role of potential groups, see David Truman, *The Governmental Process* (New York: Knopf, 1951).   [77] See, for example, *Le Monde*, October 1, 1987.

vatized, and especially the decision of the Conservative government to award controlling blocs of stock to specifically designated share-holders. The "*noyaux durs*," or "hard cores."

One of the principal concerns of the authors of the privatization program was that the lack of capital in France would privilege cash-rich foreign investors (see above). This fear of foreign takeovers became the justification for selling controlling interest in the privatized firms to specifically designated groups of French companies, who in turn were obliged to keep the stock for at least two years. The *noyaux dur* became a convenient mechanism for rewarding one's political friends. Thus, referring back to chapter 2, we would label these privatizations as tactical.

Which French companies would end up as controlling stockholders of the privatized firms was a choice left up to the government. As mentioned above, it was no small coincidence that the lucky beneficiaries of unauctioned, below-market stock had ties to the Conservative parties. On the other hand, it was highly unlikely that anyone with enough money to make such purchases would *not* have friends in Conservative high places.

Ostensibly, the 1986 Chirac government had a German model in mind. Most of the institutional participants in the *noyaux durs* were banks or insurance companies.[78] Sensitive to charges that old French oligarchy was being reconstituted ("*les Deux Cent Familles*"), Finance Minister Balladur was careful to point out that no one company would participate in more than two *noyaux durs*. Moreover, reflecting on the total number of favored stockholders, he ironized, "I don't have fifty-two friends!"[79]

This leaves aside, of course, the question of who owned the *institutional* stockholders. It is here that the results of privatization become interesting. The system of *noyaux durs* imprinted on the French political economy a new network of cross-holdings, interlocking directorates and proprietary relationships that would have made John D. Rockefeller or J. P. Morgan proud. The pioneering work of the French economist François Morin is especially revelatory.[80] Essentially Morin notes two important phenomena that emerged out of the sales of *noyaux durs*. First, the privatized firms owned each other. Second, by limiting each participant to 5 per cent or less of the privatized firms' total equity, no individual

[78] Michel Durupty, *Les Privatisations en France* (Paris: La Documentation Française, Notes et Etudes Documentaires No. 4857, 1988), pp. 117–120.
[79] *Le Monde*, September 17, 1987.
[80] The new network of ownership is traced by Morin in "Les Trois Cercles de Liaisons Financières", *Le Monde*, September 17, 1987, p. 34. We are grateful to Jeanne Laux for this reference. Morin did a similar analysis for pre-Socialist France in his *La Structure Financière du Capitalisme Français* (Paris: Calmann-Levy, 1974). For Laux's analysis of the limits of privatization, see her "Privatization and France's Aerospace Industry: The Limits of Liberalism," *French Politics and Society*, 5, 4 (September 1987), 27–34.

institutional stockholder held actual control of the firm. For him, diluting the controlling interest among several institutional stockholders had the effect of liberating the newly privatized firms' managements from the demands of any one owner. This, he argued, was a return to the traditional France: capitalists without capital.[81]

Those familiar with political sociology and business history will, of course, recognize the phenomenon as the one recorded by Berle and Means over half a century ago: management divorced from ownership.[82] However, Maurice Zeitlin has argued that the phenomenon is deceptive, because in widely held firms, as little as 2 per cent of equity is sufficient to control the firm. Thus a 2-per cent owner becomes an effective boss for management.[83]

It is here that the number of participants in each *noyaux dur* becomes important. Since the controlling bloc of stock is divided among several institutions, the relationships among these institutions becomes crucial. If they have conflicting interests, the management is liberated. It can play one owner off against another, the stockholders' only common interest being the profitability of the firm. If the owners have other common interests[84] with regard to the firm's strategies, the management's autonomy may be put in jeopardy by a close scrutiny from the stockholders. It is here that the effect of cross-holdings comes into play. If, for example, Société Générale owns a bloc of CGE, while CGE holds a similar bloc of Société Générale, they are unlikely to constrain each other. The two managements hold, in effect, countervailing vetoes. *The managements of the two groups may, indeed, work in concert.* They will certainly have an interest in doing so.

With this pattern in mind, Morin found that the privatization policies of the Conservatives created three new networks with the following foci: CGE-Société Générale, Paribas, and St-Gobain. Moreover, Morin reasoned that the second round of privatizations would consolidate the net-

---

[81] Morin, "Les Trois Cercles."
[82] A. A. Berle and G. C. Means, *The Modern Corporation* (New York: Macmillan, 1932); A. A. Berle, *Power Without Property* (New York: Harcourt, Brace and World, 1959).
[83] Maurice Zeitlin, "Corporate Ownership and Control: The Large Corporation and the Capitalist Class," *American Journal of Sociology*, 79 (March 1974), 1073–1119.
[84] The whole spectrum of managerial alternatives comes into play here. Institutional shareholders may have preferences because of the way a privatized company's strategy affects the shareholders' other properties. For example, if a privatized company had the option to invest in computer-making capacity this would create a demand for chips produced by other companies held by members of the *noyaux durs*. Thus, one would expect stockholder pressure in favor of this alternative. In the political realm, corporate financial support for a particular political candidate might also be subject to the same logic. Cf. Thomas Ferguson and Joel Rogers, *Right Turn* (New York: Hill and Wang, 1986). For a counter-argument, see G. William Domhoff, "Big Money in American Politics," *Theory and Society*, 17 (1988), 589–596

works even further, crystallizing the French economy into two major groups, one clustered around the Banque Nationale de Paris, and the other around Crédit Lyonnais.[85] Morin's predictions turned out to be partially wrong here, as Crédit Lyonnais subsequently fell on hard times. However, our point here is that mechanism for privatizing the French nationalized firms did not create an atomized market of many individual firms. Rather, it produced an oligopolized market with structural links among firms that did not pre-exist the policy. True, France is a relatively small country where the industrial and government elite already know each other and have habits of working together.[86] But it is also true that "where you stand depends on where you sit."[87] The new corporate networks create structures of dependence and interest which shape the demands of managerial elites.

In terms of political science, simply looking at the elite in isolation from their corporate group will not provide an adequate basis upon which to understand their political and economic behavior. The corporate network of which they are a part significantly influences their behavior. The corporate network becomes an *interest group* and an irreducible unit of analysis.

Privatizations: round II

When the Conservatives returned to power in the legislative elections of March 1993, privatization was once again part of their program, but it was hardly the focus of their economic policy. This lower key approach[88] could be explained by several factors. The most important was political: voters had become so disaffected with the Socialists, both because of a series of corruption scandals and the inability of the Left to bring down unemployment, that the Conservatives needed to make no promises at all and still be assured of a victory.[89] Second, the Conservatives had little to show in terms of dramatic economic change after their first round of privatizations. After all, they owed their election in 1993 to a stagnant economy, despite having privatized a large chunk of the economy in 1986. Finally, there was much less left to privatize: the French constitution pro-

---

[85] François Morin, "Privatisations: l'onde de choc," *Le Monde*, June 29, 1993, p. 33.

[86] See especially, Ezra N. Suleiman, *Elites in French Society* (Princeton: Princeton University Press, 1978). For an examination of this elite with regard to recent privatizations, see John Ardagh, "France within Sight of a New Horizon," *Director*, 41, 8 (March 1988), 124–130; and Linda Bernier, "The View from the Management *Poubelle*," *International Management*, 43, 5 (May 1988), 51–54.

[87] Graham Allison, *The Essence of Decision* (Boston: Little Brown, 1971).

[88] Eduardo Cue, "Privatization in France loses ideological flavor", *The Christian Science Monitor*, June 1, 1993, p. 8.

[89] See Harvey B. Feigenbaum, "France: Return of the Right," *The World and I*, June 1993.

Table 4.5 *Privatizations, round II*

Privatized	Revenue (in francs)
Banque Nationale de Paris	28 billion
Rhone-Poulenc	13 billion
Elf-Aquitaine	33 billion
To be privatized	
Aérospatiale	
Air France	
Banque Hervet	
Caisse cent de réassurance	
Bull	
Compagnie générale maritime	
Crédit Lyonnais	
Péchiney	
Rénault	
AGF	
GAN	
SEITA	
Société mars de crédit	
SNECMA	
Usinor-Sacilor	
Caisse nationale de prévoyance	

Source: Susan M. Scopetski, "Privatization in France and Italy: Pragmatism over Politics," unpublished paper, George Washington University, Washington DC, 25 April 1994; derived from: *The Economist Intelligence Unit Country Reports: France, 4th Quarter 1993; Le Monde,* 10 March, 1994, p. 15; *Institutional Investor,* January 1994, p. 49; *Europa Chemie,* 16 December 1993, p. 9.

hibited the privatization of utilities, and their privatization "wish list" amounted to only twenty-one companies (as opposed to sixty-six in 1986), with some candidates, such as Air France, having such bleak prospects as to be unlikely to attract buyers.[90] Table 4.5 lists the firms to be privatized and revenues obtained by the asset sales of the first three companies sold after the elections of 1993.

[90] On constitutional constraints to privatization, see Cosmo Graham and Tony Prosser, *Privatizing Public Enterprises: Constitutions, the State and Regulation in Comparative Perspective,* (Oxford: Clarendon Press, 1991); on the twenty-one companies, see John Ridding, "Rush for Balladur's winter bargains," *The Financial Times,* November 26, 1993, p. 17.

Privatizations: round III

By the time Jacques Chirac won the 1995 presidential election, the profitable state firms had all been sold. What was left were firms deeply in the red. Because they were endebted did not mean that these firms were not potentially profitable, but the government made a decision that they should be disposed of as quickly as possible. This meant offering additional enticements to prospective purchasers.

The strategy is best illustrated by the sale of Thomson, a firm producing military hardware and consumer electronics. In order to make the firm appealing, the government offered to recapitalize it to the tune of 11 billion francs and asked a purchase price of 1 franc.[91] The lucky buyer was Lagardère, a company recently created from the merger of Matra (military products) and Hachette (publishing). Lagardère announced it would spin off the consumer electronics division to Daiwoo of Korea, leaving many in France, not least of which Alsthom-Alcatel, the other potential buyer, scratching their heads. While the government claimed that Lagardère was chosen for reasons of "military industrial logic," *Le Monde* inferred that the president of Alcatel simply did not lobby effectively.[92] Long-time watchers of French politics would be less surprised, however, as the Hachette group has long and intimate connections with the Gaullist party. Nevertheless, the sale to Lagardère for a franc and the willingness to let Daiwoo capture the jewel of French consumer electronics caused an uproar, both in opposition circles and in the public at large.[93] Ultimately, the government felt compelled to refer the matter to an independent "privatization commission," which recommended rejecting the Lagardère offer.[94] Tactical privatization can lead to a backlash.

That backlash reached dramatic proportions in 1997. In that year, President Jacques Chirac called snap legislative elections rather than risk the political consequences of yet another year of economic austerity at the expected end of the parliamentary term in 1998. Chirac's gamble failed. The Left was voted in on a platform of more jobs and less (in fact, no)

[91] Philippe Le Coeur, "Le groupe Lagardère est désigné comme repreneur de Thomson," *Le Monde*, October 17–18, 1996.
[92] Jacques Isnard, "Matra l'emporte par souci de "logique industrielle et militaire," *Le Monde*, October 18, 1996; Anne Marie Rocco, "La bataille perdue de M. Séguin et de M. Borotra contre le choix du président et du prémier ministre," *Le Monde*, October 18 1996.
[93] Caroline Monnot, "Le gouvernement veut désamorcer la polémique sur la cession de Thomson," *Le Monde*, October 31, 1996.
[94] David Owen, "Paris suspends Thomson sell-off," *Financial Times*, December 5, 1996, p. 1.

privatization. Even here, pragmatism triumphed over ideology. Once in power again, the Socialists announced themselves open to the possibility of selling shares to private investors in what few public firms remained, although this would be decided on a case-by-case basis.[95] Most especially, this meant France Télécom, the jewel in the state crown.

Conclusions

As noted in the first two chapters of this book, the trend towards increasing numbers of privatizations is a world-wide phenomenon. While these may be motivated by differing concerns, both in different countries, and in different governments of the same country, the French experience is instructive. Experiments in the French public sector put the lie to some common justifications for privatization, while offering evidence as well in support of the proponents of the policy.

On the positive side, a number of observations derive from the French case. First, privatizations did not appear to crowd out other private investment and may well have tapped into savings held as less productive financial assets.[96] Secondly, privatizations provided funds for programs for which raising taxes might have been politically difficult. Further, because no utilities were privatized, no additional monopoly rents were created. Finally, the system of *noyaux durs* did have the effect of linking financial institutions to industrial corporations such that the former have an interest in the success of the latter. This created an approximation of industrial organization which has been successful in Germany and Japan.[97]

The negative side, however, suggests the extent to which privatization was actually motivated by politics, rather than economics or pure administrative concerns. First, firms need not be privatized to promote efficiency. French firms in the nationalized sector were, for the most part, more profitable than those in the private sector. It follows from this observation that privatizations by themselves, under conditions where nationalized firms are operating efficiently, will not improve the local economy.

[95] In the case of Thomson CSF, the defense arm of Thomson, they were even willing to sell a majority of the shares to private investors: "Paris ponders Thomson sale," Reuters dispatch, *International Herald Tribune*, July 17, 1997, p. 14.

[96] France has 1.2 trillion francs held in money market (*Sicav*) funds. See Ridding, "Rush For Balladur's winter bargains", *Financial Times*, November 26, 1993, p. 17.

[97] See John Zysman, *Governments, Markets, and Growth* (Ithaca: Cornell University Press, 1983). In recent years, however, both Japan and Germany have been moving away from this model.

French Conservatives had never shied from state interventionism in the past.[98] Consequently, given the economic success of the nationalized companies, that selling off these firms was neither an economic nor ideological necessity. It is, therefore, hard to see the Chirac government's privatization program as anything other than a political *tactic*. In the area of economic policy, very little distinguished the Right from their Socialist predecessors except for the former's emphasis on state asset sales. Selling the nationalized industries at below market value, the state did not recoup its initial investment and effectively subsidized the new purchasers of these firms.[99] The Conservative government neither maximized revenues from the sale, nor did it improve distributional characteristics of wealth creation by allowing less favored classes to "buy in."

Considering the short-term gains to the middle classes, many of whom resold their shares in a hurry, and the long-term benefits to the beneficiaries of the *noyaux durs*, privatization took on a new clarity. The sale of nationalized industries was, in short, simply a modern version of a French tradition: the venality of offices, popular before the Revolution, was transformed into the venality of other state assets. More politely: the policies of the conservative government of 1986–88 could be called *tactical privatizations*, using the terms of the typology established in chapter 2.

The second round of privatizations provided funds to the Conservative government that could be used for progressive programs such as employee retraining. Moreover, given the stagnation of the economy and a large government deficit, funding such programs any other way would probably have been economically difficult and politically ill advised. Thus the second round of asset sales fit our category of *pragmatic privatization*. Finally, after the cash cows were sold off, the lame ducks were left. The indebtedness of the remaining state firms required special cash enticements to potential buyers. Who better to offer juicy subsidies to than one's political friends? However, the Thomson case proves that, cynical as the French may be, there are limits to this strategy.

Taken as a whole, policies always involve trade-offs, sometimes of the most contradictory kind. Nationalized industries could be made a success only by defeating the other goals of state policy: the companies proved the need to shed employment to achieve profitability. Similarly, the privatizations could prove a success only by sacrificing the revenues which justified

---

[98] See, for example, Stephen S. Cohen, James Galbraith, and John Zysman, "Rehabbing the Labyrinth: The Financial System and Industrial Policy in France," in Stephen S. Cohen and Peter A. Gourevitch, eds., *France in the Troubled World Economy* (London: Butterworths, 1982), pp. 49–75.

[99] Cf. Harvey B. Feigenbaum, "Public Enterprise in Comparative Perspective," *Comparative Politics*, 15, 1 (October, 1982), 118.

them, or by deepening the budget deficits privatizations were meant to rectify.

This suggests a simple conclusion. Politicians choose a solution that solves the immediate problem. If the problem is overtly economic or budgetary, the solution appears as a pragmatic adaptation. Thus the Socialists pursued neoliberalism because their nationalizations had not proved a motor of the economy and closing the French economy from its international environment was not a realistic alternative. Decisions had to be made as the franc fell and the major French industries hemorrhaged. *Faut de mieux*: neoliberalism in the guise of pragmatic privatizations.

Similarly, the Conservatives needed an election plank and *faut de mieux*: privatization as a political tactic. Moreover, their rhetoric painted a vision of laissez-faire capitalism that was hardly anathema to the well-to-do supporters of the traditional Right. Once the electoral campaign was a success, it was not hard for the new Conservative government to find a rationale for rewarding their friends and allies. Eminently flexible on matters of doctrine, Chirac and company only carried their version of neoliberalism so far: one does not deregulate for the sake of deregulation and one does not harm a client for the sake of ideological purity. Likewise, the second round of privatizations answered an immediate political need for the Conservatives. The major concern of voters during the 1993 campaign was unemployment. Privatizations allowed the Conservatives to fund employment policies without raising taxes on their principal constituencies. By the third round, tactical goals came to the fore, but tolerance and cynicism had run their course and the backlash began.

Referring back to our hypotheses in chapter 1, the French case provides support for all of them. Privatization did not include a dismantling of the welfare state because there was no constituency basis for such a dismantling. Even Conservatives representing business interests were unwilling to run the risk of removing the social safety net during a period of high unemployment. Regarding our second hypothesis alleging international sources of privatization, it is clear that French Conservatives took a page from Britain, but only selectively. Neither monetarism nor the more extreme version of economic liberalism flourished in French soil. Neoliberal reforms in administration were both more modest, and actually predated those of Britain or the USA.

If any country is a classic example of the "developmental state," certainly France fits the bill. Like the other successful developmental states, incubation worked, and most industrial wards of the state became strong enough to survive on their own. However, while the economic success of most nationalized industries enabled their eventual privatization, the economic nationalism that often goes hand in hand with developmental states provided the conditions for the backlash to the Conservative privatization effort: it is politically risky to sell to strangers.

Privatization, nevertheless, left a stamp on the French economy. New alliances among corporations arose via the distribution of shares. This may have been beneficial in that it more closely linked financial institutions to the success of industry, where the highest value-added jobs are. This, for the moment remains a *theoretical* advantage. All that can be said for sure is that wealth was not obviously created, but simply transferred. What is also a certainty is that the newly created corporate networks control opulent resources. And it is, of course, only a banality to remark that "money" translates as "power."

5   The United States: co-optation of pragmatic initiatives by agents of systemic change

As a self-conscious movement with genuine influence at the national level, privatization came later to the USA than to Great Britain or France. As the concept of privatization began to creep into the lexicon of the international intellectual and policy communities, it was frequently exclusively associated with the sale of state-owned industries. The USA – with a cultural heritage of individualism, localism, and entrepreneurialism – had never developed much of an array of state enterprises. Europeans had always regarded the US version of the "welfare state" as puny and under-developed compared to theirs. In the international game of privatization, it seemed that the USA could be only a penny-ante player watching a dollar-ante game.

Beginning in the early 1980s, however, privatization in the USA moved from an intellectual fringe to become a centerpiece in contemporary public policy debates. In part, this meant defining privatization more broadly, to include not only state-owned industries but any other properties in which the government held a major stake, and to include not just outright sales, but any other means of significantly increasing the role of private actors and market forces. The Reagan Administration began to target programs and assets for possible sale early in its first term. In early 1987, the first major privatization was carried out, with the sale of the government's 85 percent interest in Conrail, a corporation established by Congress in 1976 to provide freight rail service in the Northeast. A President's Commission on Privatization, established in September 1987, proposed further efforts to increase private participation across a broad range of policy areas including low-income housing, air traffic control, the postal service, prisons, and schools.[1]

Within his first month in office, President Bush signaled an intent to carry on the privatization initiatives, speaking out in support of market mechanisms as vehicle for school reform and naming to his cabinet Jack

[1] David F. Linowes, *Privatization: Toward More Effective Government. Report of the President's Commission on Privatization* (Urbana and Chicago: University of Illinois Press, 1988).

Kemp, a leading advocate of enterprise zones and the sale of public housing to existing tenants. While the Bush administration was less inclined to adopt harsh anti-government rhetoric than was its predecessor, the 1992 campaign saw candidate Bush return to some privatization themes as a way to distinguish himself from Bill Clinton.

Nor did the election of Bill Clinton mean that the privatization balloon had run out of air. As we shall see, President Clinton incorporated privatization rhetoric and proposals in his own platform for "reinventing government." Although we will argue that the Clinton version of pragmatic privatization differed from the more ideological, systemic privatization envisioned by Reagan and his allies, it remains an open question which of the two visions is more likely to define the US agenda over the next several decades.

While Great Britain rightly is regarded as the foremost innovator and most ambitious undertaker of privatization initiatives, the US experience merits scrutiny for several reasons. First, much of the intellectual groundwork subsequently used to legitimate privatization was elaborated by American academics, primarily economists. Secondly, as the concept of privatization has been broadened to acknowledge the links between sales of public enterprises and less dramatic strategies – such as contracting out, imposition of users fees, and vouchers – it is increasingly apparent that the USA has been a leader in other respects, as well. Thirdly, because the USA begins with a less state-directed economy than most other nations, its experiments with further privatization may help to establish the outer boundaries of the privatization process; clarifying, through its example, just how far can it be taken. Fourth, because its federal system sets it apart from many of the most active privatizing nations, its experience may provide clues about the extent to which variations in political institutions account for differences in their respective privatization strategies. Finally, as this chapter will elaborate, the USA experience brings into sharper focus the distinction that we have drawn between privatization efforts that are rooted in a pragmatic approach to making government more effective and those linked to more ideologically driven crusades to dramatically shrink the state.

The evolution of privatization in the USA, it is argued here, owes something to the development of a theory of privatization. All significant public policies express theories about the relationship between state action and societal conditions.[2] Such theories have at least three common

<hr />

[2] Jeffrey L. Pressman and Aaron Wildavsky, *Implementation*, 3rd edn (Berkeley: University of California Press, 1984); Paul Sabatier, "An Advocacy Coalition Framework of Policy Change and the Role of Policy-Oriented Learning Therein," *Policy Sciences*, 21 (1988), 129–168.

components. They identify and categorize important societal conditions, which serve as dependent variables. They identify and categorize governmental actions, which serve as independent variables. They propose causal relationships. Beyond these common functions, such policy theories may differ in several ways. They may differ in their scope. Some are narrow and technical (a theory about the relationship between police visibility and the deterrence of crime); others cast a broad explanatory net over many aspects of human behavior (a theory about human nature as rational, self-interested beings). They may differ in their openness to empirical evidence, ranging from tentative theses, held on a contingent basis and readily subject to modification or rejection, to rigid ideologies. And, finally, they may differ in the extent to which they are primarily descriptive or normative in nature.

Development of the theoretical underpinnings served to advance the privatization movement in two ways. First, it served to "refurbish" a laissez-faire philosophy that had become politically *passé*. Unable to convincingly account for the rise and endurance of the welfare state, laissez-faire ideas had lost much of their capacity to explain, guide, and motivate. By applying economic principles to explain governmental behavior, the evolving theory of privatization provided a means to undercut the presumption that an expanded state reflected – and could best carry out – the pursuit of widely shared goals.

Secondly, privatization theory furthered the privatization movement by redefining preexisting local government practices. Many of the specific techniques that have come to be associated with privatization pre-dated the elaboration of privatization as a coherent philosophy. Adoption of these techniques, it will be argued, represented nonpartisan, pragmatic adjustment rather than the advance of a political program to disassemble the state. Nonetheless, in appropriating these practices through an exercise of intellectual imperialism, privatization theory helped establish the feasibility and credibility of efforts to scale back the public sector by buttressing the claim that "it works."

Development and legitimation of the idea

Marginality of the laissez-faire perspective

By the middle of this century, laissez-faire theories of the proper scope of government had lost their credence among the American public. Laissez-faire theorists saw a sharp distinction between the realm of the market and the realm of government. The former was identified with individual freedom, creativity, and progress; the latter with coercion. Central to the

failure of this perspective was an inability to account for the institutional-
ization and broad popularity of the welfare state.

A clear majority of Americans had come to accept at least the basic elements of the welfare state. Some public responsibilities were more
popular than others, of course. That government should ensure a mini-
mally decent standard of living for the "worthy poor" – elderly, handi-
capped, orphans – was broadly accepted. That fatherless children should
be included under the government's protective umbrella also was
accepted, although somewhat less widely and with some tentativeness.
After years of intense controversy, the national government's role in protecting the rights of racial minorities was generally recognized. Most
securely ingrained in the public consciousness as legitimate public
responsibilities, were a range of services traditionally provided by local
government, including police and fire protection, sanitation, street repair,
and elementary and secondary education and a more recently established
role for the national government as guardian against harsh features of
unregulated markets.

In this context, to view government expansion simply as an imposition
seemed obsolete and quaint. Counterposed to the laissez-faire perspective were two alternative explanations. One, rooted in the values of
the Progressive movement in the United States, saw government as the
legitimate vehicle for pursuing a broad public interest that transcended
individual and parochial interests.[3] The other, representing an evolution
of basic economic concepts, saw government expansion as an inevitable
response to market failures.

The broad acceptance of the outlines of the welfare state posed a political challenge to conservatives, as well as an intellectual challenge to
conventional economists. Conservative politicians had to come to terms
with this political landscape, or risk consigning themselves to permanent
minority status. The massive rejection of Barry Goldwater's presidential
candidacy by the American voters in 1964 brought this message home in
stark and convincing terms. The response was a gradual shifting in the
terms of debate. Conservatives needed to reassure the public that their
attack on the size and structure of the governmental apparatus did not
necessarily entail the wholesale rejection of the broad goals that had come
to be associated with liberalism and the welfare state.

Expanding the hegemony of economic concepts

It was in this intellectual and political vacuum that the elements of the
privatization thesis began to come together. A critical and early intellec-

---

[3] Linowes, *Privatization*, pp. 230–231.

tual step was the replacement of the notion that economic behavior and government behavior were distinct spheres of human interaction with a perspective that subsumed government dynamics as a subset of economic processes. Arguing that the behavior of public officials and governmental agencies could be explained – in much the same ways that the behavior of consumers and firms could be explained – as the result of rational pursuit of individual self-interest, economists like Milton Friedman[4] and George Stigler,[5] along with public choice theorists such as James Buchanan and Gordon Tullock,[6] lay the groundwork for an intellectual de-legitimation of the welfare state.

Much of Friedman's classic *Capitalism, Freedom and Democracy* reformulated conventional laissez-faire perspectives about the inherently coercive nature of government. But Friedman moved beyond this, explaining government through analogy to markets, not simply juxtaposition to markets. In doing so, he articulated three themes subsequently taken up by others writing about privatization in the 1970s and 1980s.

The first of these themes involved the *analogy between government and private monopolies*. Characterizing government as a public monopoly accomplished three things. First, it made criticisms of big government more accessible and acceptable to a mass public that already had internalized the association between monopoly and inefficiency, unresponsiveness, and waste. Secondly, it gave criticisms of big government an anchor in traditional microeconomic theory at the very time that the assumption that economists could provide an objective and scientific underpinning for public policy was on the rise. Thirdly, it made an important step toward expanding the hegemony of economic theory. Economists previously had based their claim to expertise upon the distinctiveness of the economic sphere; the analogy between government and private service providers suggested the possibility that government and political action might be considered subsets of economic behavior.

A second theme introduced by Friedman was the characterization of *government regulation as anti-consumer*. The expansion of governmental regulatory activities had enjoyed popular support because it had been portrayed as protecting citizens from threats to their health, safety, and general well-being that were presented by the undiluted pursuit of profit by large businesses. Friedman argued that regulation frequently represented the victory of large business or professional interests, which used their political

[4] Milton Friedman, *Capitalism, Freedom and Democracy* (Chicago: Univ. of Chicago Press, 1962).

[5] George Stigler, "The Theory of Economic Regulation," *Bell Journal of Economics and Management Service*, 2 (Spring, 1971), 3–21.

[6] James Buchanan and Gordon Tullock, *The Calculus of Consent: Logical Foundations of Constitutional Democracy* (Ann Arbor: University of Michigan, 1962).

clout to convince legislators to impose licensing and regulatory burdens on new and small providers, as a way to reduce competition.

The third theme concerned the *distinction between government responsibility and government provision*. Friedman acknowledged the nature of "public goods," and the difficulties these posed to market processes predicated on discrete transactions among self-interested individuals. Services which had "neighborhood effects" might require government to play a role, since individuals who refused to pay for such services might be able to gain a free ride. But, according to Friedman, government could address the free-rider problem, through its taxing power, and yet leave the provision of the service to private firms operating in a competitive environment.

In addition to these three themes, Friedman contributed to the theory of privatization by introducing the idea of the education voucher, as a feasible technique for putting his ideas into practice. According to Friedman, the government would ensure a minimum level of schooling by providing parents with vouchers "redeemable for a specified maximum sum per child per year if spent on 'approved' educational services."[7] Direct provision could be left to private enterprises operating for profit or by non-profit institutions. Competition among these providers would result in more efficient services and in better schools.[8]

Although widely read and discussed, Friedman's formulations had little immediate impact on national policy. This is not unusual. Kingdon argues that publics need to be ready to listen, and it may take years of softening up before a new policy idea takes sudden hold.[9] In some senses, Friedman's ideas might be seen to be ahead of the times. His early work coincided with an era of national optimism and governmental activism manifested in the War on Poverty programs of the Kennedy/Johnson years. A decade later, such factors as urban riots, defeat in Vietnam, the persistence of poverty, and fiscal crises in major cities had shaken this optimism and shaved down expectations of what the public sector could accomplish.[10] By then, as well, the theory behind privatization had been further formalized and elaborated in ways that enhanced its perceived credibility.

---

[7] Friedman, *Capitalism, Freedom*, p. 89.

[8] For a fuller discussion of the voucher idea and the subsequent evolution of the school choice movement in the United States, see Jeffrey R. Henig, *Rethinking School Choice: Limits of the Market Metaphor* (Princeton, NJ: Princeton University Press, 1994).

[9] John Kingdon, *Agendas, Alternatives, and Public Policies* (Boston: Little, Brown, 1984), p. 134.

[10] Jeffrey R. Henig, "Collective Responses to the Urban Crisis: Ideology and Mobilization," in Mark Gottdiener, ed., *Cities in Stress: A New Look at the Urban Crisis* (Beverly Hills: Sage, 1986), p. 238.

Formalizing and elaborating the theory

Friedman advanced the claim that government was best explained through the lens of traditional microeconomic theory, but it fell upon a fairly tight community of scholars coalescing under the banner of "public choice theory" to translate that recognition into a formal deductive theory and to expand it to encompass a broader range of governmental activities.

Much of the impetus toward state growth, public choice theorists reasoned, could be attributed to internally generated pressures. Rational, self-interested politicians and bureaucrats have a stake in expanding the public sector since, by doing so, they can maximize their status, power, and financial return.[11] The bluntness of the vote as a mechanism to communicate complicated policy preferences means that citizens are severely hampered in their ability to impose discipline on this process and tends to give greater voice to blocs of citizens seeking to protect or expand a single program from which they directly and substantially benefit.[12]

Others elaborated implications of the theory as it applied to governmental regulation and to local governments. Regulatory agencies, rather than watchdogs for the public's interest, were perceived to be captives of the industries they professed to oversee.[13] Local governments could be considered to be analogous to private firms, offering a product (a mix of services) in return for a price (a combination of taxes). Citizens of metropolitan areas, by the same token, could be considered consumers, shopping among local governments for that which will provide the best return for their dollar. Given the presumption that individuals start out with varied and idiosyncratic personal preferences – an assumption quite basic to conventional microeconomic theory – it could be deduced that the best mechanism for maximizing personal freedom, governmental responsiveness, and administrative efficiency was to encourage competition among many local governments offering diverse packages of services to citizens who would "vote with their feet."[14]

Perhaps as important as these substantive contributions was the added sheen of legitimacy which the public choice perspective lent to the famil-

---

[11] Gordon Tullock, *Politics of Bureaucracy* (Washington, DC: Public Affairs Press, 1965).

[12] Anthony Downs, *An Economic Theory of Democracy* (New York: Harper & Row, 1958); James Buchanan, "Why Does Government Grow?" in Thomas E. Borcherding, ed., *Budgets and Bureaucrats: The Sources of Government Growth* (Durham, NC: Duke University Press, 1977).   [13] Stigler "Economic Regulation."

[14] Charles M. Tiebout, "A Pure Theory of Local Expenditures," *Journal of Political Economy*, 64 (October, 1956), 416–424; Vincent Ostrom, Charles Tiebout, and Robert Warren, "The Organization of Government in Metropolitan Areas," *American Political Science Review*, 55 (December, 1961), 831–842.

iar argument that big government was bad government. Formal modeling and mathematical precision had recently come to be highly valued within American academic circles as methods through which the social sciences could attain the sophistication and credibility of the physical sciences. The abstract and formal presentation adopted by many public choice theorists made their work less accessible to the general public, but in return it helped to inspire and nurture a community of scholars linked by shared terminology and methodology.

Theory appropriates practice

By the early 1970s, then, much of the theoretical infrastructure for privatization had been put into place. This included a revisionist interpretation of the origin and maintenance of the welfare state that accounted for government programs and regulations by self-interested bureaucrats and politicians rather than pursuit of a public interest or democratic pressures, a formalized theory, and – in vouchers – at least one proposed mechanism for moving away from governmental provision of services without necessarily denouncing governmental responsibility.

By the early 1970s, too, the idea of privatization presumably had a much more receptive audience than had confronted early proponents, like Milton Friedman, a decade before. The "can do" atmosphere of the Kennedy/Johnson years had been displaced by a somewhat dispirited resignation to the fact that poverty and other social problems were deeply ingrained and that efforts to use government to redress inequities would entail cost and conflict. There was a sense that the national government, through the various Great Society programs, had given its "best shot," and that it had failed.

In spite of this, the emerging theory of privatization remained somewhat isolated from the mainstream of American politics and policy. While the national mood may have been one of disillusionment (President Jimmy Carter labeled it "malaise"), it was not a mood of crisis or desperation. Americans were vaguely dissatisfied with general trends in their collective life, but at the same time they were generally satisfied with many of the specifics of their individual lives. While they might not *feel* collectively satisfied, many of them were *doing* well, and they were not necessarily ready to undertake the risks attendant upon a radical policy shift. Before an idea like privatization could find broad acceptance – to move from the community of scholars and intellectuals who play with ideas into the realm of policy practice – the strain of pragmatic skepticism at the core of American culture had to be assuaged. Advocates faced the task of providing a convincing answer to the straightforward question: "Does it work?"

Reconceptualizing existing practice

Establishing the feasibility of a genuinely new proposal can present a "Catch 22" situation. Until the idea is put into practice, assessments of feasibility necessarily are speculative and hypothetical. But elected officials usually resist adopting new ideas backed only by speculation and hypothesis.

Legitimation of the idea of privatization required evidence that market forces would produce public goods, and an essential first step in producing that evidence involved reconceptualizing existing governmental practices in the United States. Privatization advocates began to build the argument that public officials, especially at the local level, already were practicing privatization whether they realized it or not.

The boundary between the public and private spheres has never been fixed or impenetrable, and the approximately 80,000 local governments in the USA over the years had negotiated a diverse, and sometimes idiosyncratic, set of public–private relations. Some were consistently aggressive regulators, some were consistently passive regulators, and some regulated aggressively in some spheres (sanitation in restaurants, for example) and not others (building code enforcement, for example). Some provided a broad range of services fully funded through general revenues; others provided a narrower range of services; others sought to limit access and defray costs for some available services by levying fees on recipients. Some sought to deliver all services and carry out internal functions using public employees; others contracted with private firms to meet some of their needs.

Privatization-as-practice, in this sense, clearly pre-dated the full elaboration of the contemporary privatization idea. The city of San Francisco, for example, began franchising garbage collection to private companies as early as 1932.[15] Users' fees for some governmentally provided services – for example, bridge and highway tolls, and fares for public transportation – had existed for as long as the services themselves.

A 1988 survey of the chief administrative officers of all cities with populations greater than 10,000 and counties with populations over 25,000 found that contracting out was the most commonly employed strategy for increasing the role of private markets in the delivery of public services.[16] Of respondents, 80 per cent indicated that their local govern-

---

[15] Linowes, *Privatization*, p. 2.
[16] Responses were received from 1,681 of the 4,870 governments to which surveys were mailed. A more detailed discussion of the methodology and results is found in Elaine Morley, "Patterns in the Use of Alternative Delivery Approaches," *The Municipal Yearbook 1990* (Washington, DC: International City Managers Association, 1990).

mental unit used private contractors to provide vehicle towing and storage services in the public safety area. Other services in which more than 40 per cent of respondents indicated they used contracting included legal services(55 per cent), street light operation (46 per cent), hazardous materials disposal (44 per cent), and the operation of homeless shelters (43 per cent).[17] Franchises, subsidies, and vouchers were privatizing strategies that were much less frequently used; almost 10 per cent of respondents, however, indicated that they were using vouchers in the areas of homeless shelters and food programs for the homeless.

These diverse governmental arrangements did *not* represent a broad but hitherto unacknowledged privatization movement, but a series of pragmatic adjustments. Table 5.1, which summarizes the responses of city officials to the 1988 survey, indicates that in many cases the local governments had *never* offered the kinds of services that privatization advocates now argue should be transferred to the private arena. Rather than a sharp increase during the 1980s, moreover, the survey uncovered a pattern of general stability, with selective signs of increased privatization balanced by evidence of growing reliance on public providers in other areas. For example, while reliance on governmental employees was declining in such areas as street repair, street cleaning, tree-trimming, crime prevention patrols and vehicle maintenance, it appears to have been increasing in such areas as solid waste disposal, utility meter readings, day care operation, and most areas of medical and public health protection.

The results, according to one review, "is somewhat surprising, given the widespread expectation of considerable increase."

It may be the case that old service delivery patterns, like old habits, are difficult to change . . . Another explanation may be that the advantages of alternative service delivery methods, although highly touted, are not yet as widely believed as proponents of these methods may think.[18]

Figure 5.1 provides some additional insight. Between 1982 and 1988 – prime years for the rhetoric of privatization – US municipalities slightly increased their reliance on direct service provision and slightly decreased reliance on contracting out. The only alternative service delivery modes that showed much proportional change were reliance on self-help and voluntarism (which increased about 105 per cent), and the use of vouchers (which increased about 170 per cent although from an exceedingly low base).

There are additional indications that the spread of privatization at the local level represented a limited and pragmatic adjustment rather than a

[17] Ibid., table 4/5.   [18] Ibid., p. 41.

Table 5.1 *Patterns in local service delivery, US cities over 10,000, 1988*

Service	Service never provided (%)	Service once provided, now discontinued (%)	Provided exclusively by local government employees (1982)	Provided exclusively by local government employees (1988)	Change in exclusive public provision (Percentage points)
Public works/transportation					
Residential solid waste collection	19	5	48	52	4
Commercial solid-waste collection	41	0	28	40	12
Solid-waste disposal	38	22	35	51	16
Street repair	1	0	65	51	−14
Street parking lot cleaning	5	2	84	77	−7
Snow plowing/sanding	20	0	79	74	−5
Traffic signal installation/maintenance	7	2	53	50	−3
Meter maintenance/collection	44	22	72	85	13
Tree trimming/planting	10	3	53	47	−6
Cemetery admin./maintenance	56	2	68	76	8
Inspection/code enforcement	2	1	82	76	−6
Parking lot/garage operation	52	2	73	74	1
Bus system operation/maintenance	75	5	24	37	13
Paratransit system	70	3	19	27	8
Airport operation	67	4	37	38	1
Public utilities					
Electricity	76	na	na	na	na
Gas	86	na	na	na	na
Water distribution	21	na	na	na	na
Water treatment	30	na	na	na	na

Table 5.1 (cont.)

Service	Service never provided (%)	Service once provided, now discontinued (%)	Provided exclusively by local government employees (1982)	Provided exclusively by local government employees (1988)	Change in exclusive public provision (Percentage points)
Sewage collection/treatment	18	na	na	na	na
Sludge disposal	32	na	na	na	na
Hazardous materials disposal	75	na	na	na	na
Utility meter reading	24	1	64	79	15
Utility billing	40	1	62	56	−6
Street light operation	25	2	30	30	0
Public safety					
Crime prevention patrol	2	0	74	68	−6
Police/fire communication	2	3	75	74	−1
Fire prevention/suppression	8	2	69	67	−2
Emergency medical service	29	6	30	47	17
Ambulance service	43	8	30	42	12
Traffic control/parking enforcement	2	1	90	86	−4
Vehicle towing and storage	46	3	7	6	−1
Parks and recreation					
Recreation service	10	4	51	53	2
Operation/maintenance of rec. facilities	6	2	58	58	0
Parks landscaping/maintenance	5	1	76	73	−3
Operation of convention centers/auditoriums	73	2	68	66	−2

Health and human services					
Sanitary inspections	55	6	49	62	13
Insect/rodent control	51	5	44	50	6
Animal control	13	5	61	64	3
Animal shelter operation	43	8	36	50	14
Day care facility operation	88	2	7	25	18
Child welfare programs	89	1	26	33	7
Programs for elderly	40	2	18	22	4
Operation/mgt. public/elderly housing	67	2	20	22	2
Operation/mgt. of hospitals	92	3	16	36	20
Public health programs	73	2	25	32	7
Drug/alcohol treatment	84	1	10	14	4
Mental health/retardation programs/facilities	92	1	13	14	1
Prisons/jails	50	2	na	na	na
Parole programs	93	1	na	na	na
Operation of homeless shelters	90	0	na	na	na
Food programs for homeless	87	1	na	na	na
Cultural arts programs					
Operation of cultural/arts programs	65	2	11	14	3
Operation of libraries	35	4	48	54	6
Operation of museums	78	1	21	25	4
Support functions					
Building/grounds maintenance	2	1	73	63	-10
Building security	24	2	85	77	-8
Heavy equipment vehicle maint./fleet mgt.	5	1	59	50	-9
Emergency vehicles maintenance/fleet mgt.	7	1	59	47	-12
All other vehicle	3	1	63	52	-11
Payroll	1	1	86	85	-1
Tax bill processing	35	6	64	65	1
Tax assessing	45	10	54	58	4

Table 5.1 (*cont.*)

Service	Service never provided (%)	Service once provided, now discontinued (%)	Provided exclusively by local government employees (1982)	Provided exclusively by local government employees (1988)	Change in exclusive public provision (Percentage points)
Data processing	9	1	64	70	6
Delinquent tax collection	37	8	59	61	2
Title record/plat maintenance	52	3	na	na	na
Legal services	18	1	29	34	5
Secretarial services	8	0	5	8	3
Personnel services	7	0	8	10	2
Labor relations	16	0	25	34	9
Public relations/information	8	1	12	14	2

Source: Adapted from Elaine Morley, "Patterns in the Use of Alternative Service Delivery Approaches," *Municipal Yearbook* (Washington, DC: International City Managers Association, 1990).

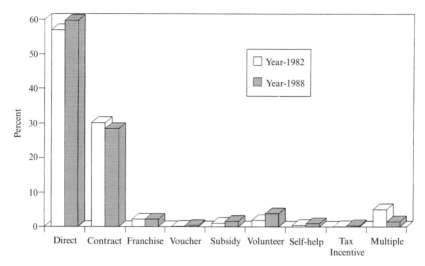

Figure 5.1 Mode of service delivery, 1982 and 1988 (for US cities with population greater than 10,000)

broad ideological reversal. A 1989 survey of state comptrollers found that only seven percent believed that privatization would be "very prominent" in providing or financing government services and facilities during the coming decade.[19] Most of the privatization carried out by the states was in the form of contracting out. Facilities privatization – in which governments turn to the private sector to "build or otherwise acquire capital facilities and then to own and operate those facilities for the government"[20] was less common; fewer than half of the states engaged in it at all, experiments were limited to a narrow range of agencies within those states, and "the value of privatized facilities is rather minimal . . ."[21] The sale of state-owned assets was even more limited with only five states reporting that they had turned to the sale of assets as a way to achieve state objectives. Robert Stein's analysis further demonstrates that local governments in the USA employ a very diverse mixture of service delivery systems and that "the service mode used is closely related to the character of the functional responsibility" – further evidence that privatization has

[19] Of those surveyed 45 per cent thought it would be "somewhat prominent" and 48 per cent expected "little prominence." The survey was conducted by Touche Ross, a private firm that itself contracts with state and local governments to provide a broad range of financial, accounting, auditing and management services. Touche Ross, *State Government Privatization in America: An Opinion Survey of State Governments on Their Use of Privatization* (Washington, DC, 1989).

[20] As, for example, when a private firm builds and manages a prison to which state courts sentence convicted criminals. Ibid. p. 15.   [21] Ibid.

been a pragmatic tool of public officials seeking the best means to meet the demands of their constituencies.[22]

Such pragmatic and selective experimentation with privatization as an administrative tool did not constitute broad endorsement of the more systemic goal of deliberately shrinking the governmental realm; as often as not it has been associated with long-standing practices, with efforts to expand governmental authority into new areas,[23] or with attempts to blunt efforts to use severe fiscal pressures as an excuse to radically redefine the boundaries of public responsibility. But in grouping these efforts together, and in defining them as analogous to the proactive changes they envisioned, privatization advocates accomplished two things. First, they addressed concerns about the administrative feasibility of privatization; obviously, privatization was technically feasible, since hundreds of governments were doing it already. Secondly, they set the stage for empirical verification that privatization not only was possible, but that it worked. The experiences of cities relying more on market mechanisms could be compared to those of cities relying on traditional governmental delivery, using systematic techniques of policy analysis.

Justification

The early and crucial evidence that privatization allowed public goals to be achieved more efficiently and more effectively primarily came from studies of cities that had contracted with private firms to provide such traditional services as fire protection and refuse collection. Two studies – one by Roger Ahlbrandt and one by E. S. Savas – are worth summarizing, both because they are fairly typical of this genre in their methodology and findings, and because they have been especially influential.

Roger Ahlbrandt investigated fire protection services in Scottsdale, Arizona, which had contracted with the private Rural-Metropolitan Fire Protection Company. He concluded that Rural-Metropolitan was providing services at a cost of approximately $3.78 per Scottsdale resident that would have cost about $7.10 if the city had chosen to provide comparable services publicly. The private firm spent more on research

---

[22] Robert M. Stein, "Arranging City Services," *Urban Politics and Urban Policy Section Newsletter*, 4, 3 (Winter 1990–1), 22.

[23] Morley notes the strong tendency for local governments to employ alternative modes of service delivery when nosing into new areas of responsibility, like provision of food and shelter to the homeless. While she links this pattern to the likelihood of lower resistance by unions and others with a stake in the status quo, it may also reflect a democratically driven ratcheting up process by which governments turn to mixed private/public provision strategies to meet newly emergent demands, then gradually incorporate these into their normal array of service responsibilities because citizens find them valuable and legitimate.

and development than public fire departments, and, accordingly, found several innovative means of minimizing capital and labor costs. These included the use of smaller fire trucks and smaller and lighter fire hoses. Rather than purchase its equipment, Rural-Metro built most of what it needed itself, or subcontracted the construction to other firms. And, rather than pay full-time firefighters to sit idly in the station waiting for a call, the company trained city workers in other departments in fire-fighting techniques. These "wranglers" worked only when needed, and were paid only when they worked.[24]

E. S. Savas compared public and private refuse collection in the New York metropolitan area. He concluded that "it costs the city more than twice as much as the private sector to collect a ton of garbage . . ."[25] In Douglaston, an area within New York City, the public sanitation depart-ment made two curbside pick-ups each week at a cost of $207 per dwelling. Whereas, in nearby Bellerose, New York, Savas found that a private firm was able to make three weekly pickups, from the back of resi-dents' homes, at a cost of only $72 per dwelling, per year.

Studies such as these found a receptive scholarly audience. A computerized search of the *Social Science Citation Index*, for example, found Savas, by wide margin, to be the most frequently cited author in articles written about privatization between 1972 and 1986. Just as importantly, they found more popular outlets as well. Savas, for example, wrote about "Municipal Monopoly" in *Harper's Magazine* in December, 1971. And an article reporting on the Scottsdale experiment – with the dramatic title "Scottsdale Slashes Spending" – appeared in *Readers' Digest* in February 1978.

From pragmatic adjustment to partisan program

Linking the emerging theory of privatization to the preexisting practices of local governments helped establish the credibility of the theory, but in the process it served to politicize the practice, with ironic results. The very fiscal, cultural, and institutional characteristics of local governments in the USA that accounted for their receptivity to privatization, to some extent had depended upon a depoliticized milieu. As privatization was brought to the national agenda, in the 1980s, it was invested with a parti-san content that undermined the atmosphere of pragmatic adjustment in which the practice initially took root.

---

[24] Roger S. Ahlbrandt, Jr., *Municipal Fire Protection Service: Comparison of Alternative Organizational Forms* (Beverly Hills, CA: Sage Publications, 1973).

[25] E. S. Savas, "Municipal Monopolies Versus Competition in Delivering Urban Services," in Willis D. Hawley and David Rogers, eds., *Improving the Quality of Urban Management* (Beverly Hills, CA: Sage, 1974), p. 477.

The local government response to fiscal constraints was primarily a managerial one. Contracting out and the imposition of user fees were part and parcel of a laundry list of responses, which included such additional tactics as hiring freezes, improved revenue collection, multi-year forecasting, and creative capital financing. The particular mix of techniques adopted may have depended in part on the ideological and partisan preferences of local officials, but it reflected in at least equal degree bureaucratic decision rules, legal parameters set by state charters and anti-tax restraints, and accommodation to localized political and economic constraints.[26] Framed as a managerial response to fiscal constraint, privatization options were publicly debated, if at all, in technical and economic terms, rather than in reference to social philosophy or political goals.

Besides the fiscal environment, two additional characteristics of US local governments help explain the spread of these initiatives in a depoliticized form. The Progressive era in American political history left, as part of its intellectual legacy, a particular view of local governments. Primarily administrative units, charged with performing various municipal "housekeeping" chores, local governments could and should be addressed in a nonpartisan manner by experts trained in applying technical criteria to maximize efficiency, instead of being addressed in a political manner by elected officials responding to interest group pressures or ideologies. The apolitical language in which the early privatization arguments were couched appealed to local officials whose roots were in that intellectual tradition.

Moreover, the legacy of the Progressive movement included more than just an intellectual heritage. The Progressives' ideas found expression in a powerful political movement, which, in the first thirty years of the twentieth century, reshaped the decision-making structures in many local jurisdictions. The resulting structural reforms were designed to insulate managers and administrators from demands by self-interested groups seeking patronage or other material benefits as political favors. These reforms included the city manager form of government, nonpartisan elections, and delegation of authority to nonelected independent boards, commissions, and special districts. This insulation gave those administrators inclined to experiment with privatization discretion that would not be available to elected officials directly indebted to constituent groups – particularly public employee unions – to whom privatization proposals represented an apparent threat.

[26] John Matzer, Jr., "Local Control of Fiscal Stress," in Gottdiener, ed., *Cities in Stress*, pp. 63–79; Irene S. Rubin, and Herbert J. Rubin, "Structural Theories and Urban Fiscal Stress," in Gottdiener, ed., *Cities in Stress*, pp. 177–198.

The national agenda – pre-Reagan

As was the case at the local level, privatization-as-practice at the national level pre-dated privatization-as-idea. The 1988 report of the President's Commission on Privatization concluded that contracting out, on a selective basis, had "been one of the government's principal ways of doing business throughout our nation's history."[27] In order to encourage and formalize contracting out by national agencies, the Eisenhower administration, in 1955, issued Bureau of the Budget Bulletin 55–4, which articulated the goal that the "Federal government will not start or carry on any commercial activity to provide a service or product for its own use if such a product can be procured from private enterprise through ordinary business channels."[28]

Even sales of national governmental assets have a long history in the United States. The Rural Homestead Act of 1862 invited citizens to stake out claims to up to 160 acres of federally owned land in the undeveloped areas of the American west. Those making a claim were required to build a structure, cultivate the land, and live on the property for at least five years. In returns for this and $26 fee, they were granted permanent title to the property. The Federal National Mortgage Association (Fannie Mae), was established in 1938 as a national governmental response to the Depression-ravaged private lending industry. The state-owned corporation would provide a new and reliable secondary mortgage market, reducing the risk to private lenders and thereby encouraging them to issue additional mortgage loans. Fannie Mae was partially privatized in 1954, and further privatized in 1968. Since then it has operated as a private, shareholder-owned corporation, although it retains a special relationship to the government, through its federal charter.

Although the anti-poverty programs of the Lyndon Johnson era were typically associated with rapid growth of the US welfare state, Smith and Stone suggest that "using private agencies to circumvent public bureaucracies was the intellectual centerpiece of the War on Poverty."[29] The Community Action Agencies assigned the responsibility to make key decisions about the implementation of federal programs at the local level, provided a forum used by private nonprofit agencies to wrest some control away from what were perceived to be self-aggrandizing politicians and entrenched local bureaucracies.

But such early efforts were predicated on different ideas than contem-

---

[27] Linowes, *Privatization*, p. 129.   [28] Cited in Linowes, *Privatization*, p. 129.
[29] Steven Rathgeb Smith and Deborah A. Stone, "The Unexpected Consequences of Privatization," in Michael Brown and Robert Alford, eds., *Remaking the Welfare State* (Philadelphia: Temple University Press, 1988), p. 235.

porary privatization proposals. Rather than representing a broad scale and deliberate effort to reduce the size and scope of governmental activity, these actions generally took place in a context of increasing national governmental growth; the privatization of Fannie Mae, for example, was accompanied by the establishment of new quasi-governmental enterprises, the Government National Mortgage Association (Ginnie Mae), which took over some of what had been Fannie Mae's mandated responsibilities.[30] And, rather than an assumption that private delivery necessarily was more efficient, initiatives to stimulate contracting out and privatize Fannie Mae primarily were based on a notion that government had unfair advantages in competing with private providers.

In the middle to late 1970s, however, this began to change. With such actions as the Securities Acts Amendments of 1975, the Airline Deregulation Act of 1978, the Motor Carrier Act of 1980, and the Depository Institutions Deregulation and Monetary Control Act of 1980, the national government showed a definite readiness to substantially reduce its regulatory involvement in the private sector. This deregulation movement was substantially influenced by the same economic theories that are used to legitimate the more expansive array of privatization initiatives on the contemporary agenda.[31]

This deregulation movement, an earlier form of privatization as we defined it in chapters 1 and 2, foreshadowed the privatization policies that the Reagan administration would propose in the 1980s, but it differed from the later privatization efforts in several respects. First, deregulation as then expressed, aimed at eliminating state-sponsored oligopolies and thus was markedly bipartisan in leadership and support. Senator Edward Kennedy, a liberal Democrat, was one of the most vocal legislative activists in the shaping of the trucking deregulation initiatives. Both trucking and airline deregulation efforts also received active support from the Democratic Carter administration. Second, the deregulation movement was exclusively focused on increasing competition, not decreasing state size nor eliminating safeguards which protected the public. Finally, the national deregulation movement of the 1970s, at least in some senses, was self-limiting; the ideas animating deregulation, and a substantial proportion of the interests supporting deregulation, were affirming an activist role for the national government at the same time that they were strategically pursuing deregulation in specific areas.

The strategic and selective aspects of this push for national deregulation

---

[30] Martin Mayer, *The Builders: Houses, People, Neighborhoods, Governments, Money* (New York: W.W. Norton & Company, 1978), p. 379.

[31] Martha Derthick, and Paul J. Quirk, *The Politics of Deregulation* (Washington, DC: The Brookings Institution, 1985).

are most apparent in the telecommunications area. The break-up of American Telephone & Telegraph (AT&T) is cited as an example of deregulation because it was accompanied by a deliberate scaling back, by the Federal Communications Commission, of efforts to supervise rates and limit the phone companies' involvement in many peripheral areas including data processing. Like trucking and airline deregulation, this was a pro-competitive position that resulted in the entry of many new firms, and the expansion of the range of options available to consumers. But the roots of this decision lay in aggressive action by the federal courts – the forced dissolution of the AT&T monopoly – that confirmed a very strong regulatory role for the national government. In the sense of chapter 1, the state was changing its *mode* of intervention, but not the degree of that intervention. The deregulation phase of American privatization did not shrink the state.

The blossoming of privatization: The Reagan agenda

The election of Ronald Reagan in 1980 marked an important shift in the political environment in which the privatization movement was beginning to unfold. National leaders prior to Reagan had celebrated the importance of the private sector. Jimmy Carter, a Democrat, had backed deregulation and emphasized a public–private "partnership" as a strategy to reverse urban decline. But the election of Reagan meant that privatization advocates, for the first time, were likely to get a more sympathetic hearing at the national than at the state or local level. Reagan's popularity and early legislative successes also suggested that privatization advocates might rapidly be able to convert their agenda into radical changes in policy and practice and move from pragmatic to systemic privatization.

Like Margaret Thatcher in 1979, Reagan had not run on a privatization platform. Rather, he had sounded more traditional anti-government themes: the need to restrain meddlesome bureaucrats, reduce taxes, unleash the entrepreneurial spirit, provide help to those who help themselves. Early in his first term, however, the White House began to formulate proposals that, in substance and stated rationale, reflected the kind of privatization already underway in Great Britain.

Several elements marked this emergence of privatization *per se* as a serious item on the US national governmental agenda. First, the Reagan administration began to formulate aggressive proposals for the sale of a wide range of state assets. Early proposals included the sale of federally owned park and wilderness lands, National Weather Service satellites, Conrail and AMTRAK, and a major petroleum reserve.

Secondly, the Reagan administration explicitly adopted the still unfamiliar term "privatization," along with the argument that privatization – rather than representing a rejection of the goals associated with the welfare state – simply represents an adoption of private means to pursue public goals. The President's Private Sector Survey on Cost Control, for example, defined privatization as an option "allowing Government to *provide* services without *producing* them."[32]

Thirdly, the Reagan administration used the term privatization to link proposed asset sales with a broad array of alternative techniques. The report just mentioned offered a "conceptual framework for the role of privatization," that identified contracting out, grants and subsidies, tax incentives, deregulation, vouchers, franchises and divestiture as techniques through which the national government could pursue public goals through private providers. In the process, the administration sought to legitimate its proposals by extending the claim that privatization had proven successful at the state and local level. "The concept of privatization in the Federal Government is a relatively new concept," the report suggested, "even though it has been applied successfully at the state and local levels." [33]

Finally, the Reagan administration drew clear and explicit analogies to the British experience. Reagan officials echoed the claim of privatization advocates that the Thatcher government already had demonstrated the economic feasibility – and political popularity – of privatization. The British example was especially important in legitimating the idea of enterprise zones and the sale of public housing units to tenants. The Heritage Foundation, a conservative "think-tank" which was influential in shaping the Reagan agenda, aggressively promoted the enterprise zones concept through publications and conferences that emphasized the fact that Britain already had demonstrated their viability. Stuart Butler, a British analyst for the Heritage Foundation, heavily drew on the British model, in his 1985 book *Privatizing Federal Spending*. In a section headed "Mrs. Thatcher Shows the Way," Butler argued that a broad range of privatization tactics had "enabled her government to make remarkable gains in her battle to cut the public sector down to size."[34]

Politicization of privatization

Along with these other developments, came another transformation. Prior to this, privatization-as-theory and privatization-as-practice had

---

[32] President's Private Sector Survey on Cost Control, *Report on Privatization* (Washington, DC: Government Printing Office, 1983), p. i.   [33] Ibid.

[34] Stuart M. Butler, *Privatizing Federal Spending: A Strategy to Eliminate the Deficit* (New York: Universe Books, 1985), p. 34.

developed relatively independently of one another; in Kingdon's terms they represented separate "streams."[35] The theory of privatization was deduced from abstract microeconomic premises; it was not induced from observation of the local government practices, although it subsequently looked to those practices as a source of legitimation. Similarly, local government adoption of privatization practices represented a series of pragmatic adjustments to an environment marked by expanding demands and fiscal constraints; it was not precipitated by a deliberate application of privatization theories, although it was sometimes explained and defended with terminology drawn from the same economics tradition.

In the hands of the Reagan administration, privatization became more than a pragmatic adjustment. It represented a deliberate attempt to use the ideas of privatization to substantially reshape the economic and political ecology. Privatization as economic theory became privatization as political strategy.

This new role for privatization got its clearest public statement from Stuart Butler. Butler took as a starting point the traditional conservative goal of shrinking the public sector, but he rejected the traditional conservative notion that the way to do so is to impose limits on taxing and spending. Such limits represent a "supply-side" strategy. And supply-side approaches were destined to fail, he suggested, because they do not appreciate the extent to which the expansion of the public sector rests upon the demand side – the capacity of government to provide desired services to specific groups, and the resulting readiness of beneficiary groups to mobilize as a pro-spending coalition.

Butler argued that the welfare state is politically resilient because it spreads costs over a large, usually unmobilized constituency, while concentrating benefits on a limited segment of the population that rallies to their defense. His explicit political strategy was to use privatization to reverse this dynamic. "Privatization involves concentrating benefits on a limited segment of the population – beneficiaries and [private sector] service providers – while the costs (assuming tax relief and other special privileges to one group mean costs to everyone else) are spread widely."[36] Contracting out and voucher programs were "politically expedient" as transitional elements in this strategy, because they allow "politicians to gain points with constituencies by promising more, not less . . ."[37] He recommended, too, that the USA learn from the British the tactic of detaching potentially powerful elements of the spending coalition: "Discounts to tenant buyers, for instance, weakened resistance to the sale of public

---

[35] Kingdon, *Agendas*, p. 90.   [36] *Privatizing Federal Spending*, p. 46.   [37] Ibid., p. 45.

housing; private garbage collectors 'bought off' public employee opposition by hiring government workers; and turning employees into shareholders was remarkably successful in breaking down obstacles to
denationalization."[38]

This notion of using privatization to reshape the interest group
environment was eagerly seized upon by some elements within the
Reagan administration. The Office of Personnel Management, for
example, in 1986 proposed a Federal Employee Direct Corporate
Ownership Plan (Fed CO-OP), which would create new, employee-
owned independent companies that would compete for governmental
contracts, initially at highly favorable terms. The 1988 report of the
President's Commission on Privatization concludes with a strong statement in favor of structuring privatization initiatives to create new interest
groups with direct stakes in accelerating the process of shrinking the size
and scope of government:

> For example, a proposal to divest a government business might suggest trans-
> ferring it to the employees . . . A proposal to divest government power-generating
> facilities might suggest giving the facilities (or selling them cheaply) to the current
> power customers . . . A proposal to divest government conservation lands might
> suggest giving it to a current conservation organization . . . In summary, if
> privatization consists simply of eliminating government programs and cutting off
> benefits, change may come at a slow pace. If privatization consists, however, of
> forming and recognizing new private rights for the beneficiaries of existing pro-
> grams, the pace of privatization could accelerate.[39]

But the aggressiveness and ideological nature of the Reagan administration's agenda of systemic privatization carried within it the seeds of a
political backlash. Most of the early candidates for sale fell into one of
three categories. Some – like public housing and the US Postal service –
had been regarded, for many years, as dreadful failures, the objects of
ridicule and scorn. Others – like Conrail, National Airport, and federal
utilities – had constituencies that were geographically limited. Still others
– like government-owned satellites and Naval Petroleum Reserves – had
benefits that were contingent on uncertain scenarios (the future production of knowledge, security in the face of potential economic and military
threats).

Rather than these politically vulnerable targets, the Reagan administration's first efforts at privatization focused on the sale of federally owned
park lands. Land was the most valuable and visible of federal assets, and
the agency most directly responsible was headed by James Watt: a strong
advocate of the conservative anti-government coalition. To those who saw

---

[38] Ibid., p. 46.   [39] Linowes, *Privatization*, p. 249.

privatization as a moral crusade, this focus was logical and appropriate. But the result was a fierce negative reaction, that dealt privatization initiatives a substantial blow.

Reaction against the sale of federal land was magnified by two factors. First, the proposed sale of government land, particularly federal park land, timberland, and oil and mineral rights, posed privatization as a threat to the environment. In spite of the public's broad support for Ronald Reagan and many central aspects of the Conservative agenda, public opinion polls make it clear that most Americans remained adamantly opposed to efforts to scale back the pro-environmental initiatives that had been launched in the previous decade. Secondly, and somewhat related, the proposed sale of government land put Secretary of the Interior James Watt into the role of privatization spokesman. Watt's outspokenness, contentiousness, and claims to a divine mission eventually turned him into a political liability. Burned on this issue, the Reagan Administration was forced to pull back from an aggressive pursuit of asset sales.

This lesson was not lost on George Bush. By nature less attuned than Reagan to an all-out assault on the institutions of governance, Bush came into office with a more modest and pragmatic orientation.

Setting the limits: reining in systemic privatization in the post-Reagan years

Ebb and flow: tactical privatization in the Bush administration

Before becoming Ronald Reagan's vice president, George Bush had been associated with a more moderate wing of the Republican Party; where Ronald Reagan sought to radically scale back the size and responsibilities of the national government, Bush's record was one of favoring restrained and yet effective government. In light of Reagan's popularity and the strategic importance of the radical conservative wing within the Republican Party, it was in candidate Bush's interest, in the 1988 election, to portray himself as carrying forth the torch of Reaganism and, for the most part, he did so. Once in office, however, the Bush administration evidenced a seemingly schizophrenic orientation toward government.

In his rhetoric and in his appointments, President Bush was less likely than Reagan to systematically degrade the enterprise of national governance. Where Reagan rarely missed an opportunity to ridicule the red tape he associated with governmental regulation, Bush, in his first Economic Report to Congress, combined his commitment to unimpeded market forces with an acknowledgment that "in some cases, well-designed regulation can serve the public interest."[40] Where Reagan frequently appointed to key posts individuals who not only lacked experience in the public sector, but who were openly hostile to the agencies they were assigned to lead,[41] Bush tended more often to turn to those accustomed to public life.

But privatization by no means fell off the public agenda. In Jack Kemp, his Secretary of Housing and Urban Development, Bush had selected one of the most dynamic crusaders for reliance on market forces to solve social problems. As a member of Congress, for example, Kemp had been a key sponsor of enterprise zones legislation. Proponents of systemic privatization, such as Stuart Butler and the Heritage Foundation, argued that the key to urban revitalization was to dramatically scale back taxation and regulation that were stifling latent entrepreneurial spirit in America's inner city communities;[42] in place of programs, like Urban Renewal and Model Cities, that sought to use governmental affirmatively to reverse decline, enterprise zones sought to achieve that end by selectively *with-drawing* the weight of government. In addition to his continued support for enterprise, moreover, Kemp was the leading national figure promoting the sale of public housing to tenants, and he made his efforts to bring this about a centerpiece in his campaign to reform HUD.

In Vice President Dan Quayle, moreover, Bush had a strong devotee of systemic privatization. Quayle's reputation as an intellectual lightweight – a reputation that much of the national media had fun nurturing – undercut his effectiveness as a public champion for privatization, but through his role in chairing the Council on Competitiveness he oversaw a behind-the-scenes effort to radically scale back federal regulations. The Council on Competitiveness worked with the Office of Management and Budget to review regulations drafted by federal agencies, and was reputed to have wielded significant influence, putting agencies on the defensive about any proposals that imposed measurable costs on mobilized members of the business community. Some members of Congress complained bitterly that the Council on Competitiveness was an illegitimate back-channel tool for the private sector to undermine responsible governmental actions, but "despite the requests of at least seven congressional committees that . . . attempted to investigate the small council staff, the council

---

[40] David E. Rosenbaum, "Bush Calls for Some Regulation," *New York Times*, February 7, 1990 (D1).

[41] For example, William von Raab, a corporate lawyer before being appointed by Reagan to head the US Customs Service, indicated "I'm not sure the government serves any other purposes" besides providing for the national defense and national security. Haynes Johnson, "Customs Chief Represents Belief in Less Government," *Washington Post*, August 26, 1986.

[42] Stuart Butler, *Enterprise Zones: Greenlining the Inner Cities* (NY: Universe Books, 1981).

... refused to provide information on who it meets and what regulations it has influenced."[43]

Nonetheless, the president's own more pragmatic style combined with changing events to apply some brakes to Reagan's privatization movement. Bush inherited a major and costly crisis in the savings and loan industry that many attributed to lax governmental oversight. Deregulation in the airlines industry originally resulted in sharp fare reductions and won widespread public support, but by the time Bush took office bankruptcies and consolidations, the elimination of some routes, and dramatic fare increases for some passengers had generated a backlash in favor of re-regulation. At the same time, Congressionally initiated studies began to document serious consequences of Reagan's efforts to cut federal employment while increasing reliance on private contractors.[44]

The Bush administration's stance on educational choice and school vouchers nicely illustrates Bush's muting of the Reagan position – and the subsequent reemergence of radical rhetoric in the context of the 1992 reelection campaign. Bush, who campaigned in 1988 on the promise to become "the Education President," generally steered clear of the kind of radical voucher proposals that Ronald Reagan initially promoted.[45] Asked early in his presidency whether it was unfair that private school parents have to pay tuition in addition to supporting the public system through their taxes, Bush indicated that it was "their right" to send their children to private schools, but "I don't think they should get a break for that."[46]

By the end of 1990, though, there were a few clues that the White House was becoming favorably inclined toward choice schemes that included private schools. Vice President Quayle was sent to Oregon to support a state initiative that would have given parents the right to attend any school in the state and provided a tax credit of $2,500 to parents if their children attended either public or private schools.[47] In announcing the launching of the new federal Center for Choice in Education in December 1990, Secretary of Education Cavazos indicated that the pres-

---

[43] Dana Priest, "Competitiveness Council is Criticized on Hill," *The Washington Post*, June 12, 1992 (A6).

[44] E.g. Jeff Gerth, "Regulators Say 80's Budget Cuts May Cost U.S. Billions in 1990s," *New York Times*, December 19, 1989 (A1); and "Congressional Study Challenges Federal use of Private Contractors," *New York Times*, September 16, 1991 (A1).

[45] A fuller discussion of this can be found in Jeffrey R. Henig, *Rethinking School Choice: The Limits of the Market Metaphor* (Princeton, NJ: Princeton University Press, 1994), ch. 4.

[46] Quoted in Albert Shanker, "A Very Hard Sell: Bush Makes the Pitch for Vouchers," *The New York Times*, January 19, 1992.

[47] Neil R. Pierce, "School Choice Takes Careful Crafting," *The National Journal*, November 3, 1990.

ident supported the new Wisconsin program that provided some low-income Milwaukee families on state support to pay tuition costs at private schools.[48] Nonetheless, such indications were quiet and indirect. The heavily publicized *America 2000* proposal, with which President Bush articulated the broad outlines of his education program in April 1991, gave very little specific attention to choice; as Harold Howe II noted, "one 85 word paragraph is all there is on the subject."[49]

Suddenly, early in 1992, the Bush administration began taking more visible and affirmative positions on market-oriented, private school choice plans. With the Senate considering legislation that might have given poorer families the right to use federal aid to attend private schools, Bush drew an analogy between proposed programs to provide government support to elementary and secondary school families attending private schools and well-established programs supporting college students. "We don't exclude [college] students who choose private schools, including religious schools," he told a group in Columbus, Ohio on January 26. The *Washington Post* article reporting the speech observed that "Education Secretary Lamar Alexander frequently has spoken of broadening the meaning of public education to include schools that are not directly controlled by local governments, but Bush has never been so direct."[50]

Coming less than one month before the New Hampshire primary, the explicit inclusion of parochial schools in the Bush administration's school choice proposals may have reflected the growing political pressure on the President to take strong stands on domestic issues, and to forestall the rising support for Patrick Buchanan among more conservative elements in the Republican party.

In January of 1992, popularity polls were still suggesting that Bush had little to fear from his potential Democratic challengers. But, as the Buchanan challenge faded later in the Spring, the surging threat from Bill Clinton loomed in its place. Clinton was a proponent of school choice, but only of choice plans that were restricted to public schools. On June 25, the president transmitted his proposed GI Bill legislation to Congress. By emphasizing the free-market aspects of school choice, Bush

[48] Lauro F. Cavazos, "Remarks Prepared for the Choice in Education Press Conference," Tuesday, December 4, 1990. The Milwaukee experiment is discussed in some detail later in the book.

[49] Harold Howe II, "America 2000: A Bumpy Ride on Four Trains," *Phi Delta Kappan*, November 1991, p. 194. But a question and answer section in the back of the prepared booklet summarizing the plan makes it clear that the preference was to include parochial schools if legally possible: "It will apply to all schools except where the courts find a constitutional bar."

[50] Kenneth Cooper, "School-Choice Idea Backed Anew by Bush," *The Washington Post*, January 26, 1992.

put himself in position to draw a stark distinction between his domestic agenda – rooted in markets and the entrepreneurial spirit – and that of the Democrats, which could be portrayed as being bogged down in bureaucracy and governmental solutions imposed from on high.

Clinton: from privatization to reinvention

Clinton positioned himself for the 1992 presidential election as a new Democrat who combined a traditional liberal's desire to use government to pursue common goods with contemporary conservatives' skepticism toward the notion that all problems can be solved by government – especially the national government – and a strong nod in the direction of fiscal responsibility. Unlike some Democrats, Clinton showed little discomfort employing the language of business and celebrating the benefits of market forces.

The juxtaposition of the language of privatization with a pragmatic commitment to making government do more and do better can be seen in the handling of two of his major domestic initiatives – health care reform and the crusade to "reinvent government." After granting health care reform the place of honor on his administration's agenda, Clinton quickly made it clear that he would not embrace a "single-payer" program – like Canada's – that would have government displace market forces as the primary actor. Emphasizing competition among healthcare providers as the primary spur to quality and constraint on cost, he portrayed government's role as one of rationalizing the market through regulation and the provision of information, and of ensuring that all citizens had a fair chance to participate in the market driven arena.

Even as governor of Arkansas, Clinton had self-consciously adopted the outlook promoted in Osborne and Gaebler's book on *Reinventing Government*. While clearly acknowledging ways in which running the government is *not* like running a business, Osborne and Gaebler recommended that public officials selectively learn some important lessons from successful business, including the benefits of competition, the need to satisfy the consumer, and "leveraging change through the market."[51]

In March, 1993, President Clinton followed up on this promise by appointing Vice President Al Gore to oversee a National Performance Review to make specific recommendations for making the "shift from top-down bureaucracy to entrepreneurial government."[52] The reinvention concept aggressively incorporated elements of the Reagan/Bush

---

[51] David Osborne and Ted Gaebler, *Reinventing Government: How the Entrepreneurial Spirit is Transforming the Public Sector* (Reading, MA: Addison-Wesley, 1992).

[52] Bill Clinton and Al Gore, *Putting People First* (NY: Basic Books, 1992), p. 1.

rhetoric. The first chapter in Gore's subsequent report to the president, titled "Cutting Red Tape," begins with a very Reaganesque recitation of the failures of the federal government. Within two pages readers are told that: "Washington's failures are large and obvious." "The federal government seems unable to abandon the obsolete." "The federal government is not simply broke; it is broken." "It is almost as if federal programs were *designed* not to work." "[P]eople simply feel government doesn't work." "We have spent too much money for programs that don't work." "[F]or more than a decade we have added red tape to a system already strangling in it."[53] Chapter 2, titled "Putting Customers First," emphasized the advantage of competition, "creating market dynamics," and "using market dynamics to solve problems." Other sections of the report emphasized decentralizing decisionmaking power, holding government accountable, eliminating waste, raising user fees, and cutting back on costs.

While tapping into the rhetoric of systemic privatization, however, the Clinton administration was seeking to return the United States' privatization energies back to their more pragmatic roots. The ultimate emphasis of the reinvention effort was on making government work better. The Gore report explicitly rejects the notion that government is structurally incapable of meeting the demands that have been put upon it. "Is government inherently incompetent?" it asks. "Absolutely not," it answers. Reagan, and to a lesser extent Bush, argued that government had usurped power, careening on its own initiative away from its sources of legitimation in the Constitution and in the values of its citizens. In contrast, Clinton and Gore took the position that the broad array of responsibilities that government had adopted represented a democratically defined consensus: "The National Performance Review focused primarily on *how* government should work, not on *what* it should do. Our job was to improve performance in areas where policymakers had already decided government should play a role."[54] All of the tools of privatization – contracting out, user fees, asset sales, market choice – could be considered and selectively employed. But the focus was on means – not ends – and the emphasis was on better governance, not less government.

An uncertain future

During its first year, the NPR apparently managed to bring about roughly $12 billion in governmental savings, and there are indications that it helped set in motion some changes in agency culture that may

---

[53] Al Gore, *Creating a Government That Works Better & Costs Less: Report of the National Performance Review* (NY: Times Books, 1994), pp. 1–2.   [54]   Ibid., p. ii.

result in further savings and improvements in performance.[55] But the enthusiasm that greeted its initial announcement did not last very long, and close observers soon raised questions about whether its impetus could be sustained.[56] The internal bureaucratic support quickly withered as it became apparent that reinvention was more likely to translate into personnel cuts than a clear and forceful reconfiguration of government to better achieve public goals. More significantly, the 1994 Congressional elections, and the capture of both the House and Senate by the Republican party posed major threats to the Clinton administration's hopes for positive reform. The radical planks of the Republicans' "Contract With America" suggested that truly systemic privatization was still a viable political dream.

During the 1996 primary, Republican candidates Gramm, Forbes, and Alexander all ran campaigns that attacked government and celebrated the marketplace and individual initiative. Patrick Buchanan's message was more complicated, combining a sharp rhetorical assault on federal bureaucracy with a wariness of free-markets when they operate in an international environment. The Republicans' nomination of the more moderate Robert Dole was another indication that the American public is not yet ready to dive head first into the pool of systemic privatization. Dole, a long-time Washington insider, adhered to a somewhat a different vision than Clinton about the substance of what government can and should do, but in portraying himself as the man who had the expertise and experience to make the government work better, he, too, positioned himself as a man who could make government work better, not as the man who would tear down its foundation. While Clinton's reelection was taken by some to represent a mandate for the pragmatic "make government work better" – and, indeed, Clinton sounded such a theme in his second-term inaugural speech – the simultaneous reelection of a conservative, Republican-dominated Congress suggests that the future shape of the state in the USA remains up for grabs.

Conclusions

Perhaps nowhere on the planet is the contrast between privatization and shrinking the state clearer than in the United States. While the country has had, in comparison to Europe, a modest welfare state which was constructed somewhat later than its opposite numbers across the Atlantic,

---

[55] Donald F. Kettl, "Building Lasting Reform: Enduring Questions, Missing Answers," in Donald F. Kettl and John J. DiIulio, Jr., eds. *Inside the Reinvention Machine* (Washington, DC: Brookings, 1995), p. 9.

[56] See all of the contributions to Kettl and DiIulio, eds., *Inside the Reinvention Machine*.

this is at least partially because the constituency for such a state has been weaker and because the political culture has been more hostile to government than elsewhere in the advanced industrial world.

However, the contrast between privatization and the reduction of public responsibility has been made clear by the shifting balance between *pragmatic* and *systemic* privatization. Pragmatic privatization occurred in the USA before the phenomenon had a name, as public officials (mostly at the municipal level) sought to provide goods and services as efficiently as possible, often with severe constrictions on financial resources. Moreover, even the movement for deregulation, conceived essentially as an antidote to oligopoly, was championed in a nonideological rhetoric by a bipartisan coalition. It was not until the rise to power of extremely conservative Republicans, led by Ronald Reagan, that we find a clear intent to use the tools of privatization to change the balance between public and private, to reduce both direct and indirect government responsibility, and in every way possible to shrink the state.

Just as we hypothesized in chapter 1, and noted in the cases of Britain and France, privatization generated a backlash. Even in a country where economic liberalism is the dominant ideology, where social democracy was stillborn, and where the poorest citizens normally do not vote, there was clearly a limit to the public's willingness to let a coterie of ideologues completely dismantle all the capacities of state intervention. Certainly, some shifts took place. But the American institutional setting can be deceptive. Often national level conservatives were content to shift redistributive mechanisms to lower levels of government, rather than to destroy those mechanisms completely. Certainly, the Republican advocates of privatization hoped that by shifting public functions to state and local authorities there might also be an absolute reduction in those functions, but part of the reason for this shift was that there was no constituency for eliminating the welfare state entirely.

The elections of 1996 seemed to indicate an ambivalence on the part of the American public with regard to privatization reforms. Both Bill Clinton and the Republican Congress were reelected. Proponents of systematic privatization argue that Republican efforts to retake the White House would have been better served by a candidate more able and willing than the political insider Dole to enunciate a strong anti-government theme. But American voters' strong negative response to the Republican Congressional leaders' willingness to shut down the federal government as a bargaining ploy during budget talks suggests that there are definite limits to the speed and degree of governmental dismantling the public is willing to countenance.

6   The boundaries of privatization

> Privatization restores government to its fundamental purpose and relieves it of burdensome functions for which it is ill-suited. This truth is finally being grasped and applied successfully throughout the world.[1]

> The fact that across the OECD ... privatisation programmes have been implemented under conservative, liberal and socialist governments points to the existence of economic and social dimensions of privatisation which transcend ideological differences and appeal to parties across a broad spectrum.[2]

To its proponents, the breadth, speed, and seeming unity of purpose of the world-wide privatization movement give it a status as a revealed truth. Its breadth is attributed to the universality of the economic laws that dictate the ultimate dysfunctionality of the modern welfare state. Its suddenness is attributed to the power of ideas and evidence to spark sharp political reversals. Rational choice theory predicted that the weight of government would dampen growth, and its extension to the world of politics predicted that government agencies would elevate their own interests over those of the public. According to the proponents of privatization, these ideas penetrated the facade of benevolence protecting the state, and opened the eyes of the mass public to the role of the state as a protector of elite privilege. The unity of purpose behind the privatization movement is attributed to the windfall of growth that privatization will spark, elevating the issue above the zero-sum politics that normally generates factionalization and maneuvering for competitive advantage.

We were drawn to our investigation into privatization by three intellectual challenges it seems to present: (1) to conventional understanding about the nature of the state, (2) to conventional understanding of the importance of domestic politics and culture, and (3) to the conventional

[1] E. S. Savas, "Private Enterprise is Profitable Enterprise," *The New York Times*, February 14, 1988, sect. 3, p. 2.
[2] B. Stephens, "Prospects for Privatisation in OECD Countries," *National Westminster Quarterly Bank Review*, May 12–25, 1992, p. 2.

premise that gradualism is the normal and expected mode of policy change. A reversal of the growth of government was anomalous in the context of theories explaining the inevitable emergence and expansion of the state. The internationalization of the privatization movement seemed anomalous in the context of political theories that give defining roles to culture, institutions, and political cleavages that varied sharply among the countries in which it was evident. And the sudden emergence on the international agenda of so radical a prescription for policy change seemed anomalous in the context of theories which suggest that interest-group politics and institutional biases make incrementalism the normal rule of the day.

These anomalies forced us to take a fresh look at the role of politics in setting the boundaries of the state, and the role of the state in shaping the landscape upon which political battles are fought. In the first section of this chapter, we draw out and amplify several themes emerging from our case studies. These relate to: (1) the contingent and politically defined nature of the boundaries of the state, (2) the gradual but incomplete globalization of the policy agenda, and (3) the mutual interactions among interests, institutions, and ideas.

In the second section we outline some basic components for a theory about the dynamics of privatization. We do not pretend to predict the future of the state; indeed, our view of the contingent nature of the process of state construction and evolution belies the possibility of doing so. But we do believe that there are tendencies and likelihoods that our conceptual approach suggests and that our empirical work supports. Based on these expectations, we conclude with some warnings about the possible consequences of systemic privatization as it is manifested in its most extreme form – in Eastern Europe and the former Soviet republics – and with a general assessment of the possible future of the welfare state.

In some respects, our investigation has led us to a more moderate view of the impact of privatization. Of the three types of privatization, systemic privatization has the greatest potential to quickly and radically alter the shape of the state. While systemic privatization has played a major role in the initial eruption of the privatization movement, we will argue here that its transition from stated agenda to implemented policy change has proved to be problematic. While tactical privatization has played an important role in the spread of the movement and in the adoption of some of its most notable victories, we suggest here that the tactical version is more likely to reallocate the costs and benefits distributed by the state than to alter its parameters. Ironically, pragmatic privatization, which is the least dramatic form, may have the greatest long-term potential to alter the character of the welfare state. But, as we shall argue, its adoption is likely to be the most incremental, its form the most responsive to national contexts, and its consequences most likely to reconfigure rather than reverse the role and responsibilities of the state.

In suggesting a more moderate appraisal of the privatization phenomenon, we do not wish to diminish to any extent its immediate implications for the way we theorize about politics. In considering the politics of privatization, we have been led to a greater appreciation of the open-ended and contingent nature of the collective enterprise through which societal interests are defined and pursued, we have been convinced that national boundaries have become more permeable and the politics of agenda-setting more globalized, and we have been reinforced in our belief that there is much profit to be gained from developing a more sophisticated understanding of the interaction among interests, institutions, and ideas.

Nor do we seek to trivialize the potential for advocates of systemic privatization to bring about changes that will significantly alter the terms on which societies set their course. While we challenge the claim that the privatization revolution represents an historical imperative that is deeply rooted and far-advanced, we do not believe, despite the possibility for backlash, that it is inherently self-limiting.

Rethinking the politics of privatization

In place of a vision of privatization as an inexorable and universal phenomenon that reflects the truth of economic laws and the power of their revelation, we offer a view of privatization as a political battleground, where outcomes remain uncertain, where victories and losses may depend on local terrain, and where ideas play an important role but not an independent one.

An ongoing skirmish

Just as analysts writing through the mid-1970s saw the growth of the state to be natural and inevitable, so too some contemporary observers have been overly quick to characterize the privatization movement as driven by broad imperatives outside the realm of public deliberation and control. But the fits and starts, the ebb and flow, of privatization programs in the nations we have considered raise questions about this model. What initially appeared to be a snowballing phenomenon, in which each success generated others in geometric proportions, has proven to be more akin to a war of attrition. Privatization thrusts are sometimes met by successful parries and counter-attacks. Rather than the unquestioned founder of a radical new regime, history may record the indomitable Margaret Thatcher as an aberration, to be followed by governments less hostile to public role in the management of economic forces. Similarly, Ronald Reagan's early efforts to adopt a systemic privatization agenda gradually fizzled out, and his administration gave birth to a more moderate and pragmatic Bush administration, which was followed by the Democrats' recapturing of the White House. In France, the Socialists lost power in 1993, but the program of privatizations launched by the Conservative government shows little sign of cementing a secure hold on control. When the Socialists regained power in 1997 the policy was consigned to only its most pragmatic applications.

Our point is not that privatization is destined to fail. Our point is that destiny is the wrong touchstone altogether. Throughout history, the state has served as both a tool of social advance and an object of maneuvering for group advantage. It is *possible* that a broadly and substantially restructured and diminished state would unleash such growth and creativity that all would benefit, but that is more hypothesis than established fact, and the broad public's willingness to entertain that argument in the course of debate has proven to be more problematic when it comes to providing a clear mandate for implementing radical change. What is more clear and more certain than the long-term social consequences, are the shorter-term costs and benefits that privatization would allocate among already mobilized publics and interest groups. It should not be surprising, in that case, that we find battles among such interests to be the most immediate predictors of the future course of events.

Global convergence and national divergence

Both the actual consequences of privatization and the political landscape within which its future will be determined are likely to depend on conditions specific to individual countries. In this sense, we believe that some of the impression of an internationalized policy agenda is misguided. It is true that the language of privatization policy has been internationalized. It is true as well that the privatization experiences of some nations are being used as points of instruction by forces within other countries, as a sources for enlightenment or as a tactical means for validating the proposition that privatization works. It also is true that some powerful international actors have used their financial leverage to force privatization onto the agendas of some weaker nations that are dependent upon them. But the convergence of language masks differences in the pace, scope, and style of privatization. Nations differ in their historical legacies in ways that are relevant to the political dynamics that privatization battles will entail. Some, like the USA, entered the 1990s with relatively few marketable assets owned by the national government. Some like Great Britain, have a stronger political tradition of working class consciousness and political mobilization. Some, like France, have a more intense culture of economic nationalism, and perhaps a greater acceptance of an ambiguous partnership between public and private elites.

Rather than vestiges of an earlier age, we see these national differences as a continued force in shaping domestic politics. Although the rhetoric of privatization seems uniform, the more concrete choices made in each of these nations seem to us to have turned on localized factors such as these.

The power of ideas: the limits of ideas

Ideas have played an important role in thrusting privatization onto the agendas of so many nations relatively simultaneously. In this sense, our analysis joins those of others[3] who have noted the power of ideas to redefine problems and redirect attention in ways that spur rapid political realignments. It is "transparently true that self interest does motivate a good deal of political behavior, and that it does affect government outcomes in important ways. But interests intimately are intertwined with ideas about what is worth doing and how the world works."[4] Privatization advocates have broadened their constituency by convincing some groups that benefits they associated with a functioning state – job security, steady economic growth, protection of the helpless, development of a transportation and education infrastructure – could be provided just as well or even better by market forces and nongovernmental initiatives.

Yet, it is important to distinguish between ideas as abstractions and ideas that find roots in existing perceptions and beliefs. The core of ideas behind privatization are not dramatically different from the theories that animated calls for laissez-faire policies much earlier in the century. Those ideas failed to take root then. Why have similar ideas seemingly taken root now?

We believe that the theories behind privatization will have effect, over the long-term, not as disembodied evidence or paradigms, and not as pure ideas carried along by their own power, but to the extent that they become rooted in a constituency that sees them as compatible with their own

---

[3] See the discussion in chapter 1.

[4] John W. Kingdon, "Ideas, Politics, and Public Policies," paper prepared for delivery at the Annual Meeting of the American Political Science Association, Washington, DC, September 1–4, 1988, pp. 2–3; Bryan D. Jones, *Reconceiving Decision-Making in Democratic Politics: Attention, Choice, and Public Policy* (Chicago: University of Chicago Press, 1994).

values and perceptions, as well as their own material interests. Many factors can influence whether ideas find an audience, and only some of these have to do with the characteristics and quality of the ideas themselves. To gain broad acceptance, however, it seems likely that a policy theory must satisfy at least three basic tests. First, it should offer an explanation of relevant history, including an accounting of the development of the societal problem and a diagnosis of the failure of past remedial attempts. Secondly, it should provide a guide to current action. This guide should include both a set of techniques and a political/administrative strategy for putting such techniques into effect. Thirdly, it should be convincing to key constituencies. Credibility, in the last sense, may depend in part upon marshaling empirical evidence. But some constituencies may respond less to rigorous studies than to whether the theory "feels right," whether its account of history and guide for future action is consistent with their understanding and experiences.

Ideas that spread rapidly but develop shallow roots are better characterized as fads than as movements. And we believe that the verdict is not yet in on how deeply the privatization paradigm has taken hold. Rather than a spiraling unraveling of public support for the state (such as one would expect if the source is the proven dysfunctionality of the state or the power of ideas), we see a gradual emergence of counter forces based on opposing values and a growing set of qualifications about the limits of privatization.

The dynamics of privatization: putting privatization in its place

Sometimes, in order to understand a thing in motion, it is necessary to regard it frozen in place. Photographer Eadweard Muybridge demonstrated as much in 1877, when he used a battery of twenty-four cameras to analyze the motion of a running horse; his series of freeze-frame pictures demonstrated that there is a moment when none of the horse's feet is touching the ground. The typology we introduced in chapter 2 imposes a kind of freeze-frame on the politics of privatization. Yet the particulars of our case studies belie such a static view. Privatization in each of the countries simultaneously reveals elements of pragmatism, the pursuit of tactical advantage, and an effort to instigate broad structural change. At various times, however, one or another of these types of privatization dominates. Moreover, each helps to create its own political dynamic, with implications for the probability that privatization will have lasting consequences. Our insights into this more dynamic understanding of privatization reinforce the distinction between shaping an agenda and bringing about long-term structural change.

From motive to consequence

The questions about privatization that have interested us the most involve its nearly simultaneous emergence across a wide variety of national settings. This explains why we anchored our typology in political motivation; it is the subjectively defined interests of influential actors, that reveal the most about the processes of agenda formation and policy initiation. Nonetheless, the possibilities are real that the consequences intended by such political actors may never materialize. They may even backfire.

Efforts to promote broad structural realignments, indeed, probably fail much more often than they succeed.[5] Hawkins, for example, argues that West Germany, in 1957, initiated a systemic privatization initiative that prefigured the Thatcher model in many respects.[6] Like the Thatcher approach, the intent was at least in part to wean a broad segment of the middle and working class into stock-ownership and, presumably, greater allegiance to capitalism and market forces, but the long-term effect on stock ownership and popular perspectives was limited.[7] But the New Zealand experience suggests that major structural shifts are possible, even though they bring considerable social costs. Even more modest objectives that do not entail systemic changes may fall short of their objectives, due either to flawed strategies or implementation by the groups pursuing those objectives or to effective counter-measures taken by opposing groups.

Such failed efforts may leave no mark at all on the distribution of power, citizens' perceptions of the state's proper role, or the capacity and formal authority of public institutions. In some cases, however, they will have consequences that simply differ qualitatively from those that the principal actors intended. Figure 6.1 extends our initial typology by incorporating those cases in which motive and consequence are not allied. The horizontal dimension represents the three types of privatization as defined by the motivation of the principal initiators; the vertical dimension represents the ultimate consequences for government, interest groups, and social classes. A brief illustration of the pattern of privatization represented is contained within each cell. Taken by itself, figure 6.1

---

[5] In spite of the high probability of failure, the magnitude of potential gain may make pursuit of systemic privatization rational for some actors.

[6] See Richard A. Hawkins, "Privatisation in Western Germany, 1957 to 1990," *National Westminster Quarterly Bank Review*, November 1991, pp. 14–22.

[7] "The Western Germany economy did not see a long-term extension of share ownership. Furthermore, Esser has argued that 'people's capitalism' is unpopular in contemporary Western Germany and does not win votes" (ibid., p. 21). Hawkins' reference in this quote is to J. Esser, "Symbolic Privatisation: The Politics of Privatisation in West Germany," *West European Politics*, 11, 4 (1988), 21.

MOTIVATION

CONSEQUENCE	Pragmatic	Tactical	Systemic
Increase efficiency and capacity of government	State or province institutes users' fees for those entering public parks; revenues are directed to improved maintenance and expansion of park facilities.	Conservative party sells public utility to "friends," but state regulatory apparatus expanded in scope and capacity.	Effort to rapidly privatize results in sharp economic decline and popular unrest, leading to gradual reassertion of state intervention.
Benefit a particular political entrepreneur, party, or interest group.	City manager contracts out garbage collection; no gain in efficiency, but private firm gains lucrative contract	Economic elites finance conservative party campaign; subsequently, those interests are prime beneficiaries of new government's privatization initiatives.	Program to privatize state enterprises in order to build a new entrepreneurial and pro-democratic class, is co-opted by pre-existing state elite.
Structural reallocation of power among classes; diminished capacity, authority, and legitimacy of the State	Developing nation privatizes as condition of international aid; increases power of indigenous privileged classes	Progressive politician adopts privatization platform in order to blunt conservative criticisms; implementation radically weakens union constituencies.	Conservative party successfully implements program to sell off state enterprises, cut-back public bureaucracy, shrink social welfare responsibility.

Shaded cells are those in which eventual consequences match the intentions of the key initial proponents.

Figure 6.1 From motive to consequence

simply reminds us that political initiatives may turn out differently than the principals imagine. Many of our readers may not need such a reminder, but in an era in which interest groups and politicians make demands for radical restructuring based on claims for certain benefits, such a call for modesty is worth making nonetheless. That said, we believe we can push further than the conclusion that "anything can happen." While not determined, the course of privatization politics contains within it some patterns and tendencies that are instructive. In drawing these out, we begin with some insights that emerge from others' research into distinctions among the various stages in the policy process.

The long road from agenda to impact

Policy analysts have noted the existence of relatively distinct stages through which policy travels on the path between concept and consequence.[8] Roughly, these stages consist of agenda setting, policy formulation and enactment, implementation, outcome, and evaluation.

Many of the factors and strategies that determine the probability of a group's success in pursuing its interests are common across each stage of the cycle; resources such as wealth, information, access, and persistence, for example, can help a group bring its issues to public attention, press officials to enact legislative or regulatory change, and keep the pressure on bureaucracies to carry through. But some resources and strategies may be more productive at one stage than another. It is this – as well as changing environments – that leads some issues that reach the public agenda to fizzle out before policy changes, and leads some policies that are formally proclaimed to prove hollow, symbolic, or ephemeral.

Prior to the 1980s, advocates of smaller government were having a difficult time getting their policy preferences onto the decision agenda in industrialized Western nations. Elites often use their informational advantages, political leverage, and institutional access to restrict the public agenda to issues that do not threaten their privileged status. According to the literature on agenda setting, relatively disadvantaged groups may face troubles in getting their issues onto the public agenda, then, unless they can expand the scope of conflict, drawing new groups into the battle as allies.[9]

[8] Charles O. Jones, *An Introduction to the Study of Public Polcy* (North Scituate, MA: Duxbury, 1977); James E. Anderson, *Public Policy-Making* (New York: Holt, Rinehart and Winston, 1979); Michael Hayes, *Incrementalism and Public Policy* (New York: Longman, 1992).
[9] E. E. Schattschneider, *The Semi-Sovereign People* (New York: Holt, Rinehart and Winston, 1960); Frank R. Baumgartner and Bryan D. Jones, *Agendas and Instability in American Politics* (Chicago: University of Chicago Press, 1993); David A. Rochefort and Roger W. Cobb, *The Politics of Problem Definition: Shaping the Policy Agenda* (Lawrence, KS: University of Kansas Press), 1994.

This highlights the potential importance of two kinds of resources and skills. The first comprises resources and skills relating to *information dissemination*; mobilizing allies may depend upon reaching individuals and groups who already share general concerns but who may not be aware of the specifics of the issue. The second involves the capacity to *redefine the issue* in order to convince individuals and groups that they have a common interest that has hitherto gone unrecognized. The former puts a premium on access to the media (broadly defined to include academic and policy communication as well as those intended for mass publics). The latter puts a premium on constructing broad appeals that allow groups with differing values to find something to identify with, or on redirecting attention to values that have not previously been part of the public debate.[10]

Significantly, tactics that succeed in propelling an issue onto the public agenda may have little pay-off at the stage of policy enactment and implementation. Indeed, at times tactics that help at the agenda-setting stage are directly counter-productive when it comes to permanently reshaping policy.[11] Exaggerated appeals – those that warn of impending crisis or promise dramatic pay-offs – may gain attention and initially broaden the constituency for a policy proposal, but a constituency so constructed may dissipate quickly as time allows a more careful assessment of conditions or as early reforms fail to meet inflated expectations.[12] Similarly, broadly framed appeals may be vague enough to allow disparate groups to identify with them, and symbolic appeals may stir deeply held values that mobilize the previously unmobilized, but constituencies made of strange bedfellows may not last past the morning, and the power of symbols to motivate can create a polarized environment in which counter-mobilizations are more likely, negotiation is seen as unprincipled and martyrdom favored over necessary compromise.[13]

Recognizing that getting privatization onto the international agenda is not the same thing as embedding it in international practice, and building on some relatively simple observations about the kinds of factors that may erode an agenda-building constituency or spur a counter-mobilization by a superior force, we now build a link to our initial typology that gives it a more dynamic element that helps to account for the patterns we have uncovered in the case studies.

[10] On the importance of shifts in attention, see Jones, *Reconceiving Decision-Making.*

[11] One of the earliest and strongest statements about this tension – which focuses on how it affects relatively powerless groups – can be found in Michael Lipsky, *The Politics of Protest* (Chicago: Rand McNally, 1970).

[12] This point is developed more fully, as it relates specifically to calls for privatization in education policy, in Jeffrey R. Henig, *Rethinking Schools Choice: Limits of the Market Metaphor* (Princeton, NJ: Princeton University Press, 1994).

[13] Murray Edelman, *The Symbolic Uses of Politics* (Urbana, IL: University of Illinois Press, 1964); Douglas Yates, *The Ungovernable City* (Cambridge, MA: MIT Press, 1977).

The unstable politics of systemic privatization: polarization and backlash

The same attributes that have propelled systemic privatization onto the international agenda contribute to an unstable and unpredictable political environment which sets the stage for a counter-mobilization which may or may not succeed. By anchoring its ideas in the ideological heritage of laissez-faire, privatization proponents helped to animate the movement with a moral vision associated with personal freedom, anti-socialism, and creativity, but in the process it attracted a zealotry and rigidity of purpose that pushed the movement to embarrassing extremes. By linking the promise of privatization to multiple and not necessarily consistent goals – including deficit reduction, lower taxes, social justice and economic growth – privatization proponents temporarily broadened their constituency, but in the process they established high expectations and set the stage for disillusionment when tough choices had to be made. And, in linking privatization strategies to a deliberate agenda to unravel the welfare state coalition, privatization proponents rallied political and financial resources committed to the conservative cause, but in the process they alerted and reinvigorated elements of the original coalition that promoted state expansion, helping to reestablish common interests that had begun to fray.

This dynamic has been more apparent in the USA and Great Britain than in France, where systemic privatization was never a dominating force. In the USA, a vision of systemic change at key junctures has led privatization advocates to choose targets based on ideology rather than practical politics and to suffer as a result. Compared to most industrialized nations, the US federal government owns relatively little, but the vision of systemic privatization encouraged the Reagan Administration to scour available holdings looking for something they could sell. As discussed in chapter 5, the Reagan administration by-passed more politically vulnerable targets, to focus on the richer and more dramatic prospect of selling federally owned park lands. The proposed sale of government land, particularly federal park land, timberland, and oil and mineral rights, posed privatization as a threat to the environment. Ideological zeal, in this instance, encouraged the administration to underestimate the backlash that would be spurred by such a sharp attack on a governmental responsibility that most Americans perceived as legitimate.

Similarly, in Great Britain, an ideological commitment to broad systemic privatization led the Thatcher government to carry the battle to the National Health Service and British Rail/the Royal Mail, targets that made some potential supporters very uneasy indeed. And in the 1990s, as noted in chapter 3, continued allegiance to privatization led the Major

government to continue down the road of asset sales even after the polit-
ical balance sheet showed that it had begun to exact a high political cost.
Opposition, initially quite muted, was greatly strengthened over water,
coal and rail privatization, not least within the Conservative Party itself.
The newspapers in Britain have carried article after article arguing that
"Privatisation goes off the rails."[14] This was equally true with Major's
plan to emulate the Dutch experiment in privatizing the mail service.[15]
The diminishing popularity of these initiatives was certainly an element
in the huge Labour victory that chased the Conservatives from office in
1997.

Promises that privatization will allow the public to enjoy lower taxes
without sacrificing personal security or social justice have proved difficult
to realize, at least in the short-term, making political support for
privatization more tenuous and volatile. It is arguable that the British
public accepted the sale of industries such as Rolls Royce, British Steel,
just as the French likewise accepted the sale of Elf-Aquitaine or St.
Gobain, on the grounds that there was no case for them remaining in the
public sector,[16] and that, in any event, such asset sales did not seem have
much impact on the citizen's daily life. However, opposition to privatization has grown as privatizations of basic utilities in some instances have
led to substantial price rises and/or a deterioration in the quality of
service. There is already disquiet in Britain regarding the price rises
imposed by the water companies and the profits being made by British
Telecom. In France, the potential sale of major corporations to foreigners
had the same delegitimizing effects as the high utility prices in Britain,
diminishing the public taste for privatization, and for the politicians associated with the policy.

Moreover, as various privatization initiatives begin to compile mixed
records of success, the broad definition of privatization that helped generate a sense of momentum in the movement's earlier days has the potential
to backfire. The maturation of the privatization theory was marked by
several publications providing overviews of privatization.[17] Each defined
privatization broadly to include the entire gamut of techniques, from contracting out to asset sales, and each offered anecdotal and empirical evi-

---

[14] *The Times*, May 18, 1993.

[15] Andrew Adonis, "Hard Battle to Privatise the Post Office," *Financial Times*, November 2,
1994, p. 7.   [16] See especially Feigenbaum, *The Politics of Public Enterprise*, chs. 3 and 5.

[17] Robert W. Poole, Jr., *Cutting Back City Hall* (New York: Universe Books, 1980); James T.
Bennett, and Manuel H. Johnson, *Better Government at Half the Price* (Ottawa, IL:
Caroline House, 1981); E. S. Savas, *Privatizing the Public Sector* (Chatham, NJ: Chatham
House, 1982); Steve H. Hanke, "Privatization: Theory, Evidence, and Implementation,"
in C. Lowell Harriss, ed., *Control of Federal Spending* (New York: The Academy of
Political Science, 1985); Linowes, *Privatization*.

dence of the feasibility and success of these approaches. These overviews tended to cite many of the same studies. With few exceptions, however, the studies cited failed to systematically or directly assess large scale, deliberate, and programmatic efforts to reduce the scope of the state. For the most part, they represented fairly simple comparisons between publicly and privately provided services, with little or no effort to control for differing economic and institutional environments. And, for the most part, the private delivery systems they evaluated were modest efforts that had emerged through pragmatic adjustment. Nonetheless, the results of these studies were presented in such a way as to provide the more aggressive elements of the privatization agenda a "halo effect." As Paul Starr has noted, "By treating these heterogeneous measures as members of the same family, the advocates of privatization use the more moderate ideas, such as vouchers and contracting out, to gain plausibility for the more radical goal of government disengagement."[18]

Some of the more deliberate and substantial privatization efforts have now developed a track record of their own. And, while privatization proponents are pleased with some of the results, that record is not without its embarrassments. In the USA, deregulation of the airlines initially seemed to lead to the competition and lower prices that proponents had promised. But airline bankruptcies, labor troubles, confusing price structures, declining service to rural areas, and concerns about safety have led some in Congress to express doubts about the wisdom of their earlier action.[19] Some of the states that launched their own enterprise zones have found them less successful than more traditional direct government subsidies as a way to stimulate economic development.[20] The Reagan administration's small-scale experiment with housing vouchers disappointed the *Wall Street Journal*, presumably a sympathetic audience.[21] Even the experiences of Great Britain and France now provide a more problematic set of lessons. British dissatisfaction with service provided in the wake of the privatization of British Telecom and British Rail, with the rapid increases in charges following water privatization, the massive pay increases and bonuses to senior executives in privatized utilities, and scandals in France involving rumored "inside deals," have contributed to an air of growing wariness regarding privatization. Arguably, this played a contributory role in the electoral defeat of the Conservative government in 1997.

[18] Paul Starr, "The Limits of Privatization," in Hanke, ed., *Prospects for Privatization*, p. 126.
[19] Martha M. Hamilton, "Eastern Strike Raises Fears of Higher Fares: Debate on Airline Deregulation is Rekindled," *The Washington Post*, March 13, 1989, A17.
[20] Paul Farhi, "Do Enterprise Zones Work? In St. Louis, Results Are Tepid," *The Washington Post*, February 19, 1989, H1.
[21] Joann S. Lublin, "Uncertain Solution: Vouchers for Housing Help Some Poor, Fail to Benefit Others," *The Wall Street Journal*, November 1986, p. 1.

Selective failures of privatization ought not discredit the broad program, any more than selective successes ought to have been taken as empirical verification that the program was universally viable. But public perceptions do not follow strict rules of evidence. Now that the more radical privatization efforts have been conceptually bound to the more modest and pragmatic adjustments, problems associated with the former can be expected to stiffen resistance even to the latter.

At the same time that exaggerated promises, unresolved tensions among goals, and growing attention to unpopular privatization efforts have begun to expose the fragility of the constituency for systemic privatization, the stark, ideological and aggressive stance of the systemic privatization loyalists has shown signs of reinvigorating the constituencies that traditionally have supported an expansive role for the state.

In the USA, the traditional liberal Democratic coalition rests on distinct constituencies: labor, minorities, and higher socioeconomic groups concerned about protecting the environment and consumer rights. Events of the late 1960s and early 1970s threatened to unravel this coalition. The shift to a service economy and the growth of public sector employment put strains upon union organizations that had their traditional base in the manufacturing sphere. Affirmative action programs drove a wedge between civil rights organizations and white ethnic union members. Environmentalists' efforts to preserve land and limit development were perceived as anti-jobs by some workers; the same efforts were seen as anti-access to civil rights organizations seeking to break down barriers to affordable housing in the suburbs.

Such strains continue to weaken the Democratic party, but privatization has provided a potential unifying device. Each element of the coalition is unnerved by different components of the privatization movement. Public service employees are particularly concerned about contracting out. Public school teachers are concerned about education voucher plans that might support private schools. Manufacturing workers worry about deregulation in areas of occupational health and safety. Civil rights organizations regard warily privatization initiatives that shift responsibility from government to self-help or voucher and user fee proposals that base their claims of fairness to the poor upon presumptions of redistributive financing mechanisms that might not materialize. Environmentalists fret about the sale of public lands; consumer activists worry about poor maintenance on deregulated airlines.

In launching a full-scale attack on the idea of a caring, progressive, and effective government, proponents of systemic privatization may be mistaking citizens' unease and uncertainty for a more fundamental aversion to government. According to one analysis of Americans' trust in government and concerns about government power from 1935–1988, the public's aversion to government is neither unambiguous nor fixed:

There continues to be some ambivalence in Americans' opinions about big government. Many Americans will agree that the national government is involved in too many issues and yet expect it to do more . . . Americans still express belief in "individualism," and many hold to their personal responsibility to surmount the obstacles they confront in life. But belief in individualism does not preclude the possibility of a helping hand from government.[22]

Belief that the federal government has too much power peaked in the period between 1978 and 1982, but then it started to decline. Experiencing the government-shrinking policies of the Reagan administration led some Americans to have second thoughts about government's place in society. By 1988, "the percentage of the public predisposed to agree with President Reagan's call for more cuts in Washington was no larger than in 1964, at the height of LBJ's popularity."[23] This same kind of uncertainty and fluidity is evident in the resurgence of the Labour Party in Great Britain. As detailed in chapter 3, privatization initiatives had become something of a political liability to the Conservative Party. The early round of asset sales did not challenge the basic legitimacy of the state as a guarantor of social welfare in the same way that would a reconfiguration of the National Health Service, for example.

Moreover, in order to assuage concerns, proponents of systemic privatization in both Great Britain and the USA frequently have had to outline an ambitious role for the public sector in monitoring private sector contractors, in regulating corrupt or unfair market practices, and in expanding redistributional activities. Ironically, this means that advocates for systemic privatization sometimes have found themselves reaffirming the legitimacy of governmental intervention in the market and staking out a strong role for government in integrating lower-income groups into the middle-class.

In Britain the sale of British Telecom and British Gas led to the establishment of regulatory authorities to avoid the potential for abuse that might tempt private utility companies. This impulse to regulate appears to be gaining more strength as various European nations begin to worry about the vulnerability of their indigenous corporations in the emerging European Union. For example, anti-trust legislation was never strong in either Britain or France, but the European Union has taken a consistent and growing interest in avoiding "the abuse of a dominant position." And in both Britain and France, privatization proponents tacti-

---

[22] Linda L. M. Bennett and Stephen Earl Bennett, *Living With Leviathan: Americans Coming to Terms With Big Government* (Lawrence, KS: University of Kansas Press, 1990): pp. 134–135.   [23] Ibid., pp. 31–32.

cally adopted a rhetoric of "peoples' capitalism," which, while intended to convince the working class that it would share in the bounty of an unleashed market, may serve to reaffirm the notion that government has a legitimate role to play in the mitigation of class differences.

In the United States the neoliberal reforms of the bureaucracy popularized as "reinventing government" were clearly adopted by the Clinton administration to reassure citizens that their taxes were not being wasted. Nevertheless, it was equally clear that the reforms were initiated to create confidence in future expansion of the state. At the state and local levels, too, proponents of the contracting out of public services have found themselves in the forefront of calls for government to take on a stronger "watchdog" role, ensuring that private contractors meet performance standards.[24] And concerns that the poor will suffer as a result of their inability to compete in market arenas have been met by proposals that housing, education, and medical vouchers be targeted specifically to increase the purchasing power of the poor.

The conventional politics of tactical privatization: circulating winners and losers

In contrast to the polarized, volatile, and somewhat unpredictable politics that is spurred by broad efforts at systemic privatization, tactical privatization engenders a continuation of conventional partisan patronage politics by slightly different means. In this context, privatization sometimes is reduced to symbolic posturing through which candidates and parties can tap into anti-tax and anti-bureaucracy sentiments, either differentiating themselves from their opponents (usually those currently in power) or blunting the thrusts of their genuinely more conservative opponents. When rhetoric translates into genuine policy initiatives, the sale of state assets and the awarding of governmental contracts often represent, in this context, little more than a new form of benefits with which those in power may reward long-time supporters and lure new ones.

Because the primary motivation in tactical privatization is to gain electoral advantage, proponents' allegiance to the goal of dismantling the state is contingent upon contemporaneous political currents and fortunes. After initially gaining control of the governmental apparatus, candidates and parties that campaigned on privatization themes may feel compelled to "deliver the goods." But the simple fact of being in control alters the tactical calculations in some very real respects. The same

---

[24] Ruth Hoagland DeHoog, *Contracting Out for Human Services* (Albany, NY: State University of New York Press, 1984).

groups that see an authoritative government with the capacity to act forcefully as a juicy target when they are frozen out of power, may begin to see it as a valuable tool when they get their hands on the levers. Privatization activities that directly benefit supporters, as seen in the *noyaux dur* patterns in France, make tactical sense. Where an ideological commitment to systemic privatization might lead to an aggressive hacking away at the most significant forms of state power, however, a tactical orientation points toward a more surgical carving that may eliminate programs and agencies with historical ties to the opposition, while at the same time retaining, or even bolstering, state power in areas that can protect and expand one's core constituency.

Because both parties can play the game, tactical privatization is less likely to spark ideological polarization, and is also less likely to give a primary role to the politics of ideas. Here, ideas serve as rationalizations for actions rather than as genuine reasons for action. While the competition among interests may be intense, in this context it is less likely to gain the emotional edge and resistance to compromise that marks the politics of systemic privatization. Somewhat paradoxically, the recognition that both sides are maneuvering for their own benefit, and the atmosphere of tolerant cynicism it engenders, can make it easier for minority and majority parties to negotiate and strike bargains.

The politics of tactical privatization is more likely than systemic privatization to leave in place the fundamental boundaries of the state, but it is conducive to turnover in leadership. Like systemic efforts, tactical privatization has the potential to lead to a backlash. In each of the case countries, revelations about selective benefits to political supporters have occasioned minor scandals that political opponents have seized upon to discredit the party in power. In the previous section, we speculated that backlash against systemic privatization *could* stimulate a resurgence of a broad coalition supportive of an expanded role for government. It is possible that revulsion to cynical, tactical manipulation of privatization, similarly could lead to a reassertion of state power – for example, in such areas as campaign finance reform, conflict of interest legislation, and the like. But the backlash to tactical privatization scandals is just as likely to be limited to a more short-term and selective effort to "throw the rascals out" – one which limits itself to replacing one set of rascals with a new set.

Tactical privatization can make the transition into systemic privatization, however, if it serves to create new interests that add their political muscle to the battle to dismantle the state. As noted in chapter 4, the privatization of French national firms may be producing new corporate networks that will generate new and powerful demands for their own policy agenda. British efforts to use the sale of council housing to turn

Labour renters into Tory voters have proven less successful than initial reports suggested,[25] but it remains possible that these types of initiatives – including the efforts in both Britain and France to turn the masses into (presumably more conservative) stock-holders, will bear fruit over the long term. In the USA, conservative Republicans are making a major effort to allow households to opt for private insurance in lieu of Medicare and Social Security, at least partially motivated by the tactical calculation that this will detach the wealthiest, most educated, and most politically motivated from the constituency that so far has stymied efforts to sharply scale back these governmental entitlements.

The unpolitics of pragmatic privatization: ongoing adjustment

Pragmatic privatization offers the least grandiose claims but may ultimately have the greatest impact on the amorphous relationship between society and state. Pragmatic privatization is deliberately selective; rather than a broad program to fit all circumstances, it presupposes that details and specifics matter. While some state-owned enterprises may be sold at social profit, others should be retained because to do so will protect national economic independence, provide a counter-weight to large private suppliers, soften the impact of free market forces, or generate revenue that can be reinvested in other ways. While some services may be provided as well by private contractors, others should be kept in the public sector, because there are not enough private providers to generate genuine competition, because public goals are too complex or ill-defined to be contractually stipulated, because monitoring of private performance is not possible, or because a activity is so centrally tied to the legitimacy of the state that it cannot be entrusted to private providers no matter their expertise.[26]

Partly because it is selective and attentive to specifics, pragmatic privatization tends toward incrementalism. Rather than a sudden and wholesale abandonment of public responsibility, for example, privatization made inroads in the United States through a gradual process. Sometimes privatization has represented a pragmatic effort to increase revenues or decrease costs during short-term fiscal crises; when public revenues rebound the government sometimes reasserts its role, at other times it does not. Frequently, too, techniques like user fees and contract-

---

[25] Ray Forrest and Alan Murie, *Selling the Welfare State: The Privatization of Public Housing* (London, Routlege, 1991).

[26] For a thoughtful consideration of the conditions under which privatization may and may not be advisable, see John Donahue, *The Privatization Decision* (New York: Basic Books, 1989).

ing out have been adopted simultaneously with the expansion of public responsibilities to new areas; in deciding to add new tennis courts at a public park, for example, state or local authorities might opt to institute sign-up fees rather than fight the political battle that would be needed to impose that cost upon the general taxpayers. In some cases these funding arrangements not only become institutionalized, they become models that are copied by other jurisdictions and other agencies within the same jurisdiction, but in other instances it appears those services later migrate back to the more conventional funding through general revenues.

Pragmatic privatization tends to be depoliticized. Its promoters and overseers frequently are career administrators rather than elected politicians. And its attention to details and specifics reinforces the notion that this is an area that calls for technical expertise rather than popular mobilization. Partly because it is promoted quietly, by career administrators, pragmatic privatization initiatives are much less likely to spark sharp public backlash. They are instituted without much of a constituency, and they do not need much of a constituency to be sustained.

It is due to these factors – selectivity, incrementalism, low visibility, and bureaucratic sponsorship – that pragmatic privatization may ultimately bring about more substantial and sustainable changes in the character of the welfare state. As we noted earlier (chapter 1), the boundaries between state and society exist across multiple dimensions, including financing, delivery, responsibility, and decisionmaking. Rather than a sharply dual system, in which services are parceled out in one or the other sectors – government or market – most services in complex industrialized nations are the product of an ill-defined, largely *ad hoc,* and generally fluid assignment of responsibilities across both spheres. Pragmatic privatization leads us toward a state that directly delivers fewer or different services. But if, at the same time, it leads us toward a state that more aggressively and effectively monitors private providers and more authoritatively intervenes when necessary to promote social values such as justice and equity, such changes would be better understood as a reconfiguration than a repudiation of the state.

Our hypotheses revisited

It is useful, as we begin to draw conclusions from our review of privatization in Britain, France and the USA, to recall the hypotheses discussed in chapter 1. Our first hypotheses, that the effect of privatization policies on the size of the state is a consequence of the nature of the constituency that has gained power, is clearly supported by the three cases. While pragmatic privatization policies were adopted by both left- and right-wing governments, those privatization policies which were most likely to shrink the state, that is, *systemic* privatizaton policies, were only adopted by conservative governments.

Our second hypothesis, that developmental states create the conditions for their own shrinkage is supported in the case of France, the only developmental state we have studied in detail. The role of nationalized industry is typical of a developmental state, where the state creates enterprises to solve the problems of market failure. Firms which were created to pursue functions in the absence of private entrepreneurs, such as Elf-Acquitaine,[27] or which were previously uncompetitive as private firms, were brought back to profitability through state ownership. Their new-found profitability made them candidates for privatization, when conservative governments came to power and were seeking state revenues other than taxation. That developmental states often expand in response to economic nationalism,[28] was illustrated in the negative by the resistance to privatization engendered by the French government plan to sell Thomson Multimedia to Korean investors.

Our third hypothesis, that state shrinkage is rooted in external factors is supported in two ways. First, it is clear that conservative governments in both France and the United States were influenced by the earlier experiments of Margaret Thatcher in Great Britain. Thus, the internationalization of ideas and the power of transnational learning are evidenced in both cases. Secondly, more indirectly, the world-wide stagnation engendered by the oil crises of the 1970s, which brought conservative governments to power in Britain and America, led to many of the budget deficits privatization was intended to correct. Also, more indirectly, increasing competition from low-wage economies as world markets became ever more integrated, served as a credible reason for governments to reduce taxes to employers whose profitability was challenged by world competition. Such revenue reductions created incentives for state asset sales, and encouraged governments to reduce expenses. Beneficiaries of the welfare state became vulnerable constituencies in such a deflationary climate.

Our fourth hypothesis, that shrinking the state could generate a backlash against privatization as groups discovered that such policies put their interests in jeopardy seems to be occurring in all three countries as we write. Indeed, this backlash may be even more important elsewhere in Europe. We turn now to the political impact of privatizations where such policies have been most dramatic.

---

[27] See the discussion in Harvey B. Feigenbaum, *The Politics of Public Enterprise* (Princeton: Princeton University Press, 1985), ch. 3.

[28] Alexander Gerschenkron, *Economic Backwardness in Historical Perspective* (Cambridge, MA: Harvard University Press, 1962).

A speculative parenthesis on privatization in Eastern Europe[29]

The focus of this book has been on the advent of privatization in advanced capitalist countries, with special attention to the policies of Britain, France and the United States. However, the most far reaching privatizations have occurred in the formerly Communist countries of Eastern Europe. We started our research well before the Berlin Wall fell in 1989 and therefore can, perhaps, be forgiven our Western focus. Nevertheless, as we intended our three-fold typology introduced in chapter 2 to be generic, we would be remiss if we did not consider the implications of the events in the countries east of the Elbe River.

It will come as no surprise that we consider the reforms currently underway in the former Communist countries to best be characterized under the rubric "systemic privatization." Systemic privatizations are the most ideological in their origins, and the most widespread in their impact. Rather than being the technocratic solution to a discrete number of specific problems, systemic privatization aims at permanently changing class relations.

Proponents of rapid and radical privatization in the formerly Communist states are willing to risk deprivation and disruption in what they assume to be the short term. Their expectation is that the introduction of market principles and forms will reinforce shifts in power, perceptions, and institutions that are conducive to further democratization and, perhaps even more emphatically, that will serve as a backstop against the potential for reversion to former practices.[30]

The most naive among these privatization proponents see the unleashing of the ideas of markets and personal freedom to be sufficient to put these countries on paths of modern and efficient production, and to permanently inoculate them against the possibility of the old Communist institutions being resurrected. The recrudescence of ancient nationalisms and ethnic hostilities have given pause to the general optimism, but these clouds on the political horizon have tended to be de-emphasized in face of the belief that the storms can be averted if priority is given to accelerating economic reform.

---

[29] An extended version of this argument first appeared as "Privatization and Democracy," in *Governance,* 6, 3 (1993), 439–453.

[30] As the *Financial Times* put it: "the fall of the communist regimes throughout eastern Europe . . . has opened the way for privatization of state-owned enterprises and assets on an unprecedented scale. With it has come the promise of greater prosperity but above all the chance of creating a property-owning middle class to underpin democracy and guarantee the irreversibility of the escape from totalitarianism." Anthony Robinson, "Not as Easy as it Looks," *Financial Times*, Survey: Privatization in Eastern Europe, July 3, 1992, III-2.

Somewhat more cautious observers recognize that market concepts will not suffice unless they are coupled with institutional changes. These include institutional changes intended to establish a legal and regulatory framework within which market transactions can be protected and enforced, as well as broader economic institutions, such as a functioning stock market, lending institutions, and the like. While more sophisticated, this view, too, is ultimately optimistic that economic reforms, once rooted into place, are sufficient to bring about a lasting democratic reform.

It is our view that privatization policies do not necessarily lead to such propitious outcomes. Following our analysis of the USA, Britain and France, we believe it is useful to consider how the realm of political interests is affected in the East by policies, for the most part, designed in the West. It is logical to assume that the shape of state/society relations in Eastern Europe, as in the West, will depend on an open-ended battle among competing groups with differing interests and world views. A state that is democratic, responsive, and accommodating to personal freedom must be created and nurtured; it is not the tail that wags inevitably at the back end of the market dog.

Like the most optimistic of the privatization proponents, we believe that broad economic reforms can set into motion political forces that will not readily be reversed. Unlike them, however, we believe that the causal connection between markets and democratic practices is hardly as direct and certain as the proponents of widescale, and rapid privatization seem to believe. Rather, as we have stressed, the relationship between political and economic change is a contingent one. The conclusions that we have drawn from the experiences of Western countries, remind us that it makes a difference what *kinds* of markets one creates, and more specifically, the manner in which the emerging markets are shaped by – and interact with – the legal, cultural, and political fabric of the diverse societies in which they appear. Even in the more established democracies, privatization policies may lead to the re-creation of the political landscape in ways that limit the state's capacity to innovate or implement policy. Especially, where democratic norms and practices are less well ingrained, some economic choices may lead to long-term incentives for political repression, and may introduce and nurture anti-democratic forces.

Since the privatizations of Eastern Europe have most closely approximated our *systemic* category, where class relations are deeply affected, it is worthwhile to apply the lessons of historical sociology. As others have before us, we suggest that the emergence of modern democracy depended upon the development of a strong and independent middle – or "bourgeois" – class.[31] No one underlined the fact more dramatically than Barrington Moore whose famous four words state the case succinctly: "No bourgeois, no democracy."[32] Moore suggested that the pro-democratic sentiments of the bourgeois class rested on its concrete interests, rather than on principled commitment to the abstract notions of human rights or popular control. It had an interest in the defense of property rights, individual liberty, and equality before the law (over aristocratic privilege). Moreover, in countries which had industrialized early, this class had a preference for limited government over large and intrusive states which meddle in markets and demand the support of taxes.[33]

Sadly, the nature of the alliance between the industrial and commercial middle classes and pro-democratic forces has proven to be contingent on the conditions that characterized particular nations in a particular era; the link is not assured. Most problematically, the interests of industrialists in countries which were late economic developers have often tended more toward a preference for authoritarian rule to keep wages low in the face of international competition.[34]

Privatization in Eastern Europe is similarly likely to result in the creation of a new bourgeois class, but there is no guarantee that it will be one with the will and capacity to nurture and sustain democratic institutions and values. As we elaborate in greater detail elsewhere,[35] the historical alliance between this class and democracy that characterized several Western industrial nations, including the USA, Britain and France, is made more difficult in the contemporary context, wherein an internationalized economy may preempt the development of an indigenous alliance of analogous function.

Most of the economies of eastern European countries seem to be living museums of archaic technologies. Consequently, political elites in the former Communist states are desperate for transfusions of capital so as to modernize, or if modernization is impractical, to create new industries. Not surprisingly, privatization has seemed a pragmatic solution to their capital shortage. To the extent that the introduction of markets and foreign capital can help to shake out old inefficiencies and jump start economic production, we, too, see it as a potentially progressive force. It is

[31] Louis Hartz. *The Liberal Tradition in America* (New York: Harcourt, Brace, 1955); Seymour Martin Lipset. *Political Man* (New York: Anchor Books, 1960); Alexis de Tocqueville, *Democracy in America*, ed., Richard Heffner (New York: Mentor, 1956).
[32] Barrington Moore Jr., *Social Origins of Dictatorship and Democracy* (Boston: Beacon Press, 1966), pp. 418. Moore, however, in the preceding sentence, credits Marx with the insight. [33] Perry Anderson, *Lineages of the Absolutist State* (New York: Verso, 1974).
[34] Gerschenkron, *Economic Backwardness.*
[35] Feigenbaum and Henig, "Privatization and Democracy."

our contention that foreign investment not only creates jobs and transfers technology, it transforms the political landscape in ways that complicate the long-term outlook for democracy.

Even in the USA and Western Europe, the veneer of consensus surrounding the privatization movement masks underlying tensions between indigenous firms and foreign investors, between free-market ideology and economic nationalism. Chapter 4 illustrated this most clearly. In the developed world, business interests are diverse in objective interest and orientation toward the costs and benefits of unregulated markets. For instance, neither US airlines, nor semiconductor firms have been enthusiastic about dismantling the state, while the huge, more globally sourced firms have pushed for greater market freedoms.[36] In less developed countries, and in the former Communist states, the indigenous industrial and commercial class is in a fledgling state, politically as well as economically, and may be unable to withstand competitive international pressures on its own. And the high mobility, force and speed of international capital make it improbable that such indigenous groups will have the same opportunity to mature and exercise a stabilizing and progressive influence that the Western equivalent enjoyed in an earlier era. Moreover, foreign investors do not always have the same political stakes as the locally based middle class: in the past the former have been willing to accommodate many of the world's most repressive regimes.[37] This is especially true when foreign firms are primarily interested in a low-wage labor force to produce for export markets.

The various factors that moderate the impact of ownership shifts in the West are likely to be more attenuated in Eastern Europe, and the clout of external versus internal interests disproportionate. Prior to the serial revolutions, the national state out-muscled indigenous business interests, to the extent such business interests existed at all. But the newly formed states are saddled by a legacy which discredits the use of governmental authority. And, posed against the external financial interests, the national governments are puny and inexperienced.

The newly privatized economies are, however, confronted not just by the problem of control by foreign investors whose interests may diverge from those of the citizenry. The consequences of producing for foreign (versus domestic) markets, in open (versus closed) economies, are equally political. Firms in the former "Socialist Bloc" maximized produc-

---

[36] Thomas Ferguson and Joel Rogers, *Right Turn* (New York: Hill and Wang, 1986).

[37] Peter Evans, *Dependent Development* (Princeton: Princeton University Press, 1979). Richard L. Sklar, *Corporate Power in an African State* (Berkeley and Los Angeles: University of California Press, 1980).

tion rather than profits.[38] This had beneficial employment effects and was in this sense, at least, politically benign. The problem for the new democracies is that cost conscious firms confronting a stagnating world economy, where many of the most dynamic competitors draw on cheap labor, may find themselves with the same incentives to repress wages as in Germany of the inter-war period,[39] or as in some of the bureaucratic authoritarian regimes within the Third World. There is, we think, a very important distinction between firms which produce for export markets and those which produce for domestic markets, and there is a significant difference between firms which are relatively sensitive to labor cost and those which are less so.[40]

To state the overall argument in the language of class, democracy has its best chances for survival where the capitalists have an interest in a prosperous working class. Producing for the domestic market means the firms want their customers to be well paid, although preferably by other firms.[41] Even though newly privatized firms may wish to pay their workers as little as they can get away with,[42] collectively, if they are producing for the domestic market, they have no common interest in government assistance to keep overall wages low.[43] If, on the other hand, the post-Communist governments invite investment from companies attracted by Eastern European wage differentials, whose products are oriented toward

---

[38] Janos Kornai, *The Economics of Shortage* (Amsterdam: North Holland Publishing Co., 1980). Both socialist and capitalist firms have an incentive to control backward linkages (vertical integration): socialist firms wish to assure themselves of resources while capitalist firms wish to control costs.

[39] James R. Kurth, "The Political Consequences of the Product Cycle: Industrial History and Political Outcomes," *International Organization*, 33, 1 (Winter 1979), 22–24.

[40] Thomas Ferguson, "From Normalcy to New Deal: Industrial Structure, Party Competition and American Public Policy in the Great Depression," *International Organizations*, 38, 1 (Winter 1984), 41–94; Peter A. Gourevitch. "Breaking with Orthodoxy: The Politics of Economic Policy Responses to the Depression of the 1930s," *International Organization*, 38, 1, (Winter 1984), 95–130; James R. Kurth. "The Political Consequences", 1–34.

[41] Ernst Mandel. *An Introduction to Marxist Economic Theory* (New York: Pathfinder, 1970). Mandel sees this as a fundamental "contradiction" of capitalism. Regrettably, Marxist analysis tend to see most conflicts of interests as contradictions which inherently lead to implosion, rather than as conflicts which may end in compromise. This latter view, of course, does not mean that, as neoclassical economists assume, the system will always tend toward equilibrium.

[42] Modern management, of course, does not operate quite like the stereotype of *Das Kapital*, for wages rise not only with productivity, but to assure loyalty and reduce absenteeism. Nevertheless, wages which rise in the twentieth century cut into profit margins as they did in the nineteenth.

[43] J. Pool and S. Pool, *Who Financed Hitler?* (New York: Dial Press, 1978); Kurth, "Political Consequences."

export markets, the citizenry of these countries may find themselves to be saddled with employers who have little interest in their employees' relative wage gains. Sustaining worker acquiescence in such circumstances may eventually require coercion.

Capitalism means change, and with it a changing array of interests and actors who exert their respective influences upon the state and upon the future. But change need not be in only one direction, and this is especially true of political change.[44] Ironically, the pro-market advocates of rapid and radical privatization recall the tenets of the nineteenth-century socialist thinkers, who saw History as a process of teleological evolution and subscribed to what became known as the "Doctrine of Progress."[45] Our cautions are not meant to discredit the potential for the selective use of privatization to serve a progressive function. We endorse the attempts of the Eastern European countries to create a strong, and pro-democratic middle class. However, we must underscore the potential of indiscriminate privatization to fuel reactionary trends. As a policy directive, our argument suggests that privatization strategies need to be *managed* rather than *unleashed,* and that they need to be guided by a sensitivity to the nurturing of *political* habits and constituencies, not simply *economic* values and forms. The introduction of market forces into Eastern Europe should be cautious and conditioned, lest those forces undermine, rather than encourage, the budding democracies east of the Elbe.

Conclusion: the future of privatization and the state

The mixed record of privatization policies has served to underline the weakness of claims that such policies represent a "natural" evolution of advanced industrial economies. Privatization proponents explain its eruption on the national government's agenda by reference to objective economic interests of the state, linking it directly to goals of efficiency, competition, innovation, and deficit reduction. But an exclusive focus on economic forces obscures the intensely political nature of the privatization movement. Privatization initiatives are political because they redistribute costs and benefits among diverse and competing groups. And portraying privatization as a necessary adaptation to fiscal constraints fails to acknowledge the considerable range of alternative responses open to governmental actors and the extent to which selection of policies

[44] Samuel P. Huntington, *Political Order in Changing Societies* (New Haven: Yale University Press, 1969).
[45] Karl Lowith. *Meaning in History* (Chicago: University of Chicago Press, 1949).

within that range may reflect partisan tactics and pressure from mobilized interest groups.[46]

The vision of privatization as a revolution of ideas portrays the state as a vestigial remnant – a concentration of power that has illegitimately buffered itself and gained leverage but which is ready to be toppled because it lacks genuine constituency and because its public philosophy is outdated. We agree that institutions which are not rooted in interests are fragile, but we foresee a strong resilience to the state in general, and the welfare state in particular – not just because it helps shape the playing field, but because it has interests (and supportive ideas) as well.

The privatization movement as a revolution in ideas is significant because it represents a deliberate effort to redefine both economic and political interests. And it has been successful, at least in the sense that it has reshaped political discourse. Governmental options are conceived and talked about differently today. The differences shift expectations and the burden of proof against those who would argue for an authoritative governmental role.

We have suggested, however, that the forces underlying the explosion of privatization as a visible item of public discussion and public debate differ from those that would explain its formal adoption and lasting implementation. Discussion of privatization and implementation of privatization proceeded on two fairly distinct tracks and, somewhat ironically, practices associated with privatization have proven most viable when least visible.

Among the three types of privatization, only systemic privatization entails a fundamental attempt to shrink state. But, with the exception of Britain and New Zealand, and the difficult case of Eastern Europe, systemic privatization at this point remains more a vision than an accomplishment. Much of what has occurred to date has been shaped by pragmatic and tactical motives, and, as we have suggested, may prove to be self-limiting, as the constituency for a backlash strengthens. The coalition that has carried privatization forward is more diverse and disunited in motive and interest than the rhetoric of the privatization revolution acknowledges. And the constituency that believes the state – albeit, perhaps, a reconfigured one – has important responsibilities, a legitimate role, and a capacity to act authoritatively on behalf of the public good remains, we think, broader and deeper as well.

The extent to which the new language of public policy will be trans-

---

[46] Henig, Hamnett, and Feigenbaum, "The Politics of Privatization"; John Vickers and Vincent Wright, "The Politics of Industrial Privatisation in Western Europe: An Overview," *West European Politics*, 2, 4 (1988), 1–30.

lated into substantial and lasting alterations in the political/economic landscape, then, remains problematic. In some instances, ballyhooed privatization initiatives represent rather conventional actions, relabeled for reasons of expedience. In some cases, proposed initiatives have been stalled by unforeseen political and economic constraints. And in still other cases, genuine initiatives have mobilized opposing constituencies that, turning some of the ideas behind privatization to their own advantage, have begun to pare down and possibly reverse the privatization trend.

We began this book with an examination of the growth of the welfare state and in many ways the growth of privatizations represents the obverse. We see several possible scenarios. Briefly, they may be stated as: (1) an increase, or even an acceleration of privatization policies if the policies are viewed as successful and are widely imitated, but then declining because there is little or nothing left to privatize; (2) a backlash leading to rejection of further privatizations, perhaps including an expansion of the public sector; or (3) a transformation of the methods of state intervention, but a maintenance of the functions of the state, including the welfare state. For example, some industries may be sold-off, but the proceeds used to finance other public programs, as occurred in France. There may be a decline in public ownership, but an increase in regulation, as happened in Britain. These are not, of course, mutually exclusive scenarios. Privatization may expand in some countries while contracting in others. Moreover, there would more than likely be significant variations across countries. In some cases there might be versions of each scenario going on coterminously as a country might privatize for pragmatic reasons in one public sector area while expanding the role of the state elsewhere.

The evidence in this book suggests that shrinking the state may be more problematic than the proponents of privatization have assumed. Despite the best efforts of those who favor its dismantling, the state may not be so much wrecked as transformed, with new constituencies reacting in unpredicted ways. Action leads to reaction just as policy reshapes circumstance. Privatization transforms the arena in which political conflicts mutate – and continue.

Index